NICK BARRATT'S BEGINNER'S GUIDE TO YOUR ANCESTOR'S LIVES

FAMILY HISTORY FROM PEN & SWORD BOOKS

Tracing Your Yorkshire Ancestors
Rachel Bellerby

Tracing Your Royal Marine Ancestors
Richard Brooks and Matthew Little

Tracing Your Army Ancestors
Simon Fowler

A Guide to Military History on the Internet
Simon Fowler

Tracing Your Northern Ancestors
Keith Gregson

Your Irish Ancestors
Ian Maxwell

Tracing Your Air Force Ancestors
Phil Tomaselli

Tracing Your Jewish Ancestors
Rosemary Wenzerul

NICK BARRATT'S BEGINNER'S GUIDE TO YOUR ANCESTOR'S LIVES

Pen & Sword
FAMILY HISTORY

First published in Great Britain in 2010 by

PEN AND SWORD FAMILY HISTORY

an imprint of
Pen & Sword Books Ltd
47 Church Street
Barnsley
South Yorkshire
S70 2AS

Copyright © Nick Barratt 2010

ISBN 978 1 84884 056 0

Typeset in 10pt Palatino by Mac Style, Beverley, East Yorkshire
Printed and bound in the UK by the MPG Books Group

Pen & Sword Books Ltd incorporates the imprints of Pen & Sword
Aviation, Pen & Sword Maritime, Pen & Sword Military,
Wharncliffe Local History, Pen and Sword Select, Pen and Sword
Military Classics, Leo Cooper, Remember When, Seaforth Publishing
and Frontline Publishing.

For a complete list of Pen & Sword titles please contact
PEN & SWORD BOOKS LIMITED
47 Church Street, Barnsley, South Yorkshire, S70 2AS, England
E-mail: enquiries@pen-and-sword.co.uk
Website: www.pen-and-sword.co.uk

CONTENTS

Section One

TRACING YOUR FAMILY TREE

INTRODUCTION

In this section I'll take a look at the main sources available for constructing your family tree, which forms the basic component of your personal heritage – the skeletal frame on which to hang the historical context of your background. Each chapter in Section One will explore how to work further back in time, adding names to your tree and finding clues along the way to help you investigate each ancestor, in the process finding out more about real people who formed part of your history.

In particular, I will explain:

- How to take your first steps – you don't have to rush straight to the nearest computer to access the Internet, despite all the hype that suggests you simply log on and download your family tree! You need to do some basic detective work first, using your family and their treasured possessions as your evidence …
- How to build your first family tree, and use it to map out the research trail you will follow, both online and in archives across the country. This will form the backbone of your research, and show you at a glance all the people that you are related to, and their place in the nation's history.
- How to locate, obtain and interpret the main 'building block' sources that you'll need to expand your family tree – duplicate civil registration certificates, census returns, parish registers and probate documents such as wills. By using these sources in combination, you can quickly expand

the number of direct ancestors you're related to, generation by generation, and build a much bigger family tree.
• How to take the clues from your family tree and explore your personal heritage in more detail, with particular reference to places of residence and occupations – in other words, putting flesh on the bones of your initial research.

But all journeys start with one first small step, and in the case of genealogy the initial preparation you make at the beginning of your research will stand you in very good stead later on. You'll need no special tools, only a pen or pencil, a sheet of paper – and plenty of patience …

Chapter One

GATHERING INFORMATION

The aim of your initial research is to construct your first family tree, as it will become a vital way of organising your data and showing you, at a glance, the names and vital statistics of the people who are your ancestors – as well as the areas in which you'll need to do further research. So where do you begin? The easiest place is with yourself, and what you already know about your family. Simply record all relevant details about your immediate family, from your date of birth to your parents' names, dates of birth and marriage, your grandparents' names and biographical data, and so on. See how far back you can get from memory alone – it's probably not as far as you'd imagine, bearing in mind you need to record accurate data on dates of birth, marriage, death and also where these events happened, as well as the full names of each person. Most people manage grandparents, and then start to struggle – so don't worry if you haven't got that many names written down at first! It might be worth looking for paperwork that may be squirreled away at home, such as original birth, marriage or death certificates stuffed in envelopes, lying forgotten in dusty cupboards or drawers. Don't forget to include siblings at all levels of the tree as these names may help to narrow down searches when you come to locate the family in original documents, as well as your own children or grandchildren. Continuing the tree and passing on the legacy you've created is an important part of personal heritage, and many of the activities I'll be suggesting can form part of fun education projects with the younger generations.

It's important to write down as much as you can remember about everyone in your initial tree, including where they lived, whether they moved around, the dates they lived in certain places, and their various occupations. These extra details will help to enrich your personal heritage when you come to undertake much deeper investigations in the archives and learn more about the local and social history of the areas where your roots lie; or possibly help solve any difficulty identifying a relative with a common name, for example. Even the most trivial snippets of information can become surprisingly relevant later on, so make a note of everything you can think of, and where possible start to construct a mini timeline for the life of each person you're related to.

Researching personal heritage is about discovering the truth behind family stories that have been passed down through the generations, and putting flesh on the bare bones of the names that make up your skeleton tree. If you've been told that your grandfather fought in France during the First World War you'll be able to hunt down any service papers that might survive, so make a note of any similar stories for each person on your preliminary tree. Write down what you can remember of the stories and who told them to you, so that if you need to verify some information during the course of your research you'll know who to turn to. Making a note of the origin of any family rumours, even if the person from whom the rumour originated is no longer alive, is equally important. If your great-grandmother is believed to have told a family story to her children, which was passed down to their children, and then to you, this chain of events may become relevant when you are looking into the truth of the tale, particularly bearing in mind that the facts could have been distorted over three generations of story-telling.

Crucially, from day one of your research you should record every detail you come across and its source, whether on paper, in a computer document, or using a Dictaphone or similar new media recording device, to make sure you have an accurate research trail of everything you've found. The basic family tree built from your own knowledge (and with the help of your immediate family) will quickly highlight the areas on which your research plan will focus, as it will remind you where there are gaps in your knowledge and which details need to be verified against original or official sources. Therefore it's vital to make sure your notes and family tree are clear and easy to understand. There will be more tips on how to organise your research in the following pages, but here's a recap of what needs to be written down when building your basic tree:

- Your full name, dates of birth and marriage, names and dates of birth and marriage of your descendants

- The names and vital details of your siblings
- Your parents' names, dates of birth, marriage and death if applicable
- The names and vital details of your aunts and uncles (the siblings of your parents)
- Your grandparents' names, dates of birth, marriage and death if applicable
- The names and vital details of your great-aunts and great-uncles (the siblings of your grandparents)
- Anything you know about your great-grandparents, their siblings, and anyone who came before them
- Family stories and where they originated.

Oral History – Talking to the Family

Now that you've exhausted all your own personal knowledge of the family history with the help of your immediate family and any documents in your possession, it's time to think about casting the net a little wider. Your extended family and relations may be an untapped mine of information, full of stories of ancestors who have long since departed, but if they're not asked to share their memories then these stories may never be told. Don't forget family friends as well – they'll have their own stories and impressions of your nearest and dearest, and can often provide some welcome perspective on events, people or stories.

Organising an informal reunion is the perfect way to get a general picture of who knows what, which are the most fascinating family stories, and who is willing to talk about them. Easter and Christmas holidays are the most natural times for families to get together and for family gossip to start creeping into conversation. You'll probably have heard most of the tales time and time again, but these are good opportunities to dig out stories you've never heard before, if you ask the right questions. You'll be amazed at how much your family members have never told you, simply because they think their everyday stories wouldn't be interesting to you – by asking a few questions that might seem out of the ordinary in day-to-day conversation you can gain a wealth of knowledge about your family that may make you see them in a whole different light. How did they react during the Blitz? How did your great-aunt feel about working in a munitions factory during the war? Asking unexpected questions can uncover whole chapters of your family's past, and finding out about your own family's experiences of major historical events can give you a new perspective on your personal heritage.

Although you may be eager to get started, talking to the wider family may need to be a gradual process as some people could be wary of giving away too much if aspects of the family's past have never been talked about before. It might take time for some people to come round to the idea of having the family's heritage investigated. You'll probably discover that others are just as interested in your research as you are though, and will be surprised at how much they can help. Make a special effort to encourage the older generations to open up about their memories of their parents and grandparents. Older relations may know the names of people in your direct family tree that you'd never heard of before, and this will save you time and money when you start your archival research looking for ancestors in the civil registration indexes and on census returns.

Once you have a general idea of who the best people are to talk to about the family's heritage, it's a good idea to arrange separate interviews with each so that you can talk to them uninterrupted and have time to prepare a list of questions, topics and people you'd like to find out more about. Your list of questions needs to be clear and concise, and during the interview you should focus the conversation on one family member at a time so as not to cause any confusion. When and where was your father Liam born? Was he christened Liam or William? So, he was born in Ireland and immigrated to England, but when and where did he marry?

Try to establish the full name (and maiden name) of every key person who is mentioned during the interview, as well as their dates and places of birth, marriage and death, and their occupations. These are the basic components of a family tree and will help you to identify that person in original records. Once you have all the biographical detail you need and your relative has relaxed a little, you can move onto more revealing questions, exploring what that person was like and how their life evolved. Why did Liam leave Ireland and how old was he at the time? Liam emigrated in the 1920s, so do you think this had anything to do with the Troubles at that time and the Civil War in Ireland? Did Liam ever talk about his life in Ireland before he left for England?

When interviewing people about their memories of other relatives, you should ask just as many questions about your interviewee's own upbringing, memories of growing up, and their working life as well. Day-to-day life has changed so much during the last fifty years that even the smallest details may seem unexpectedly interesting to any younger generations who listen to the recording in the future: they are living archives of memory and experience, and it's easy to lose sight of the fact that their everyday life becomes more interesting with the passing of time to the next generation or two down the family tree.

It might seem natural to talk to family members about the past, but when interviews are being recorded it will probably be more difficult for your relative to relax and talk openly. Give the people you talk to enough time to reflect on what they're going to speak about and the confidence to talk at length by showing an obvious interest in what they have to say. On the other hand, you may have to exercise some diplomacy if they start to ramble on or go off at a tangent, as people sometimes do! Sticking to the points in question is vital if you're going to get all the information you need.

Using the list of family tales that you've compiled as a guide, ask your interviewee if they can embellish those stories with any more detail. Have you recalled what you were told accurately? On the other hand, people may not feel comfortable talking about all the issues you'd like to raise, so tread carefully at first, trying to ignore the burning desire to find out everything there is to know about a deep-rooted family secret. If you sense that it's a touchy subject, then move to safer ground. It's easy to forget in the twenty-first century that matters such as illegitimacy, adoption and divorce that occurred years ago can still be hurtful to talk about. If your interviewee feels pressurised to talk, they may be less inclined to help with other queries you have, and you never know, if the matter is dropped they may decide to open up at another time when they feel more comfortable.

The more people you're able to talk to, the better. You'll no doubt find that different people's versions of the same story will differ, but when you come to verify facts in the archives it usually helps to be aware of all the possible scenarios of events, as a story passed down verbally through many generations will rarely be completely accurate. Be wary of believing everything you're told as fact, as time can play tricks on the memory. Oral historical accounts are invaluable, but people love to exaggerate their story to captivate their audience. It's best to cross-reference the stories you're told with lots of different family members, then it's up to you to distinguish the truth from the myths where possible, using primary sources in the archives.

Errors may also crop up in the basic information you're given in the course of your interviews. Gathering dates and places of births, marriages and other key events from interviews with relatives is useful to speed up your research in the archives, but don't assume that the information you're given by relatives from memory is always correct, even if your source is adamant that they're right. These are simply guidelines for you to follow. Everything should be verified using official documentation where possible, such as civil registration certificates. Your relative may also be unaware that the name by which they knew your ancestor was not their official name. Granddad Liam was actually christened and registered with the name Patrick William, but he chose to use his second name, and then shortened that. The use of second names in preference to official first names used to be common practice. When looking for relatives' documents in the archives it's essential to know their official name because you'll probably need it to locate their records in alphabetical indexes. Nevertheless, if a relative was known by more than one name it helps to be aware of the various options, so you have an alternative to look under if you don't find them with their official name.

Beware of false relationships planted among the information you receive from other family members. 'Uncle Jim' may have been a close family friend rather than a blood relative, and 'Cousin Sarah' may actually have been your Gran's aunt, but because there was such a small age difference between them, they were brought up more like cousins rather than aunt and niece. Make sure you gather the specifics about exactly how each person is related so that your research is not misguided.

How to avoid early errors:

- Interview as many relatives as possible to cross-reference stories, names, dates, places and events
- Establish exact relationships and find out everyone's full names and nicknames
- Don't rely too heavily on second-hand information from relatives – use it as a guideline for your research
- Be ready to substantiate everything with primary evidence.

Recording interviews for posterity

Oral history creates a living link with the past and is invaluable to genealogists and historians. It's essential to record the oral evidence you gather, because as time passes there will be fewer people to speak to who remember a way of life that will never return, and who can tell stories about colourful characters that would otherwise be forgotten. It's obviously important to ask your interviewee for their consent for the interview to be recorded first, and to discuss the method you're thinking of using. If possible, make the most of the opportunity to video-record the conversation using a camcorder or digital camera. You could then find a way of incorporating this material into a digital presentation once you've finished your research. Tape recorders and Dictaphones are just as good for capturing the tone of the interview. At some point you may have to explore a way of transferring your audio or video recordings to a new medium as technology progresses, so it's important to keep up to date with the best ways of doing this before it's too late and your old media format is obsolete. There are many commercial companies, both online and in the high street, which can re-format and digitise older forms of media, such as cine film or videotape.

Whichever media you eventually settle on to record your interviews, it's always a good idea to have a practice run to make sure the sound quality is adequate – there's nothing more disappointing than spending an hour getting some really good footage and gems of information only to find you can't properly hear what was said when it's played back.

Unfortunately some people leave it too late to ask older relatives for their help, or may not have any living relatives to rely on to fill in the gaps for them. If this is the case, it's still possible to start your family history from scratch using the information on your birth certificate to find your parents' marriage and births, and then work back from there using the basic sources. These processes will be explained later in Section One. It's also possible to extract information about your relatives from any personal mementos and documents that might have been passed down to you, which can aid you just as much in your search for further primary evidence in the archives.

Personal memorabilia

Personal memorabilia is invaluable for putting some colour into the lives of the people who, up to now, are simply names on your provisional family tree. Discovering these dusty, long-forgotten items can give you a real urge to want to find out more about the people they once belonged to. Perhaps you've found a letter from a set of relatives who emigrated to the Colonies a hundred years ago and you want to find out who the author 'Alf' could have been? A postcard or an old love letter can tell you so much more about the individuals concerned than any document you're likely to find in the archives, so it's well worth taking the time to seek them out.

Personal memorabilia can come in all shapes and sizes – school reports, military medals, badges and uniforms, ration books, identity cards, insurance policies – the list is endless. All these types of memorabilia can fill in the gaps that are no longer within living memory. If you stumble across family heirlooms and are unsure to whom they once belonged, ask other people in your family who might know. You're bound to find old photos and not be able to name one single person in them, so why not scan them and e-mail a copy round to the rest of the family to see if they can help?

Personal details found on official documents such as old passports and employment papers can also save you time when searching for relatives on census returns, as you might already have found where your relative was living at certain points in time and what their occupation was. Most people are unaware of or forget just how much information they have about their family's history sitting right under their noses until they start actively looking for it. Have a dig around in the loft, in relatives' chests of drawers and in old family albums to see what can be found, and get the wider family involved in the search. Family heirlooms are often passed down to the eldest surviving child, so ask if any descendants of the older generations have some interesting objects you might be able to have a look at. Army medals reveal the campaigns that the soldier fought in, and an old wedding photo might have names and a date on it – these clues can lead you to further official sources.

A surprising amount of documentation created during the two World Wars still survives in people's homes, and can provide clues to finding supplementary material from that era deposited in archives. Letters granting exemption from compulsory conscription, or military discharge papers, medals and uniform apparel were sometimes kept by soldiers as a souvenir. Any evidence that your ancestor was in the Army, Air Force, Navy or Merchant Navy before or after the wars will give an indication of where to start looking to find any more documents that may be held in the archives for them. Most medals were awarded for service at a particular time or for specific battles or events, so if you do find medals around the house then consult a published guide to help you examine the design and identify what they would have been awarded for.

A wealth of civilian material also survives from the wartime era, such as ration books, letters to and from loved ones separated by conflict, and telegrams from the Army informing next of kin of the death of a soldier, illustrating the strained conditions under which your ancestors had to live. Civilian documents issued during peacetime are equally informative, e.g. passports with a person's photo, vital details and stamps from the places they visited, or identity papers and naturalisation certificates if they immigrated to Britain during the nineteenth or twentieth centuries as did so many people in search of work and stability.

For hundreds of years letters were the main form of correspondence between family and friends who lived apart. The Internet, e-mail and mobile phones have radically changed the way we communicate, so that correspondence with loved ones can be instantly deleted or kept completely private in a way that was not possible with good old-fashioned paper and pen. Therefore old letters that have survived can be of tremendous use to family historians, providing names and addresses and conveying your ancestor's personality through their writing style. Correspondence gives an insight into people's day-to-day lives, their feelings and their hopes. Postcards from family holidays can give you an idea of your ancestor's social life and class. If they travelled abroad before cheap aeroplane fares made foreign tourism a common phenomenon, you'll know that they were probably well-off. These days, round robin Christmas letters are often kept, and provide an annual snapshot of family events.

General everyday items found when hunting in the attic or through drawers, such as theatre tickets, museum entrance receipts, dinner bills, ballet or opera reviews, football season tickets and magazines, provide a wonderful insight into your relative's personality and values. These ordinary objects might seem like hoarded junk, but if your relative believed they were worth holding on to, then that is an obvious clue to what was important to them. The kind of things you find are also key indicators as to what your ancestor's lifestyle would have been like and the amount of disposable income they must have had. A whole stash of opera tickets from the 1930s would suggest the person who purchased them was probably well educated and lived comfortably, as well as having an appreciation for a particular style of music!

Birth, baptism, marriage, death certificates and memorial cards are the most common personal documents to be found stashed away in drawers. Not only can they be used to verify information you've been told by relatives; finding these original copies will also save you the cost that would otherwise have been incurred ordering duplicate copies from the General Register Office. Any other official records that may have been kept, such as wills, deeds and legal documents, are a great stepping stone for your research, perhaps supplying more names to add to your tree, as well as giving addresses of buildings and homes linked to your family's past. Wills are particularly useful because they usually name members of the extended family and explain how they were connected to the person who wrote the will.

It was once common practice to keep a family Bible in which details of births, baptisms, marriages, spouses' names, deaths and special family events were written. If your family kept such a Bible that survives, it may contain names and dates going back way before the official registration of births, marriages and deaths began, as will be explained later in Section One. Usually only one copy of the family Bible would have been produced, as they are invariably hand-written documents, so it's worth asking cousins and extended family whether a Bible was passed to their side of the family if you do not have one. As with all the sources you find, it's wise to verify every piece of such information the Bible contains using official records, and try to establish if the Bible was written retrospectively or whether it was updated at the time of each event. Family Bibles that were added to at a later date from memory or hearsay are more likely to contain discrepancies, but they can still be useful as a guide to your research.

Unusual first or middle names passed down through a few generations can suggest that name was a maiden name of one of the women in your tree, passed down to her descendants as a Christian name so that it was not completely lost after she took her husband's surname. Keep an eye out for distinctive name patterns among the documents you uncover and see if you can locate the original source of the name when you start your research in the archives. Name patterns can also be used for tracing more common first and middle names – for example there may have been a long line of John Thomases mentioned in a series of documents that could make locating public records for any earlier generations a bit easier, going on the theory that there may have been more men by the name John Thomas in the line. This type of speculative research should not be used as a rule, but can be a handy way of confirming the results of traditional research methods.

Cuttings from local newspapers of birth, engagement, wedding announcements and descriptions of the big day are often kept and treasured, which will give you names, dates and places for these events. Perhaps somebody in your family did something that deserved special comment in the local paper, or was involved in a local disaster or crime that was reported. If one of your ancestors was well respected within the local community an obituary may have been written about them shortly after their death, and their funeral may also have been reported. Newspaper articles can be the unexpected source of old photographs supplied by the family to the journalist.

Most people will come across at least a few black and white photos in the family's collection, which provide a fascinating insight into our relatives' sense of fashion, their expressions and surroundings. Some photos may have had names, dates and places of the shot written on the back, but even if you can't name the majority of people in the frame it's always interesting to try to work out when the picture was taken and who the people might have been. If any of your pictures don't have names or a date written on them, show them to as many elderly relatives as possible to see if anybody recognises the faces or locations. Ask for permission to make scans or digital copies of any old photographs you find in relatives' houses, so you can add them to your research collection and write on the back of the paper copies each time you identify a new face. Making sure there are extra copies of valuable old photos will ensure the younger generations of your family get to appreciate these family heirlooms in the future in case the original is ever lost or damaged. There are special preservation services available from many specialist photo developers that can prevent old photos from fading and restore scratched or damaged images. Most people in the Victorian and Edwardian periods couldn't afford a camera of their own and would have visited a photographer's studio or had their picture taken at a photographer's stand at a fair. Photographic studios frequently printed the company name and address on photos, so you can trace this in trade directories to establish when that studio was in business and to work out whereabouts the person in the photo must have lived. Your local archive or museum may also be able to help you date the clothes or background in an old photo.

Personal memorabilia to search for:

- Civil registration and religious certificates confirming births, marriages and deaths
- Wills, deeds and legal documents
- Newspaper cuttings and obituaries
- School reports and photos
- Family Bible and name patterns
- Letters and postcards
- Military, Naval, Air Force and Merchant Navy documents, medals and uniform apparel
- Civilian wartime letters, ration books, identity cards
- Employment papers and letters
- Passports and citizenship documents
- Old receipts, magazines, tickets to the theatre or to football matches
- Photographs.

Personal heritage is not only about the past, but also about preserving the present for the future. Compiling your personal heritage should be as much about recording the details of your own life as your ancestors' lives – your children, nieces, nephews and grandchildren will eventually want to learn about their personal heritage, and you are as much a part of that as any of the people you uncover in your research. Instead of always e-mailing or texting friends and family, take the time to write letters – or print out and preserve the communications of others where they relate to family matters.

It will become apparent while trawling through boxes of unnamed photographs just how important it is to start writing down the names of the familiar faces in your own family albums, as well as the dates the photos were taken, so that people will be able to identify you and your loved ones in the future. Consider keeping a few everyday items that may seem inconsequential today but will help to illustrate some of the defining events of your life in the future; or put together a time capsule every five or ten years, showing how society has changed.

Why not take the opportunity before you start your archival research into the past to write a biographical account of the key events of your own life, and the things that are important to you, including all the information about yourself that you wish you knew about your forebears? Diaries, journals and even scrapbooks are a great way to record information which will be fascinating to your descendants in the years to come. You might decide to use this as an introduction to your research once the project is complete, explaining to your audience why you wanted to investigate your personal heritage and why it's so important to you. Advice about personal archiving in the digital age is provided in Section Four of this book.

In the meantime, the following chapter will explore the technicalities of family trees in more detail, and examine the various ways in which you can store your family history research and organise your findings as the project progresses.

Overview of questions to consider from home before entering the archives:

- What do I know about my ancestors?
- What do my relatives know about our ancestry?
- Are there any family mysteries to clear up?
- Is there any personal memorabilia to give me some clues?

Chapter Two

YOUR FIRST FAMILY TREE

Terminology

If you are new to genealogy and personal heritage research it's a good idea to familiarise yourself with some of the terms you'll come across before embarking on your project. Your family tree will provide the basis for your research plan, showing at a glance what you know already and what you still need to find out. Understanding the official terms that describe the relationships between everybody in your tree, and the various ways a family tree can be arranged, is a fundamental starting point before you begin your research in the archives. It should help you to map out the names you've gathered from your initial research at home and with the family so far. A family tree is a diagram that allows you to see at a glance how everybody you are related to is connected, but there are many different ways of drawing family trees. Listed below are some terms you will come across in the course of your genealogical research and the technical terms used to describe relations from your immediate and extended family tree, followed by tips on the various methods of arranging your tree.

Glossary of Terms

ancestor	someone in the past who is related to you
bachelor	unmarried man
base child	see 'illegitimate child'
bastard	see 'illegitimate child'
biological	relationship through blood, whereby two people share the same genes
deceased	dead

generation	group of people who were born around the same time as each other
illegitimate child	child whose parents were unmarried when they were conceived/born
maternal	female side of the family, usually meaning the mother's side
natural child	see 'illegitimate child'
paternal	male side of the family, usually meaning the father's side
predecease	to die before somebody else
predecessor	see 'ancestor'
sibling	genderless term to describe a brother or sister
spinster	unmarried woman
spouse	genderless term to describe a husband or wife
widow	woman whose husband has died
widower	man whose wife has died

Glossary of Relationships

Direct Line

Your 'direct line' simply means your parents, grandparents, great-grandparents, their parents, and so on. In other words, these are all the people who have been biologically crucial to your creation. Every time you find another generation in your direct line the prefix 'great' is added to their relationship status to you. Therefore the parents of your grandparents are known as your great-grandparents, and the parents of your great-grandparents are your great-great-grandparents, and so on.

A simple family tree showing only your direct line of ancestors can be drawn as you add more names to the tree through your research. This type of tree saves space because it includes the minimum number of names, and is useful for seeing at a glance where each new surname infiltrates your heritage. A tree showing only your direct line would not include your siblings, nieces and nephews, aunts and uncles, cousins, the siblings of any of your grandparents, or any other extended branches.

Every time you search for another generation in your direct line you'll need to look for double the number of people as the generation that came before that. This is because we all have two parents, who each have two parents so that we have four grandparents. These four grandparents have two parents each, which means we have eight great-grandparents, and then sixteen great-

great-grandparents. This is why it can be easier to have a tree just showing the names in your direct line once the research has progressed a little!

Nieces and Nephews

Most people will know that nieces and nephews are the words used to describe the children of your siblings. Niece is a female child and nephew a male child. Any subsequent children of your nieces and nephews would be your great-nieces and great-nephews, and another 'great' is added to the prefix when the next generation is born.

Uncles and Aunts

Your uncles and aunts are the siblings of your parents. The siblings of your grandparents are known as your great-uncles and great-aunts, and each further generation you go back another 'great' is added to the prefix. Therefore, the siblings of your great-grandparents would be your great-great-uncles and great-great-aunts. Some people use the word 'grand' instead of 'great', or would describe these relatives as 'great grand uncles and aunts'.

Cousins

Your cousins are the children of your aunts and uncles, and these make up the extended branches of your family tree. The children of your immediate aunts and uncles are known as your first cousins. Any subsequent descendants of your first cousins are described by how many generations they are 'removed' from you. If your first cousin has a child, this child is your 'first cousin once removed'. If your first cousin has a grandchild they would be your 'first cousin twice removed'.

First, second and third cousins can only be used to describe cousins who are of the same generation. Therefore if you had a child, and so did your first cousin, the relationship between these two children would be second cousins. This means that while you refer to your cousin's child as your 'first cousin once removed', your child would call them their 'second cousin'.

The cousins of any previous generations to yourself should be referred to as the cousin of whichever person in your direct line with whom they share the same generation. This means that the parent of your second cousin should be called your 'parent's first cousin', the parent of your third cousin would be your 'parent's second cousin', and the grandparent of your third cousin would be your 'grandparent's first cousin'.

The relationships between cousins are confusing and very often in documents such as wills and census returns, which will be used in the course of your research, people use the word cousin to describe a range of distant relatives without qualifying exactly how they're related.

Step-relations

Step-relations are people who are part of the same family through marriage only, instead of being blood relations; therefore they don't share any biological characteristics. If your biological parents separate and divorce, or if one of your parents has died, they may choose to marry another person and their new spouse would be your step-parent. If both your biological parents marry other people, you could have two sets of parents – your two biological parents and their respective spouses, one being your stepfather, the other your stepmother.

If either of your step-parents has children from a previous relationship to marrying your biological parent, these children become your stepbrothers and stepsisters because neither of their parents are biologically related to you. Your biological parent would describe these children as their stepsons and stepdaughters, just as you would be your step-parent's stepchild.

Half-relations

The word 'half' is used to describe a relationship between children who share only one biological parent. If your biological father or mother has a child with your step-parent, this child would be your half-brother or half-sister. Alternatively, you may have half-brothers and half-sisters from a relationship your biological parent had before you were born. For example if your father's first wife, with whom he had children, died and you were the child of his second wife, the children from the first relationship would be your half-brothers and half-sisters because you share one biological parent.

In-Laws

When two people marry, they become relations 'in-law' to their partner's immediate family through the legal contract of the marriage. Therefore the father of the groom is the 'father-in-law' of the bride, and the groom would be described as the 'son-in-law' to the parents of the bride. Equally, if either the bride or groom has siblings, these are the brothers- and sisters-in-law of the respective parties.

Below are some abbreviations that you will find in other people's family trees, and that you might choose to use in your own to keep as much space available as possible:

Glossary of Abbreviations

b.	born
m. or mar.	married
=	married
2.	second marriage
d.	died
ob. or obit.	died
d.s.p. or o.s.p.	died childless
d.v.p. or o.v.p.	died before father
l.	left descendants
bapt. or bp.	baptised
chr.	christened
bur.	buried
lic.	licence (marriage licence)
MI	monumental inscription
c.	circa or about
?	uncertain or unknown
o.t.p.	of this parish
w.	wife
s.	son
s. and h.	son and heir
dau.	daughter
g.f.	grandfather
g.m.	grandmother
g.g.f.	great-grandfather
g.g.m.	great-grandmother
inf.	infant
spin.	spinster
bach.	bachelor

unm.	unmarried
div.	divorced
wid.	widow
wdr.	widower
mat.	maternal side of the family
pat.	paternal side of the family
Distaff	female side of the family
Spear	male side of the family

Designing your First Family Tree

In bygone days the aristocracy kept family trees as a way of documenting their illustrious heritage and proving their connections to royalty. Fantastic illuminated manuscripts on scrolls of parchment were commissioned by the great and the good to display pedigrees showing coats of arms, heraldic beasts, miniature portraits of famous ancestors and all the key names in order of descent. There has never been a standard way to draw up a family tree, but these early designs have provided inspiration for genealogists today who now have a wide range of template trees available to choose from. The method of drawing up your tree that you eventually decide upon will most likely depend on which you find easier to read and use.

Your first family tree will probably be manageable enough to include all the names you gathered when talking to your relatives, including each person's vital biographical details (their dates of birth, marriage and death). As you start adding more names to the tree through your research you may need to look at different ways of arranging it, perhaps not including all the names of your distant cousins, so as to make room for the new names you're uncovering in your more immediate branches. There will undoubtedly be large gaps in your first tree and details you're unsure of, but this is part of the purpose of drawing it all out as opposed to having lots of lists – so you can see at a glance where there are holes in your research, and what needs verifying. It's easy to lose sight of the detail when you're faced with a long narrative of notes, so drawing everything out into a diagram with uniform data sections for everybody on the tree really helps to keep things clear. Now that you have a full grasp of the relationships between everyone in your tree, pulling all of your notes together into a diagram should be a quick process. Making sure you add the same data for each individual (dates and places of birth, marriage and death for example) will make it obvious where any of these details are missing. If you put question marks next to anything on your tree that you're unsure of, then you can see quickly what has been verified already and what is still to be done. Another way of doing this is to write anything that is absolutely certain onto your tree in pen, while putting anything that is yet to be confirmed in pencil, so it can be written in pen once the relevant documentation has been found.

There are a few popular methods for drawing family trees, and you can use whichever you find easier to read, add to or draw out. This is your personal heritage project, so whatever design you go for, your family tree should have your name as the starting point. All the names on your tree should be written in full using the name each person was registered with at birth, which would be the maiden surnames of all the married women in your family. If this is done for everyone in your tree, then anybody who wants to verify your research in the future will be able to do so easily. Where someone was known by a different name, or had a nickname, this can be put in brackets after their full name so they can still be quickly identified.

A traditional diagram tree, or 'drop-line tree', will show the generations in your family tree connected with horizontal and vertical lines that form the branches of your tree. It makes sense to add all the names you have to your first family tree, including those from the extended family, so that you can see all the information you have so far. As your research progresses you can create smaller trees showing sections of the family who are immediately related to each other, so that more can fit onto a page and to make the size of the tree more manageable.

A drop-line family tree showing your extended family members will have your name in the middle of the tree, with your brothers and sisters (or siblings) either side of you in chronological order connected by a horizontal line, starting with the eldest. This branch makes up your generation. Below you will be your children's names, linked to you with a vertical branch, and below each of your siblings will be a vertical branch extending down to the names of their children (your nieces and nephews), followed by any grandchildren and great-nieces and great-nephews on the next generation down. Where possible, generations should be drawn on the tree at a similar level to indicate they were all alive around the same time, though this may be impractical as the tree becomes more sprawling. If you are drawing a tree showing just your ancestors and none of your descendants (the offspring of your generation) then you should place your name towards the bottom of the page to allow more room at the top for ancestors' names. Above you and your siblings' names will be your parents' names with a vertical stem linking their names to yours. Alongside each of your parents will be their siblings' names (your aunts and uncles). Above your parents, aunts and uncles will be a vertical stem leading to your four grandparents' names, each above the names of their own children.

Spouses' names are traditionally written next to each other with the man on the left and the woman on the right. Underneath each person's name you should write 'b.' followed by their date of birth, and if they have died you can write their date of death underneath their date of birth, signified by a 'd.' in front of the date. In between the names of married couples an 'm.' or = sign should be written with the date of their marriage underneath, followed by a vertical line leading to the names of the children from the marriage. Where possible, all siblings should be placed on a horizontal line starting with the eldest first and ending with the youngest, though this may be more problematic the further up the tree you go and the less space you have. For some of the earlier generations you may find it best to put the names of your direct ancestors at the beginning or end of the horizontal line linking their siblings, so they can be placed next to the name of their spouse more easily. Some family trees have dotted lines linking parents and children, which can mean that the child was born out of wedlock, or they were adopted and are not blood relations. Dotted lines are most commonly found in the family trees of members of the aristocracy, where keeping a record of the legal bloodline was important for determining inheritance at a time when being an illegitimate child meant there was no legal entitlement to the family fortune.

The aristocracy, who have a long tradition of recording family trees to prove their distinguished roots, often favoured pedigrees showing minimal detail, sometimes just the key names leading back to the most prominent ancestor in their heritage. If you have aristocratic roots in your bloodline you may find a ready-made family tree has been deposited at the College of Arms in London. Ancestral pedigrees tend to only show a direct line of ancestors, and run from top to bottom, with the earliest ancestors at the top of the tree running down to the most recent generation. A pedigree that shows all sixteen great-great-grandparents (or 2 x great-grandparents) of the youngest generation is known as a *seize quartiers*, and one that goes as far back as the thirty-two great-great-great-grandparents (or 3 x great-grandparents) is a *trente-deux quartiers*.

As you uncover more names to add to your family tree you might find it easier to work with a diagram that only shows your direct line of ancestors. Printed template trees, which run from left to right leaving gaps for you to fill in each person's name and vital details, can be found online or can be obtained from the Society of Genealogists and other record offices. The Microsoft Office website has a number of family tree templates that can be downloaded for free via the Templates link on their website at http://office.microsoft.com. Type 'family tree' into the search box to choose from a number of options, which you can print out and take to the archives with you. These types of trees are practical for carrying around, but a full version of your tree should always be kept as well, which will be discussed in the following pages.

Family trees published in books where space does not permit a large diagram tree to be printed, such as *Burke's Peerage* or *Debrett's*, are sometimes written using indented paragraphs without the need to link each generation using lines. 'Narrative indented pedigrees', as they are known, are not the easiest to follow for the untrained eye, but it is a practical method to learn and use if you want to type up your tree using word-processing software on the computer (such as Microsoft Word), with which it can be tricky to draw lines. This type of pedigree starts with the earliest known ancestor, and can include extended family members. Numbers and indented spaces are used to indicate which generation a name belongs to. Abbreviations are vital when describing relationships and each person's place in the narrative indented pedigree, as illustrated by the following example:

William Brown *m*. Mary Simons. Had issue:
1. John *b*. 1849. *dsp*.
2. Michael *b*. 1852 and *m*. Jane McBride. Had issue:
    a. Grace *b*. 1875
    b. George *b*. 1877 who *m*. in 1900 Bridget Rees. He *d*. 1950 leaving issue:
        i. Bernard *b*. 1901
3. Mary *b*. 1855

This narrative indented pedigree illustrates that William Brown had three children with Mary Simons, whose names were John (born 1849 but died without issue), Michael (born 1852) and Mary (born 1855). Their second son Michael married Jane McBride and had two children, Grace (born 1875) and George (born 1877). George, the grandson of William Brown, married Bridget

Rees in 1900 and died in 1950. George and Bridget had a son called Bernard in 1901, who was William Brown's great-grandson. The position of each name indicates which generation that person belongs to – John, Michael and Mary are all of the same generation, therefore their names are directly in line, even though other names separate them. Equally, Grace and George are of the same generation, and Bernard is in the next generation down from them.

These are just some of the styles of family tree that are used by modern-day researchers and genealogists. In the course of your research you'll come across many more formats, though they all have the same aim – to organise the data and convey it to the reader in a clear, easy to understand way. Whatever style you go for, there hopefully won't be room on your family tree to include all the information you uncover about each person in your personal heritage story. Your family tree will display the backbone of your research, but your investigative work should uncover much more about the personalities of each individual, so in the next few pages we'll look at ways to organise all your findings and keep track of the extra material you discover.

Family trees online

Most people start drawing out their first family tree by hand, but as your research progresses you'll probably want to explore some of the more practical ways of storing your findings on the computer. This will save you time when you need to update your tree and edit any mistakes, rather than having to draw out a new tree from scratch, and means you won't have to search through lots of paperwork to find what you need. Moving your findings from a single piece of paper to a computer offers so much more scope for keeping a ton of information about each individual in one place, so you can see all the dates, documents and photos you've got for that person without having to rummage around in a box of notes. Using an online or computer package to store your research is also a professional way to present your final research findings to other members of the family, as some of the packages on the market include publishing software that can be used to turn your personal heritage research into a book.

There are various options for storing an electronic copy of your research. There's a multitude of genealogy websites that offer subscriptions where you can enter the details of your family tree into a template and store it online. These are usually data-sharing sites, so your family tree may be accessed by other users of the site who might want to contact you to compare research notes if you have a common ancestor. However, some of these websites give you the option to keep your tree completely private, or to e-mail a link to the tree to family and friends so only they can see your research. If you choose not to make your online tree available to other general users of the site then you might miss out on some of the advantages this has to offer, which are analysed in the coming pages.

The alternative to using the templates provided by online subscription sites is to upload a specialist family history software package onto your computer and keep your tree on your PC rather than online. Some of the most comprehensive packages offer more features than the online subscription sites and are especially useful for personal heritage projects, as there are sections for each person in your tree where you can record not only their name and vital details, but also their nickname, details of their education and religious background, their occupation, addresses and a story section where any interesting family tales can be included. Some software allows you to upload photos, videos, audio recordings and document images linked to the relevant people in your tree.

Specialist packages are really versatile, letting you display as much or as little information as you need to view at a time, while at the click of a button you have instant access to all the information you've uploaded. You can usually display your tree using a variety of different diagrams and report formats, which can be printed out and taken with you to the archives as a reminder. Most of the trees give the option of uploading a photo to each name on your tree, so you can print out a family tree incorporating the faces of your relations, helping you to spot any similarities between the generations.

Specially designed family history software enables genealogists to share trees by saving and e-mailing them as GEDCOM (Genealogical Data Communications) files, which can be opened by any software that accepts GEDCOM. Both websites and purchased software packages accept GEDCOM files, so you can normally switch between different packages and import your old file to the new software without having to re-type your data every time. This is particularly useful if you record your research on your PC using a software package but decide to also put a copy on one of the websites for other researchers to see. There's a huge choice of family tree building tools on the market, such as online trees available at www.myheritage.com, software packages like Family Tree Maker and Family Historian, and below are summaries of further popular websites and packages, some of which can be used for free.

Ancestry
www.ancestry.co.uk

It's free to build a family tree on the Ancestry.co.uk website, either from scratch by adding the names and vital details of the people in your tree, or by uploading an existing GEDCOM file. Photos, stories, audio recordings, videos and record references can be added to each person in the tree, and the data is automatically compiled into a timeline of events and can be displayed in a drop-line or pedigree tree. The website searches for the names and dates in other Ancestry members' trees to see if you have any relatives in common, so you can choose to upgrade your subscription and contact other users if you'd like to find out more about their research. Ancestry.co.uk also has access to a wealth of digitised historical records, which will be explored in future chapters.

Genes Reunited
www.genesreunited.co.uk

Genes Reunited is the sister site to Friends Reunited, so they work on a similar basis, helping people with the same interests to get in touch. It's free to upload your family tree onto the website, which forms part of a database of names and dates along with trees belonging to other users. The site searches through its members' trees to see if there's a match between your tree and the 8 million others that make up the database, so it's an excellent resource for discovering new ancestors and finding lost relatives. Subscription members can contact other users with common ancestors and can share full family trees if permission is given. Some of the major online historical resources are also available on Genes Reunited, which can be searched to add data to your tree.

Personal Ancestral File
www.familysearch.org/paf

Personal Ancestral File (PAF) is a family tree building software package published by the Church of Jesus Christ of Latter-Day Saints (LDS). PAF is less sophisticated than some other packages on the market, as its diagram features are less flexible than other providers, but it can be downloaded completely free of charge. PAF software allows you to create your own customised templates for uploading individuals' data. You can cite the source of each piece of information, upload multimedia files, such as photos, and attach these to individuals' records. Interactive scrapbooks and slide shows can be created using your videos, audio recordings and pictures. As with most other packages, you can design and print out reports using the statistics you have entered by asking the package to find only individuals that match certain criteria, such as the number of people who died in a given date range, or a list of the people whose dates of birth are unknown – these are useful for taking into the archives with you to organise your pending research. Your findings can be shared with others on the Net by adding your PAF file to the www.familysearch.org database of Ancestral Files and Pedigree Resource Files. The PAF program is easy to use and navigating around your tree is straightforward.

Family Tree Maker
www.familytreemaker.com

Family Tree Maker (FTM) 2009 is a software package that can be bought online or in the shops for storing your research on your computer. It has a choice of formats for presenting and printing your tree, from drop-line trees and fan charts to hourglass trees and timelines. This software is integrated with the digitised historical records available on Ancestry.co.uk so you can quickly search and transfer data straight from the website into your tree. You should ensure that you purchase the version of FTM that is compatible with Ancestry.co.uk though, and not one of the Ancestry sites for another country (such as Ancestry.com, which would be more useful for finding American ancestors). The latest version of FTM has an interactive map facility so you can see a geographical spread of where your ancestors came from, and has a feature that creates timelines integrating your key personal heritage dates with world events. You can upload video and audio files as well as photos, pictures and scanned copies of documents to each individual's file in your tree.

Roots Magic
www.rootsmagic.co.uk

Roots Magic Version 4 is a great piece of computer software for storing your findings on the PC because you can add a list of sources and footnote where each piece of information was found. As well as the usual features that most of the packages have, it also has a Publisher feature that guides you through creating your own personal heritage book by combining multiple reports and charts into a single document with photos, cover pages, supplementary text and a list of sources. The Publisher creates a table of contents and an index for your book, giving it a professional finish. It's easy to share your research with other members of the family who don't have genealogy software by printing out a copy of your book or giving them a customised Shareable CD containing a read-only version of Roots Magic with all your research uploaded to it. There is also web space provided for your tree, with instructions on how to turn your data into a user-friendly and attractive website. The Roots Magic website has a free trial version of Version 4 that can be downloaded to get a feel for the software before you buy the full version.

Posting online

Whichever family tree building program you opt for, you should consider posting your tree online for other researchers to see, as this is an invaluable way of finding out more about your personal heritage from others who may have been researching the names in your tree for many years already. The websites mentioned in previous pages that let you upload your tree to the Internet and search the trees of other users normally give you the option of choosing your own privacy settings, so you can decide whether or not you want other users to be able to see your family tree and be able to contact you. It really is worth opting to put your tree on the Net for potential distant relatives to see, because there might be stories that were passed down through distant branches of your family that were never told to your direct ancestors. Equally, someone from another branch of the family may be able to fill in the gaps of stories you have been told. Contacting other researchers online is also a great way to acquire copies of photographs for members of the family you've never seen before.

You can upload what you've discovered so far from your research at home, even if you've only just started. This way you'll know immediately if parts of your tree have been researched already, because the website should spot any matching details in your tree with the names and dates in other people's trees. If you find what looks like one of your ancestors in another online tree, you should be sure when sending a message to the other researcher to include as much extra information as you can, in order for the person you're contacting to determine whether or not the relative you're enquiring about is indeed the person you think them to be. This includes names, dates and places of birth, and details of their parents. The matches found by these websites may not always be accurate, so as much detail as possible should be cross-referenced with the other researcher to ascertain whether or not there is a correct match.

Joining forces with another researcher who is tracing the same ancestors as yourself can hasten the research process, and if you broach the subject of splitting the associated costs, both of you can save some money. It can be costly ordering birth, marriage and death certificates and paying for photocopies in the archives and for database subscriptions, so it's worth investigating whether another researcher is prepared to share the burden by each of you taking on a separate branch of your mutual tree. Some researchers who have completed their project may be kind enough to impart their findings to you free of charge. Having said that, it's vital to bear in mind that other people's research may contain errors, so where possible you should ask if they can tell you their sources and double-check all the data you're given with original records until you're happy that it's accurate.

Forums and Mailing Lists

Even if you're not lucky enough to find anyone who's already researching a branch of your tree, joining genealogy sharing sites, forums, mailing lists and message boards are other worthwhile ways of posting information about your personal heritage project online because you'll meet people with common interests who may be able to help when you're stuck. If you find that you've come to a difficult patch in your research and don't know how to move forward, a member of the online genealogical community may have the answer to your query or will at least be able to point you in the right direction. As a researcher yourself, you'll probably find after a while that you're able to assist others who are facing difficulties.

The very nature of personal heritage opens up many avenues of research interest. These interests can take on a variety of forms, be it surnames, locations, occupations or ethnic groups. There's an extraordinary number of genealogy websites on the Net that have forums and mailing lists covering a vast range of historical topics. There are sites dedicated to researching religious groups, surnames, occupations, local history and more, so you're bound to find other people who are just as interested in, say nineteenth-century Yorkshire mining, as you.

Forums are subject-specific areas on websites where members post messages and files for others to read, and people can reply to conversation threads. There are all sorts of discussion forums relating to genealogy topics, and they're particularly useful for finding helpful researchers who can give advice on any query you might have. Most of the major genealogy websites have a section dedicated to forums, including those sites already mentioned such as Ancestry and Genes Reunited. On the forums pages in these websites you'll find a list of topics and can browse the messages already posted by others or you can post a message of your own by registering with the site, which is usually free to do. The most popular search engines, such as Google and Yahoo, are also able to search the messages that have been posted in numerous website forums by using their keyword search engine. This way you may find your research query has already been asked and answered by other users in a forum, saving you the time of posting a new message and waiting for a reply.

The British Genealogy website has a large coverage of forum topics at www.british-genealogy.com/forums, from occupations and surnames to emigration and Jewish roots, as well as local history forums for all the British counties. GenForum at www.genforum.genealogy.com hosts thousands of forums devoted to personal heritage research: simply find a forum that's relevant to your research by typing a keyword into the Forum Finder. Roots Chat is another site to try if you're looking for a forum dedicated specifically to UK and Irish genealogical topics, which can be found at www.rootschat.com, or for those looking for tips on tracing Scottish roots, visit www.talkingscot.com.

Mailing lists are another great place for social networking, chatting online to other like-minded people who share your interests, and gaining research tips. Mailing lists are also subject-specific, but work differently to forums in that you sign up to join a group of people who share the same research interest, and you all receive regular updates by e-mail that let you know what's been posted on the mailing list by other members of the group. This ensures you don't miss a conversation thread that may be really interesting to your research. If you wish to send a message to the group you do so by posting your message to a single e-mail address that will then deliver your message to the subscribing members of that list. Rootsweb is home to an extensive list of mailing lists covering around 30,000 topics at www.rootsweb.com.

Online Directories
www.cyndislist.com

Cyndi's List is an online directory to an extensive collection of genealogy and heritage web resources sourced from all over the world. The resources are indexed alphabetically, by country and region, or by subject, to help you find the site that is best suited to your needs. If you'd like to find any online research communities and websites that are relevant to a particular subject, such as prisons, prisoners and outlaws, then you can use Cyndi's List's alphabetical subject index to find links to genealogical resources concerning that topic, including mailing lists and forums where you can contact other researchers who are interested in the same subject.

www.genuki.org.uk

Genuki is a directory to websites containing historical information for every county and most towns and parishes in the British Isles, as well as providing general information on UK and Irish genealogy. Its resources can be searched by place but also by topic. If you wanted to know where to find out more about a particular topic such as military records, Genuki lists the web resources relevant to this topic and provides links to external websites. Genuki also supports a number of newsgroups and has links to mailing lists from around the world devoted to various subjects. The various lists have the topics covered in alphabetical order and links to mailing lists for other countries.

Keeping track of research

Researching your personal heritage generates a lot of paperwork, even if you decide to keep a record of your findings on the computer or online. Piles of birth, marriage and death certificates, copies of parish registers, wills, census returns, maps and employment records will soon mount up. Organisation is key to saving you time and ensuring your research is effective – there's nothing more frustrating than being sure that you found a record a few months ago, but able to find no trace of it in your notes or copies. You should keep a master copy of your findings to date, whether it be a hand-drawn tree, a word document, a spreadsheet, or using the family history software already mentioned. Make an effort to update your master copy after every archive visit while your findings are still fresh in your mind. This way, you'll know exactly what you have, each time you go back to do further research.

If your master copy is on paper, then it will probably be impractical to take it with you on every archive visit as your research progresses and the tree takes up more space, so you'll need to make duplicates of smaller sections of the tree as a reminder of the dates, names and places you're looking for while you're in the archive. This is where it really helps to have a copy of your tree on some form of computer software, because family history packages allow you to print out smaller sections of the tree at the click of a button. If you have a laptop, then you can take your digital notes with you into the archives and update them as you go along, rather than having to write them down on paper first, then copy them up at home.

It helps to cite the source of each piece of information on your master copy so you have a record of how many documents provide evidence to back up each detail in your tree. This will also remind you how reliable your facts are, and where more work should be done. It's equally important if the origin of your information has come from another user via a genealogical website or from a member of the family in an interview, that you make a note of this so that you're reminded that piece of data may need verifying with original sources. Keeping the names and contact details of any researchers or relatives that help you out is always a good plan, so you can get in touch with whoever provided the information if you struggle to find the evidence you need.

While you should update your research notes regularly and weed out any old irrelevant information, try to hold on to former versions that can still be referred to in case any mistakes are found in the future – your old notes may reveal where you went wrong. Making a note of the records that you've searched even if nothing was found is a good idea, as your project could span many months, or even years, so you won't always remember what you've looked at and what you haven't. You might decide to keep a research diary so you have a record of all the archival visits you've made, what you searched for on each trip and what you found.

In tandem with keeping an up-to-date master copy of your notes, you should establish a method of filing all your document copies that makes it easy to locate a record when you need to find it, and make sure you're disciplined and stick to whatever method you decide upon! Otherwise you run the risk of losing loose bits of paperwork and may need to return to the archives to get duplicate copies. Filing your original copies away after the information they contain has been added to the master copy of your research notes also keeps them in good condition. Some people choose to keep the records pertaining to one branch of the family together, putting the documents in each family file in chronological order. You might want to keep different types of records separate, perhaps having a folder for parish register entries kept in chronological order, and a folder for all your wills kept in alphabetical order.

You don't have to clutter your house with boxes of paper photocopies if you have the facility to make digital copies of all your original documentation using a scanner or digital camera. Most archives now allow digital cameras into the reading rooms, so it's possible to save yourself the cost of paying for black and white photocopies by taking colour digital copies of the originals instead, but always check with the archivist first. Then it's easy to arrange these into folders on the computer and keep them on a CD. If you've uploaded your research notes into a family history software package you may decide to attach digital copies of all your documents to the relevant individuals in your computerised tree so they can be easily found. Filing your research in this way digitally or online is a great way to save space and time, as information can be retrieved instantly, but it's not infallible – most computers have a relatively short lifespan and are susceptible to viruses, so make sure you back up your work regularly and keep several copies so you don't lose years of hard work if something does go wrong. Either way, it's important you make and retain copies of all the documents you find so that you can prove the accuracy of your research, and have the fruits of your findings for the rest of the family and future generations to read. After all, it's the original historical material you find in the archives that will really bring the people who make up your personal heritage to life.

Chapter Three

WHERE TO FIND THE BASIC SOURCES

Once you've gathered all the background names, dates and stories known about the various branches of your family tree from your relatives, and all the information you've gleaned has been organised into a family tree, you should be able to see which areas of your research you need to concentrate on. Your first family tree should help you to establish a research plan, but first you need to learn about the types of records that are available to help you discover more about your personal heritage, and where you can find them. When you've got a good understanding of the basic sources, it'll be easier to move forward and establish some goals for your research. Nevertheless, since you've told relatives about your project you've doubtless heard about some family tales you'd like to get to the bottom of, so write those down and bear them in mind as you read about the main archives and their holdings in the chapters to come.

Throughout your project you should be creating a paper trail to back up your findings. Archival research is much like the work of a detective – just as the prosecution in a trial wouldn't be successful without substantial evidence, so every detail in your family tree should be supported with as many reliable sources as possible. There's always the danger that if one piece of information (such as a place of birth) is assumed to be correct without any proof, it could lead to you following an incorrect family in earlier documents. The key to ensuring that your research is accurate is to cross-reference everything with at least two different documents where possible. This includes the data you've got from your initial investigations at home, and may mean ordering duplicate birth and marriage certificates where these haven't survived. I'll shortly take a look at the main sources you'll need to use to verify your family tree and work even further back.

The Victorians started recording information about our ancestors at a level that had been inconceivable before. Subsequently we have a wealth of sources to help us discover all about our forebears, from where and when they were born, how many siblings they had, and when they married, to how many children they had, where they lived, what they did for a living, when and how they died. Civil registration certificates recording births, marriages and deaths from 1837 are the major building blocks used by historical researchers to trace a family line in England and Wales back to the beginning of the nineteenth century. Civil registration began in Scotland in 1855 and in Ireland in 1864, but research in these countries follows the same basic principles. Information found in civil registration certificates needs to be compared and used in conjunction with the evidence in census returns, which are available every ten years between 1841 and 1911, and wills that can be found right through to the twenty-first century yet stretch back to the medieval period. To find your ancestors prior to 1837, church and ecclesiastical records such as parish registers can be consulted to trace baptisms, marriages and burials.

The records fit together like a jigsaw to create your tree – as you methodically work your way back through time, finding as many of these records as possible for each person in your direct line, you'll find new clues to help you locate the next piece of information. Don't treat any of the documents you find in isolation – keep checking back over what you've already found and remember how you have reached the point you're at now. Every document you unearth should give names, places, dates and occupations to add to your tree or confirm what you've already been told. Compare as many records as possible to ensure all these details tally up and contain identical, if not very similar, data for each person. Only then can you be sure that you're tracing the correct line of ancestors.

When the basic information in your ancestral lineage has been proven and you've got some background detail regarding the occupations and places that compose your personal heritage, you can consult more complicated records and do some in-depth research to inject some colour into the data provided by the basic sources. There's a surprising amount of historical material that's survived from employers and local communities, such as land ownership documents, workhouse records and Armed Forces service records, which have been deposited in archives across the country. First we'll take a look at how the administrative history of the United Kingdom will shape your research, along with some of the major repositories you'll need to consult throughout the course of your personal heritage project, and then analyse the records they hold in more detail.

Administrative districts

Where They Lived: The United Kingdom
Historic changes in administrative boundaries affect where records are kept, how they are arranged and what types of records survive, so researchers need to keep these in mind when looking for documents. Today, the United Kingdom is divided into the major administrative regions of England, Wales, Scotland and Northern Ireland, but the administrative geography of each region has changed several times. Great Britain was formed in 1707 with the Union of Scotland, England and Wales. In 1801 Ireland joined the union to create the United Kingdom of Britain and Ireland, but a major change occurred in 1922 with the creation of the Republic of Ireland and Northern Ireland. Only the six counties in Northern Ireland remained under the administration of the United Kingdom after 1922. England was the central point of administration for the United Kingdom, therefore some Irish and Scottish records will be found in English repositories, while each territory also maintains its own central archive.

Counties have defined the major administrative boundaries in England since the Normans, in Wales since the sixteenth century, in Scotland since the twelfth century, and in Ireland since the nineteenth century, though the county boundaries have not remained the same. In England and Wales the Ancient Counties had sub-divisions known as Hundreds, Divisions and Wards that were used in census enumeration up until 1851. In 1889 a new system of Administrative Counties was established in England and Wales to replace the Ancient County boundaries, with sub-districts known as Municipal Boroughs, and Urban and Rural Districts, which were governed by County Councils. This new system created ten more counties, bringing the number up to sixty-two. By 1965 the total number had decreased to fifty-eight, at which time the boundaries of Greater London were established. Each county has at least one County Record Office where records relating to the history of the county are deposited. Therefore when looking for records relating to towns that are now in Greater London but before 1965 were deemed to be in Essex, Kent, Hertfordshire, Surrey or Middlesex, you may need to consult more than one County Record Office. The Administrative County boundaries were abolished in 1974 and replaced by six Metropolitan Counties and thirty-nine Non-Metropolitan Counties.

English and Welsh counties have been sub-divided into many different administrative units in the past, the most important of which for family historians include parishes (civil and ecclesiastical), manors, Poor Law Unions, Parliamentary constituencies and civil registration districts. Many of these administrative sub-divisions have overlapping boundaries. The smallest types of administrative units relevant to most family historians are parish boundaries. The Poor Law Union boundaries of England and Wales replaced the system of Gilbert Unions, which had grouped together several parishes that maintained their poor in one workhouse. The Poor Law Unions were used to form civil registration district boundaries in the nineteenth century, which were also used when compiling the census from 1841 to 1911, after which point census enumerators used local government districts. The Poor Law Unions were abolished in 1930 and replaced by the Administrative County Councils.

Local history societies have published pamphlets explaining how the counties have been administered at different points in time. There are publications that detail various types of boundaries across the British Isles. *The Phillimore Atlas and Index of Parish Registers* by Cecil R. Humphery-Smith has maps for the counties of England, Wales and Scotland showing the parish boundaries and the dates these were established, along with an index of parishes and the civil registration districts they came under after 1837. There are also maps of England and Wales published by the Institute of Heraldic and Genealogical Studies showing where the registration district boundaries were for the periods 1837–51, 1852–1946, and 1946–65.

In the seventeenth century, Scotland was divided into Counties and Burghs, which were ancient urban settlements given trading privileges by the Crown. There were Burghs of Barony granted by the Crown to some landowners, Royal Burghs that were mainly sea ports, and Police Burghs that adopted a town council to take control of policing, paving, lighting and cleaning. The number of Burghs increased over time and their boundaries moved. Separate valuation rolls and electoral rolls were compiled for Royal Burghs and Police Burghs until 1975, so burgh boundaries are important for tracing Scottish records. Burghs also produced court books, guild records, registers of deeds, financial accounts and records of Burgh institutions such as schools and libraries. 'County Landwards' and 'Parish Landwards' were the areas of land within a county or parish that did not fall within a Burgh. In 1975 Burghs were replaced by district councils, and then by local authorities in 1996.

Key Archive Locations

Technically, a record office or repository is where collections of original documents, known as an archive, are stored and preserved for the benefit of the public and for future generations; but most people refer to these places of deposit for historic manuscripts as 'the archives'. There are hundreds of archives across the United Kingdom where anyone can look at original material for research purposes free of charge. Each territory within the UK has a main repository for the records of central Government and public bodies. In addition to the principal repositories described in the following pages, there are hundreds of smaller archives dedicated to conserving documents of special importance to the history of the local area. Every county has at least one main archive known as the County Record Office (CRO) where records of local government, family estates and companies are held, and some large towns or regions also have a Municipal Archive or Local Studies Library where further material might be found, such as rate books, trade directories and maps. In addition to the secondary resources one would expect to find in a local library, such as local history books and biographies for local dignitaries, a lot also hold contemporary sources including newspapers, electoral lists and deposited research notes. Aside from government-funded archives, many universities, museums, large companies, institutions and family estates have their own archives with manuscript collections, which can be accessed by members of the public for specialist research purposes.

The archives you need to use will depend largely on the areas your ancestors came from and what they did; however, the major archives described here will be useful for some aspects of your research regardless of the places you're researching. You'll more than certainly need to visit more than one archive, so after the summary of the main repositories you'll find some general guidelines on how to work in archives, which can be applied to whichever institution you visit.

The National Archives
www.nationalarchives.gov.uk

The National Archives (TNA), based at Kew in West London and formerly known as the Public Record Office (PRO), is the main repository for the records created by central Government departments in England and Wales and the United Kingdom, but its collections also cover records from all over the British Isles, the British Empire and the countries of the Commonwealth. Its collections are varied in content and date from the Domesday-book right up to the most recent Government records. Government departments created a wealth of administration concerning ordinary individuals, so if your ancestor was a railway worker, applied for British citizenship, was a convict transported to the colonies or spent time in a debtors' prison, you may be able to find out more fascinating detail about their lives from the records kept at Kew.

TNA has a large range of material covering occupations in the Army, Royal Air Force, Royal and Merchant Navy, Coastguard, Metropolitan Police, Railway, Customs and Excise and Civil Service, some of which include individual service histories for recruits. It also stores many trial and court records, prison records, bankruptcy cases, information about dissolved companies, some surviving divorce case files, passenger lists for immigrants and emigrants and land records. In 2008 the Family Records Centre for England and Wales closed down and microfiche indexes to births, marriages, deaths and duplicates of other genealogical indexes such as probate records, plus microfilm copies of the census, were transferred to TNA for safe-keeping. Digital images of civil registration indexes and census returns are now available online, but can be accessed for free when using on-site computer terminals at TNA.

The collections at TNA will be analysed in more detail in chapters to come, but there are also subject Research Guides on The National Archives website explaining how to find the records you're looking for. The National Archives online Catalogue contains a brief description of every single one of the 10 million documents held there, and can be searched by keyword. Each document has a unique reference, which is needed to order up the original copy. The records have been arranged in the Catalogue according to the Government department from which they originated; therefore the first part of the document reference is the departmental code to which the record belongs. For example, all records pertaining to the Foreign Office have a reference with the prefix FO.

The online Catalogue has its limitations, as the search engine can only locate words in the brief document summary. This means if the word you're looking for doesn't feature in the document description, the record won't be found using the online Catalogue. You'll need to use research guides provided by

TNA and the subject advice found later in this book to help you locate hidden records. Some of the most popular documents at TNA are gradually being digitised and indexed by name so people can access them online from home for a small fee (or free of charge when using TNA computers on-site). First World War British Prisoner of War interviews, Victorian Prisoners' Photographs, Death Duty Registers, First World War Campaign Medals, Second World War Seamen's Medals and Alien Registration Cards are among the many records already available to download on the Documents Online pages.

British Library
www.bl.uk

The British Library, in St. Pancras, London, has a copy of almost every book, journal and pamphlet ever published in England and Wales, and has a large manuscript collection. While most researchers will not need to visit the British Library until their project is in its advanced stages, the records of the India Office and the East India Company at the British Library will be needed by researchers tracing British families in India. The British Library is a good place to find published transcriptions of parish registers, lists of society and institutional members, directories or occupational registers, as well as other specialist guides for tracing specific aspects of your personal heritage. It has duplicates of historical electoral registers from around the country, and a large collection of maps and plans covering Britain and the rest of the world. The map collection and local history publications make it worth visiting for local history research. If you don't live near London, there is a Boston Spa Reading Room near Wetherby in West Yorkshire where over 7 million records belonging to the British Library can be viewed.

The British Library's newspaper collection is located in Colindale, North London, where an enormous number of regional and national historical newspapers dating back to the earliest publications can be browsed. Many of these and additional local papers are also available in local study centres, but the archive in Colindale is a central repository where media resources from all over the country can be consulted in one place. A digitisation project is gradually making some of the major historical papers available to search by keyword and date online, and free access is provided on computers at both the reading rooms in St. Pancras and Colindale. The digitisation project means that the original newspaper collection will eventually be transferred to the reading rooms at St. Pancras and the Colindale branch will be closed down. The British Library's newspaper titles and published sources can be searched by keyword using the Integrated Catalogue on the website, which is also host to a variety of more specialist online catalogues providing references needed for ordering the material at the British Library.

National Library of Wales (Llyfrgell Genedlaethol Cymru)
www.llgc.org.uk

The National Library of Wales (NLW) in Aberystwyth, west Wales, has a large collection of material for researchers tracing Welsh roots, including newspapers, maps, books, manuscripts, pictures, photographs, archives and electronic resources. The NLW has begun a digitisation project and its electronic records, many of which are for genealogical and local history research, are free to view on the website. There are various types of online search engines available from the website to search the NLW collections. Indexes to criminal records, wills, marriage bonds, photographs and maps can be found on the Family History and Digital Mirror pages, and the 4 million records comprising the library collection can be searched by keyword on the Library Catalogue.

Scottish Record Offices
Scotland, like England and Wales, has a local record office for each county that preserves historical records for its jurisdiction and records of local government. The main central archive for Scottish records is The National Archives of Scotland (www.nas.gov.uk) or NAS, based in Edinburgh, which keeps records created by the Scottish Government, private records created by courts, businesses, estates and ecclesiastical material. The majority of the NAS Catalogue can be accessed online using a keyword search engine. Some documents for the Scottish are held at The National Archives in Kew including Army, Navy and Air Force service records after the Union of Scotland and England in 1707, ship passenger lists from 1890 and immigration papers. The National Library of Scotland (www.nls.uk) or NLS, also located in Edinburgh, holds legal deposits, manuscripts, maps and Scottish newspapers. Some maps have been digitised on the website, and some of its catalogues can be searched online. The General Register Office for Scotland keeps family history records, including civil registration indexes and census

returns. The records can be accessed at the ScotlandsPeople Centre in General Register House, Edinburgh (www.scotlandspeoplehub.gov.uk).

Irish Record Offices
The central repository for the majority of Northern Irish records is The Public Record Office of Northern Ireland (www.proni.gov.uk) or PRONI, in Belfast, where the records of Government departments, the courts, local authorities, non-departmental public bodies and private depositors are held. The central repository for documents relating to the rest of Ireland is the National Archives of Ireland (www.nationalarchives.ie) or the NAI, in Dublin. In 1922, when Northern Ireland and the Republic of Ireland were created as separate entities, some records for the northern counties formerly held in Dublin were transferred to Belfast. However, some records relevant to Northern Ireland that pre-date 1922 may still be found in Dublin, and some Irish records are also kept at The National Archives in London, including records of the Royal Irish Constabulary prior to 1922 and First World War Army attestation papers. Fewer records have survived for Ireland than for other areas of the United Kingdom because of the island's turbulent history, and a large number of records dating back to the thirteenth century were destroyed by fire at the Four Courts during the Civil War in 1922, exacerbating the problem for researchers.

Family History Library
www.familysearch.org

The Family History Library was established in 1894 by the Church of Jesus Christ of Latter-Day Saints in Salt Lake City, Utah, USA to gather genealogical records from around the world, and is now one of the largest libraries of its kind holding millions of microfilmed and microfiche parish, civil registration, census and other genealogical records, books, periodicals and electronic resources. The library has set up thousands of Family History Centres worldwide that hold duplicates of most of the microfilm and microfiche available at the Family History Library in Utah. There are nearly eighty Family History Centres in England alone, and records can be ordered in from Family History Centres elsewhere. To find the one nearest to you, visit the website.

Family trees and deposited works held at the Family History Library can be searched online by surname. The Family History Library's major electronic resources are available to search online free of charge and include Ancestral Files and Pedigree Resource Files uploaded by other researchers, and the International Genealogical Index containing transcriptions from thousands of parish registers. The website is useful for researching ancestors who emigrated, because it contains a large transcribed collection of overseas records. Anything found on the website should be checked against the original records where possible, as the transcriptions and family tree files may contain inaccuracies.

Society of Genealogists
www.sog.org.uk

The Society of Genealogists' Library is located near the Barbican in London. There is a daily charge to visit and use its facilities for non-members. The library holds published pedigrees, family trees and research notes deposited by other researchers, a wealth of records from county sources including copies of parish registers and indexes, poll books, directories, local histories, the International Genealogical Index on CD-ROM, Scottish civil registration indexes and some overseas records, particularly for the British Empire. The Society's catalogue can be searched online from its website via SOGCAT, which contains descriptions of everything in the library except the Document Collections. It's best to consult SOGCAT before you pay to visit the Society of Genealogists to ensure they have material relevant to your research. There's also an online Library Index that describes some of the collections held for various areas of research, like the study of surnames, wills or overseas records.

Working in Archives
You may find that some of the archives you'll need to visit will be a long way from home, so it's important to make sure you're fully prepared before a visit so your time there isn't wasted. Contact details for most repositories in the UK can be found by using the ARCHON directory via The National Archives website at www.nationalarchives.gov.uk/archon. ARCHON contains addresses, telephone numbers, e-mail addresses, opening days and times, website links and street maps for archives all over the United Kingdom, and can be searched by place or by the name of the archive.

Planning your visit

Genealogy and local history is now so popular that some of the smaller archives get booked up quickly, so ring in advance of your visit to find out whether you need to make an appointment, otherwise you may be turned away if you show up unannounced on a busy day. The archivist will be able to explain how to use the indexes and archives when you arrive, but it's a good idea to give them a rundown of the types of documents you'll be looking for in advance of your visit, to ensure they're all stored at that archive, and so the necessary preparations can be made for you. You may have to book a microfilm reader for the day if there are limited machines available, or some of the documents you need to see may be held in off-site storage and take a few days to be transferred to the reading rooms.

Most archives require proof of ID to issue a reader's ticket to new users, so check what you'll need to take with you. Many County Record Offices have joined the CARN (County Archive Research Network) card scheme, and registering for a card at one archive provides access to all the other participating archives. You might also need to take cash with you to pay for any photocopies of records found if the archives don't have a card machine. If you have a digital camera, find out whether you're allowed to take photos of documents in the archive, and whether a camera permit needs to be bought for this. Using a digital camera is sometimes cheaper than paying for paper photocopies, depending on the archives' copying policy.

Archives are designed to preserve documents for generations to come, and everyone who uses the resources in our archives has a responsibility to ensure the material is respected and does not get damaged. Each archive has its own set of rules, which will be found printed around the reading rooms, but document handling guidelines are roughly the same across the board.

Do:

- take a pencil and notepad to make notes. Laptops are also allowed in most reading rooms.
- wear protective gloves when handling photographs or old manuscripts. These are available on request, free of charge in most archives.
- use paperweights, book supports and clear plastic map covers provided in reading rooms.

- lock your bags, coats and other belongings not required in the reading room into any lockers provided. Most archives now require personal belongings to be locked away while readers are in the archives.
- carry your research notes and pencils in a clear bag if these are provided by the archive.

Don't:

- take pens, rubbers, scissors or anything that might deface the documents into the reading rooms.
- eat or drink in the reading rooms in case anything should spill on the documents.
- put documents on the floor if there is not enough room on your desk – someone could easily tread on and damage them.
- overly touch photos or documents, or run your finger across the pages when reading, which wears the material out.

Chapter Four

USING THE BASIC SOURCES

Civil Registration

On 1 July 1837 the first official birth, marriage and death certificates were issued in England and Wales. The civil registration of births, marriages and deaths for people of all religious denominations was introduced partly so the Government could monitor population trends. Prior to this, baptisms, marriages and burials had only been recorded at the church or religious institution where the ceremony took place, and there was no central record of these. The Government therefore had no accurate statistics regarding the population before the advent of civil registration, which was important to tackle issues such as overcrowding in towns and infant mortality.

Quarterly alphabetical indexes were produced containing the names of everybody in England and Wales who was registered as having received a birth, marriage or death certificate. Duplicate copies of all the certificates ever issued can still be ordered today, and with a centralised index for the whole country these are a valuable source for genealogical researchers. Each type of certificate, which will be described in this chapter, gives different information about the individuals concerned. We'll look here at how the system worked, how it changed over time, and how to go about locating a certificate and ordering a copy.

The civil registration system

England and Wales were divided into twenty-seven registration districts in 1837, each one served by a Superintendent Registrar, which were further sub-divided into smaller districts administered by local registrars. Initially it was the responsibility of the local registrars to travel through the districts collecting information about births and deaths, so during the early stages of civil registration some births and deaths were accidentally missed out. Churches and other licensed religious places of worship sent details of all marriages that took place there directly to the Registrar General for England and Wales. The Births and Deaths Registration Act of 1874 decreed that families were responsible for registering their own births and deaths at the Registry Office closest to where the event took place, so there are far less people missing from the indexes after this date.

The local registrars forwarded the returns of births and deaths every quarter to the Superintendent Registrar, who compiled an index for the whole district. This was then sent to London to the Registrar General for all of England and Wales, so it could be incorporated into a nationwide index. The Registrar General's records are now held by the General Register Office (GRO), part of the Office for National Statistics (ONS), and once you've found a reference in the indexes a certificate can be ordered online from www.gro.gov.uk. Copies of the original returns also survive in local Registry Offices if you can't find a record in the national indexes, in instances where there may have been an error when the information was transferred across. However, in the majority of cases you should be able to find what you're looking for in the central index.

It helps to find out which registration district administered the village or town where your ancestors lived, because this will enable you to whittle down the possibilities you find in the indexes, particularly if you're looking for common names. In 1852 the registration districts were reorganised and increased to thirty-three, and another reorganisation took place in 1946, so even if your family stayed in the same place for generations the registration district that administered their births, marriages and deaths may have changed at these times.

What will the certificates tell me?

Civil registration certificates for all parts of the United Kingdom provide roughly the same type of information, although early Scottish certificates are more detailed than their English and Welsh counterparts. The certificates will be your main point of reference for working your way back through the generations of your family in the twentieth century, as the most recent census returns available for public inspection are those of 1911. Throughout the twentieth century and for most of the Victorian period you can order birth certificates to find out a child's parents' names, then work back to find the parents' marriage certificate to discover their ages and fathers' names, and use this information to locate their birth certificates so the process can be repeated again and again to get one generation further back each time. It's important to make sure you apply for full certificates rather than the cheaper shortened versions, because the shortened certificates won't contain enough information needed to build your family tree.

Birth Certificates

Birth certificates for England and Wales are useful to historical researchers because they provide the child's date and place of birth, but crucially a full certificate gives the parents' names and the mother's maiden name, helping you work back another generation. Along the top of the birth certificate will be details of the registration district and sub-district, as well as the county in which the birth was registered. Then there are several fields that the person registering the birth was required to fill in:

- *When and where born*: The exact date and place of the birth. Early registrations sometimes only give the name of the village or street, but later registrations give full addresses. If the time of the birth is also given this may indicate the child was one of twins or triplets. You can search for the siblings' births in the indexes by looking for any other children with the same surname who were registered in the same district with the same registration reference code.
- *Name, if any*: This should give the child's first and middle names, though if the parents hadn't decided on a name the birth may have been simply registered as male or female under the parents' surname.
- *Name and surname of the father*: The first names and surname of the father. It's assumed the child took the father's surname, therefore this equates also to the surname of the child. In some cases the father's name is blank, which usually means the parents were unmarried. In these instances the birth should have been registered under the mother's surname.
- *Name and maiden surname of the mother*: The mother's full married name, followed by her 'former' name. Her former name is usually her maiden name, although if she was married before then her previous married surname may also be given. This information is needed in order to trace the maternal line back.

- *Rank and profession/Occupation of father*: This tells you what job the father did at the time the child was born, and is useful for cross-referencing with any other information you find about him so you can be sure you've got the right person. It's also useful to establish how his career progressed, for example his rank may have changed from certificate to certificate, for when you look for employment records. If the father's name is blank on the child's birth certificate then this section will also be blank.
- *Signature, description and residence of informant*: This is the name of the person who registered the birth, their relationship to the child and their address. The informant was usually a parent, so if the address they give is the same as the place the child was born then you'll know that child was born at home. If the name is marked with an X this means the informant could not write.
- *When registered*: The date the informant went to the Registry Office to register the child's birth. This could be up to six weeks after the birth occurred, so you may find the birth was registered in the quarter after the child's date of birth.
- *Signature of registrar*: This is the name of the local registrar who registered the birth.
- *Name entered after registration*: If the child's name was later changed, the birth may be registered under both the first and the new name, and details of the change would be entered in this column. Equally, if the child was later adopted the date of the Adoption Order may be given here, though the child's new name will not be given for identity protection reasons.

Marriage Certificates

Marriage certificates give details of the bride and groom and where and when the marriage took place. The marriage will also be recorded in the parish register of the church or place of worship where the ceremony was held, but there isn't a centralised index to these. Once you've found the birth certificate of a child, providing you with the parents' names and the mother's maiden name, your next step should be to search for the parents' marriage. The marriage certificate will give you the bride and groom's fathers' names and help you work back yet another generation. Marriage certificates contain the name of the church, parish and county where the ceremony took place along the top, followed by the information below:

- *When married*: The date the marriage occurred.
- *Name and surname*: The full names of both the groom and bride.
- *Age*: The ages of the groom and bride should be given, although you may come across entries that say 'full age', which means they were over 21, or 'minor', meaning under the age of 21. This may make it more difficult to find birth entries for these people, although evidence in census returns can help.
- *Condition*: This column states whether the groom was a bachelor (unmarried), widower or divorcee, and whether the bride was a spinster (unmarried), widow or divorcee.
- *Rank or profession*: The occupation of each party will be given here, though until the twentieth century the bride's occupation (if she had one) was rarely given.
- *Residence at the time of marriage*: The addresses of the groom and bride are given here. It used to be traditional to marry in the bride's parish; however, the groom had to have also been living in the parish for at least a month before the wedding, so his may be a temporary address.
- *Father's name and surname*: The fathers of the groom and bride are usually listed here. If this column is blank for one party it may mean the bride or groom were illegitimate, and either may not have known who their father was or didn't want to disclose his name. Alternatively the father may have died, though it is more usual if this is the case for '(deceased)' to be written next to his name.
- *Rank or profession of father*: The fathers' occupations or social status should be given here. Those of the upper class might give their rank as gentleman, though it was possible to overexaggerate one's status. If the father had died then 'deceased' may be given in this column.
- *Type of marriage*: The type of religious ceremony through which the marriage was performed is given underneath the details of the bride and groom, which is useful for finding out whether your ancestors were Catholic, Methodists, Quakers or Jewish, for example. It will also say whether the marriage was condoned by licence or by banns. Marriages performed after banns means that the wedding was announced in the parish for three consecutive weeks before it took place to ensure nobody had a reason to object to the marriage (for example if one party was married already and their spouse was still living). A groom might seek a licence instead if the couple wanted to marry outside of their home parishes, or did not want the publicity of banns being read.

- *Signatures of two witnesses*: At least two people are required to witness the ceremony. If the witnesses had the same surnames as either the bride or groom you can assume they were probably related (perhaps a sibling) and use this as another clue to cross-reference with information in other documents you find. Next to the witnesses' signatures are also the bride and groom's signatures – if any of these are marked with an X it means that person could not write.

Death Certificates

It's not essential to order death certificates for people in your family tree in order to trace your lineage; however, they can be useful for cross-referencing information at the start of civil registration when fewer records are available, or if you're researching a very common name and need as much information as possible to be certain you're tracing the right line. You might be keen to order a death certificate to clear up a family mystery, or to find out why one of your ancestors died young. Death certificates can open up new lines of enquiry, as they indicate whether an inquest was held, or the cause of death can tell you whether the person died in unusual circumstances, which would give you cause to check local newspapers to see if further details were reported. However, death certificates don't contain as much useful data as birth and marriage certificates for tracing your heritage back another generation, as will be seen from the information they contain:

- The registration district, sub-district and county where the death was registered are given along the top.
- *When and where died*: The date the person died and the location. In some instances this may give you a fresh line of enquiry: for example, if your ancestor died in a workhouse then the name of the institution will be given and you can find out whether any workhouse records about their admittance and burial survive in a local record office. If an address is given, this is not necessarily where the deceased person lived, because they may have died while out visiting people.
- *Name and surname*: The full name of the deceased is given here.
- *Sex*: Whether the deceased was male or female.
- *Age*: The age of the deceased person is useful to work back from if you've been unable to find any other information for them – if they died shortly after the start of civil registration but before census returns are available, then you'll be able to use the age on the death certificate to start searching

for a baptism in parish registers. However, ages on death certificates are more prone to be inaccurate than on other documents, because proof of birth was not required and the person who registered the death may not have been certain how old the deceased was.

- *Occupation*: This is helpful for cross-referencing with other data you've found, so you can be sure you've got the right person. It will also help you to trace employment records. Women's death certificates usually give their marital status and the name of their husband and his profession if they were married, so again you'll know whether you've found the right woman.
- *Cause of death*: Most early death certificates give quite vague descriptions for the cause of death compared to modern certificates that provide a medical breakdown – for example, 'natural decay' simply indicates the person died of old age, rather than specifying their final illness. Meanings of some antiquated terms for illnesses we may not recognise now can be found by looking up a specialist online dictionary such as www.antiquusmorbus.com: for example, consumption was the commonly used name for tuberculosis in the nineteenth century. The name of a doctor who confirmed the cause of death may also be given after 1874, as it became compulsory to have a doctor's certificate before a death certificate could be issued.
- *Signature, description and residence of the informant*: An informant is usually a person who was present at the death, most commonly a family member, which is useful for cross-referencing information as their relationship to the deceased person is given. If an inquest was held then the Coroner will be listed as the informant and the date of the inquest should be given here, which would help you locate a corresponding newspaper report and find out whether the Coroner's full report survives at the local record office.
- *When registered*: The death should have been registered no more than five days after the event: however, if it was registered by a Coroner there may have been a significant delay.
- *Signature of registrar*: The signature of the local registrar who registered the death.

How do I find a certificate?

To order a certificate you first of all need to find the name you're looking for in the General Register Office index. The index will provide you with a reference code needed to order a copy of the full certificate from the GRO. Copies of the centralised birth, marriage and death indexes for England and

Wales are available to search free of charge in many locations, including on microfiche at The National Archives, in most central libraries and local studies centres, and via the local indexes held by Register Offices. The complete collection from July 1837 has now been digitised and is also available to search online via a number of subscription websites, including Ancestry (www.ancestry.co.uk), Find My Past (www.findmypast.com), Family Relatives (www.familyrelatives.com), The Genealogist (www.thegenealogist.co.uk) and BMD Index (www.bmdindex.co.uk). Free BMD (www.freebmd.org.uk) is another website set up by volunteers, which is completely free to use and contains partial transcriptions of the indexes from 1837 up to around 1925.

There are three separate indexes for the births, marriages and deaths in England and Wales. The original indexes available on microfiche at archives and libraries are arranged chronologically, with each year split into quarters up until 1984 when there is just one index for each year. The index for each quarter (or year after 1984) is then arranged alphabetically by surname. Therefore to search for a name you may need to look through several quarters if you're not sure exactly when the event took place. The quarters are divided as follows:

March quarter – covers January, February and March
June quarter – covers April, May and June
September quarter – covers July, August and September
December quarter – covers October, November and December

Remember that you won't always find an entry in the quarter that covers the date of the event. For example, a child's date of birth may have been 30 November 1871, but the family had six weeks to register the birth and did not do so until January 1872, therefore the birth would be located in the indexes in the March quarter of 1872 rather than the December quarter of 1871.

It's possible to locate an entry in the indexes, even if you have no idea on what date it happened. Simply use logic to work out a time frame for your search, so if you've found the birth certificate for a child in January 1915 you can work backwards from that date in the marriage indexes searching under the parents' names until you find a match for them there. This may mean a search of ten or more years, but once you've got the hang of the indexes your searches will speed up. A search over a large space of time will probably throw up more than one possibility in the indexes, particularly if you're looking for common names, so you'll need to write a list of the most likely ones you find and start with ordering the most likely based on geographic location and middle names or initials if the couple have any.

Some of the birth, marriage and death indexes available online are organised in exactly the same way as the microfiche copies: they've simply been digitised and you need to browse through the scanned pages until you find the entry you're looking for (such as at BMD Index). The online indexes are quicker to use than the microfiche copies because the search engine will automatically find the pages you need to search for a particular surname.

Other sites have transcribed parts of the indexes so a database can search for name, date and registration district matches within the indexes, saving you the time of scrolling through the pages quarter-by-quarter (this is true of all the records on Free BMD). It should be remembered that any errors made in the indexes (such as a name spelled slightly differently) won't always be picked up by a transcription database, so a more thorough search of the digitised indexes is recommended to ensure you find all the possibilities.

To order any type of certificate you need to know which year and quarter the event was registered, the name it was registered under (either the bride or groom in the case of a marriage certificate, which would have been registered under both names), the registration district where it was registered, and the volume and page number references that the GRO need to be able to identify the correct certificate. In some cases the indexes provide more information than this, but these are the basic details that are essential to have before a certificate can be ordered. The contents of the birth, marriage and death indexes for England and Wales, and how to use them, are described more fully below.

Birth Indexes
To begin a search of the birth indexes you need to know roughly when (and preferably where) the child was born, as well as the name they were registered with. The person's age might be found on their marriage certificate, death certificate or on a census return or employment record, and the latter two should give details of where the birth might be registered. This will give you a starting point for your search if you don't already know the date of birth.

The quarterly birth indexes from September quarter 1837 until June quarter 1911 provide the following information:

- Surname, followed by the child's first name (in alphabetical order)
- Any births registered without a first name will be found at the end of the list for each surname, denoted by 'male' or 'female'
- The registration district where the birth was registered
- A volume and page number.

The indexes from September quarter 1911 onwards also show the mother's maiden name, making it much easier to identify the correct entry in the indexes, though you don't need to know the mother's maiden name to order the certificate. The addition of the mother's maiden name also makes it possible to trace your family tree forward from marriages found from 1910 onwards. If you find a marriage after this date you can search from the date of the marriage onwards for the births of any children with the groom's surname who have the same mother's maiden name as the bride's former surname.

When you've found the correct entry in the birth indexes, you need to make a note of the following details from the index to be able to order a copy of the certificate from the GRO:

- The year and quarter in which the birth was registered
- The first name and surname of the child
- The registration district in which the birth was registered
- The volume and page number of the entry.

Marriage Indexes

A marriage search will usually commence once you've located the birth of a child from the marriage, whose birth certificate will (usually) provide you with both parents' names and the mother's maiden surname. The parents' marriage can then be searched from the date their child was born back through time. Information in census returns can help to narrow down the search, if you make a note of the age of their eldest child and work backwards from the year they were born. A census return or employment record may give the age of one of the parties to the marriage, so you can limit the year range of the search even further based on the earliest possible year they could have married, depending on what the age of consent was at that time. The age of consent in England and Wales was 14 for boys and 12 for girls as long as they also had parental consent, until 1929 when it rose to 16. The age for marriage without parental consent was 21 until 1969 when it was reduced to 18.

Marriage indexes up until March quarter 1912 provide the following information for the name the search was conducted under:

- Surname, followed by first name
- The registration district in which the marriage took place
- The volume and page number.

If you conduct the marriage search under both the bride and groom's names, you'll know you've found the right people if they are registered in the same year and quarter, and have matching registration districts, volume and page numbers. Alternatively, there are websites with databases of transcribed index entries that can cross-reference transcriptions to find names before March quarter 1912 that have matching marriage references (such as Free BMD). The marriage indexes from March quarter 1912 onwards provide the surname of each person's spouse, making it far easier to spot the correct entry.

To order a copy of a marriage certificate, make a note of the following information from the index:

- The year and quarter in which the marriage was registered.
- The full name of at least one of the people on the marriage certificate. If you know only the bride's first name and surname, or only the groom's full name, this will be sufficient.
- The registration district.
- The volume and page number of the entry.

Death Indexes

As with the other searches, you'll need to have a rough idea of when a person died to begin a search for their death certificate. This may be deduced from two consecutive census returns if the person is living on the earliest return, but by the following census return a decade later their spouse is described as widowed. Equally, if a father is described as deceased on their child's marriage certificate then you'll know they died sometime between the child being born and the date of the marriage. This gives some parameters for your search, but to narrow down the results it also helps to know roughly where they were living and might have died, and also their age if you're conducting a search after 1866.

The death indexes from September quarter 1837 until December quarter 1865 provide the following details:

- Surname, followed by the first name of the person who died
- The registration district in which the death was registered
- The volume and page number.

The death indexes between March quarter 1866 and March quarter 1969 also give the age of the person who died, making it much easier to identify the correct entry. After June quarter 1969 the death indexes are more detailed still, showing the date of birth of the person who has died rather than just their age. This can be a quick way of finding a relative's birth if you know when they died in the last thirty-two years.

To order a copy of a death certificate from the GRO make a note of the following information from the index:

- The year and quarter in which the death was registered
- The first names and surname of the person who died
- The age at death or date of birth if given, but this is not essential
- The registration district
- The volume and page number of the entry.

How do I order a certificate?

Once you've found the entry you're looking for in the indexes, you can order the full certificate either online by visiting the GRO website at www.gro.gov.uk and completing an online application form with your card details, over the phone (0845 603 7788) or by post. Certificates ordered from the GRO website will be posted to you after three working days of receiving the order at a cost of £7 per certificate. Alternatively, there's a 24-hour processing service that costs £23. To order a certificate by post you need to either collect a form from your local central library or Registry Office, telephone the number above and ask for the form to be posted to you, or send an e-mail to certificate.services@ons.gov.uk requesting a birth, marriage or death ordering form to be posted to you. Fill the form in and return it to GRO, PO Box 2, Southport, Merseyside, PR8 2JD with a cheque, postal order, or your credit card details filled out for the correct payment.

Ensure you complete the form for a full copy of the certificate and not a short copy, as the latter will give you very limited information. There are boxes on the form for you to enter the information you've noted down from the indexes, but you may also choose to include checking points if you know of any extra information the correct certificate should contain, such as a father's name on a birth certificate. If the certificate you've ordered from the indexes does not correspond with the checking points you've put on your order form, the Office for National Statistics will not produce a certificate and will give you a £4 refund, so you need to be sure that your checking points are absolutely correct before putting any on the form.

Civil registration in Scotland

Civil registration began in Scotland on 1 January 1855, and was compulsory for all religious denominations as soon as it was introduced. The General Register Office for Scotland (GROS) Statutory Registers are more detailed than the English and Welsh GRO certificates, particularly for the first year of registration when a lot of detail was asked of the informants. The original indexes can be accessed at New Register House in Edinburgh; however, www.scotlandspeople.gov.uk is the official Government website that holds genealogical data for Scotland. It contains online indexes and images of the Scottish GRO Statutory Registers for births from 1855 until 2006, for marriages from 1855 until 1933 and for deaths from 1855 until 2006, and digital images of paper records from New Register House are continually uploaded. The indexing system works in a similar way to the English and Welsh GRO, and certificates can be ordered from the Scotland's People website once the correct entries have been located in the index.

Civil registration in Northern Ireland

The civil registration of births, marriages and deaths for all religious denominations began in Ireland on 1 January 1864, although the registration of non-Roman Catholic marriages started on 1 April 1845. The age of consent for marriage was 14 for boys and 12 for girls as long as they also had parental consent, until 1975 when it rose to 16. Records from 1845 to 1921 for the whole of Ireland, and Northern Irish records since 1922, are held at the General Register Office (GRONI) in Belfast and can be consulted using computer terminals in the offices on Chichester Street (see www.groni.gov.uk).

The indexes for 1845 to 1958 have been transcribed by the Church of Jesus Christ of Latter-Day Saints (LDS), which can be searched via the Family Search website at http://pilot.familysearch.org/recordsearch. You'll need to locate the Irish indexes by selecting European records from the drop-down list and scrolling down to find the records for Ireland. Microfilm copies of some of the Irish indexes can be consulted at your local LDS Family History Centre (see www.familysearch.org to find your nearest one), or alternatively each county in Ireland has a local Heritage Centre that offers fee-paid search services. Many of the Heritage Centres, including Derry, have database transcriptions of their local registers. The Irish birth and marriage indexes are not as detailed as those for England, Wales and Scotland (that is to say they don't provide mothers' maiden names or spouses' names), but the certificates contain much the same information. Once an entry has been found in the indexes you can order a certificate from the General Register Office of Northern Ireland for £6 either online, in person from the GRO, or by telephone, post or fax. Contact GRONI on +44 (0)28 9025 2000 to find out more.

Census Returns

Census returns are fantastically informative sources for personal heritage researchers, the only drawback being that you need to trace your family back to 1911 before you can begin using them. Census returns provide a snapshot of the population on a single night, showing everybody in each household and the relationships between them. You can find out your ancestors' ages, where they were born, where they lived, whether they had a disability, their family set-up, and guesses can be made as to their social status based on their professions and the number of servants they employed. The information found in census returns will lead you to a wide variety of other sources, as will be explained in later chapters. Using census returns in conjunction with civil registration indexes you can trace your family tree right back to the beginning of the nineteenth century, as the available census spans eighty years, so you should find up to three or four generations in your tree.

The first census of the English and Welsh population was taken in 1801 to find out how many men could be conscripted into the Army should Napoleon invade the British Isles. Since then a census has been taken once every decade; however, the returns up until 1841 didn't record names, although some records for 1821 and 1831 note the name of the head of the household – local archives can provide information where such data survives, since they have usually been transcribed by Family History Societies or other groups. The census returns from 1841 onwards gradually became more detailed as the State wanted to learn more about the population. The 1841 census was the first to provide the names and ages of everybody in each household, and the 1851 census was even more detailed, with further questions asked of each household every decade. There is a 100-year closure rule on census returns; however, the 1911 census has been opened to the public early following a successful appeal under the Freedom of Information Act. This means researchers are now able to access the eight census returns for England and Wales taken every decade between 1841 and 1911. Collecting census returns became the responsibility of the General Register Office (GRO) in 1840, and all the returns for England and Wales have been deposited at The National Archives in Kew.

Understanding the census returns

The census returns were all taken on a Sunday night on the following dates:

- 6 June 1841
- 30 March 1851
- 7 April 1861
- 2 April 1871
- 3 April 1881
- 5 April 1891
- 31 March 1901
- 2 April 1911

A few days before the census return was taken, the census enumerator delivered the forms, or schedules, that needed filling in by each household in his enumeration district. On the night the census was due to be taken, every householder in the country was supposed to fill in the schedules detailing who was in the house at that time, their relationship to the head of the household (from 1851), and their biographical information. This included any visitors, lodgers or servants, so people weren't always recorded at their home address. The enumerator sometimes had to help people fill in their forms during the nineteenth century when illiteracy was widespread, which may account for some errors (such as surname spellings) found on census returns.

The enumerator collected all the household schedules the following day, the originals of which no longer survive before 1911. He transferred the household information into his enumerator's book, which was arranged street-by-street and household-by-household. Any empty houses were also noted in the enumerator's book. It's these books that we use today to find out about our ancestors. The census enumerators' books can contain errors because the information has been copied from the original schedules, but on the whole they are an invaluable source.

The returns from 1841 to 1901 are handwritten in the enumerator's handwriting, but the schedules from 1911 survive and we can see digital copies of the originals in our ancestors' own handwriting. Unfortunately the enumerators' books for 1841 were written in pencil and some are badly faded. The enumerators and statisticians who analysed the books made notes on them, which have obscured the odd word. However, some of the markings made by enumerators also help genealogists interpret the data. In particular the enumerators put a small double slash between each household living in a separate property, a useful clue when just the street or village name is given at the top of the page with no breakdown of house numbers. A single slash between groups of names indicates separate households living in the same property, such as a house converted into flats.

The enumerators' books for each year are split into registration districts based on the area covered by each enumerator. The original returns are arranged by county, then by enumeration district, and further divided into sub-districts. The census returns are now online and every name they contain has been indexed so you can find individuals easily. Prior to the creation of name indexes, you needed to know where your ancestors were living before you could search for them. Unfortunately the 1841 returns for some districts have been lost, but details of the missing books for each county can be found on the Ancestry website. All the enumerators' books contain a description of the district they cover at the start of each book, giving the road names or hamlets in the order the enumerator entered them into the book.

The 1841 enumerators' books contain the following information:

- Along the top of each page is the city, town or parish covered. Alongside each household is the street, area or house name where the family lived. House numbers were not provided in this census, and in many cases didn't exist.
- A note was made in a column whether each building was inhabited or uninhabited.
- In the houses that were inhabited, the names of all the people who had slept in the property on the night of the census were recorded in a list,

starting with the head of the household. However, the relationships between these people weren't given.

- The age and sex of each person was given in the next set of columns, though ages above 15 years were rounded down to the nearest 5 years, which is worth bearing in mind when entering ages into a website search engine.
- A column was provided for people to enter their profession, trade, employment, or whether they were of independent means. The last option was sometimes abbreviated to 'I.S.'. Other common abbreviations found in this column are F.S. for Female Servant, M.S. for Male Servant, and Ag. Lab. for Agricultural Labourer.
- There was a column where the enumerator needed to enter N (no) or Y (yes) to indicate whether each person was born in the county of the enumeration district, and the last column was filled in if anyone was born in Scotland (S), Ireland (I), or Foreign Parts (F).

Later census returns were even more detailed. The 1851 census was the first to describe how everybody in the household was related to the head. It also asked people for their marital status, their accurate age, exactly where they were born, and whether they were blind or deaf and dumb. The disabilities column was extended in 1871 to include imbecile, idiot or lunatic. From 1891 people were asked in the professions section whether they were employed or an employer, and from 1901 whether they carried out their work from home. The 1891 census for Wales and Monmouthshire also asked whether each person spoke English only, Welsh only, or both languages. 1911 is the most revealing survey yet, asking how many years every married woman had been married, how many children were born to the marriage, how many had died and how many were still living. The occupational information is still more detailed, providing the name of the company employees worked for. This increasing quest for knowledge about the population was driven by the State's desire to better understand the communities they were governing, and their usefulness to family historians is just a happy coincidence.

In many of the later census returns for each household, the family's house number, street name and village or town where they lived are given, so you can follow up the address using maps and street directories to find out if the house still exists and visit the property to take some photos. The research steps for tracing the history of ancestral homes are explained in greater detail in Section Two. You should cross-reference the address where you find your relatives living in the census returns with the addresses given on certificates you order for them, to make sure you've found the same people. The census is also useful for narrowing down searches in the civil registration indexes, as has already been explained, providing you with ages and places of birth from which to work. Find out which civil registration district covered the village or town where your ancestors are found living on the census and you'll be able to pick out the correct names from the birth, marriage and death indexes. Look out for any people described as relatives-in-law to the head of the household, because their surnames may be a clue as to the maiden name of the head's wife. You might also discover that one of your ancestors had been married previously if you find them living with stepchildren on the census. If one of your ancestors was not living at home with the rest of the family then they may have been in an institution or aboard a vessel. Special returns were filed for vessels and institutions from 1851, though these sometimes only give people's initials rather than their names to protect their identities. They are also indexed online in the same way as the normal census returns.

Accessing the census returns

The original returns for all the censuses have been deposited at The National Archives, and are available either in digital or microfilm form. The records for each census year have been allocated a document reference by The National Archives, and you'll need to understand the referencing system to be able to find a return when you're not using the online name indexes, but also for your own records when you do find a return online so the image can be found quickly again.

The Home Office administered the 1841 and 1851 censuses, so these have both been given the classification code HO 107. The 1841 census returns for parishes were grouped into hundreds, which were given piece numbers forming the next part of the document reference. The hundreds were grouped together to form an enumeration district book, and the books of five or six enumeration districts were put together and given another reference number, the book number, forming the third part of the census return document reference. Within each book a folio number was stamped on every other page, which is the fourth part of the reference, and the last part of the document reference is the exact page number where the information can be found, which is printed on every page of every book.

Example:

HO 107	1841 census
HO 107/534	1841 census for the hundred of Salford, Lancashire
HO 107/534/5	1841 census for the hundred of Salford, and book 5 for the enumeration district of Great Bolton East
HO 107/534/5 folio 5, page 18	Unique reference for page 18 of the 1841 census for Great Bolton, covering households on Cook Street

The enumeration system changed in 1851, using registration districts and sub-districts to organise the returns. This created shorter document references, as each sub-district was allocated a piece number to go after HO 107, followed by the folio and page numbers. In 1861 the census returns started to be filed under the Registrar General (series RG). The prefix for 1861 census returns is RG 9, for the 1871 census it's RG 10, for 1881 it's RG 11, and so on. The reference number after the RG code is still relevant to the sub-district as in 1851, followed by the precise folio and page number for each page of the book. The first part of the reference for each census return is displayed on a reference slip to the side or bottom of each page, and the individual folio and page numbers can be found printed at the top of the page.

All the census returns up to and including 1911 have now been digitised and can be searched by name or place online, which is by far the easiest way to access the records. Several commercial websites provide access to the censuses so you can search the indexes and scanned pages at home by subscribing to one of these genealogy sites, but most local libraries and record offices have subscribed to the Ancestry Library Edition, which is available to search for free using computer terminals in the library. The National Archives provides free access via its on-site computer terminals to the Ancestry website for searching the 1841–91 census returns, as well as 1901censusonline.com and 1911census.co.uk. However, if you'd prefer to search from the comfort of your own home, you can access transcriptions and digital images of all the censuses between 1841 and 1901 by paying for a subscription to www.ancestry.co.uk. Most other genealogy websites provide access to some parts of the census in either transcription or image form, or both. www.1901censusonline.com has the complete collection of returns for all returns between 1841 and 1901, except for the 1881 returns, and sections of the census returns for 1841–91 are being transcribed at http://freecen.rootsweb.com, which is free to use. The only website that currently provides access to the 1911 census is www.1911 census.co.uk, although credits and vouchers can be bought from www.findmypast.com that can be used on both websites. Find My Past has a large online census collection for the previous years, though this is not complete.

Each website has a unique search engine, but most have the option to search by name, age, place of birth and place of residence for the person you're looking for. There's usually a search tool for locating the digitised page of a specific reference, and address searches can be carried out for some of the censuses including the 1911 census, the 1901 census on www.1901 censusonline.com and the 1881 census at www.ancestry.co.uk. It helps to enter as little detail as possible into the search engines to get a fuller list of possibilities, and making use of the age-range options and phonetic search-finding tools are good ways of locating entries that might contain slightly different data to what you were expecting. Every website has a page explaining how to get the most out of their search engine, and tips on what could be done differently if at first you can't find your ancestor.

Various name indexes for some census returns and regions were compiled before the digitisation projects, particularly by local family history societies for returns covering their area. These will be available at the local record office, and some can be found at TNA. The 1881 census has been fully transcribed by the Church of Latter-Day Saints and these transcriptions can be searched by name at www.familysearch.org.uk. The name indexes provide the full reference number of the census return so you can track down the original page. If you can't find your ancestor's name using the online indexes, it is worth checking the old name indexes before searching the census enumerators' books for the area in which you'd expect to find them living.

Prior to the digitisation of the returns, microfilm copies had to be consulted at the archives. The entire collection of census returns for 1841 through to 1901 can still be accessed on microfilm at The National Archives, and duplicate microfilms for local regions are also kept at most County Record

Offices. You may need to consult the microfilm copies if you can't locate a name using the online indexes, which do contain errors. The microfilm copies at TNA are arranged by reference number and there are index books and finding aids in the Reading Rooms to help you locate the correct film for the place you need to search.

Missing ancestors

There are a number of reasons why you might not be able to find an ancestor using the online census returns. The data has been transferred several times from handwritten material, so there's plenty of room for human error. Firstly the original schedules were copied into the enumerators' books, then the information was transcribed into a modern database. In most cases the entry was probably wrongly transcribed and you'll just need to play around with various spellings and data entered into the search engine until you find what you're looking for.

Your ancestor may have given inaccurate information, perhaps recording their nickname rather than the name under which they were registered at birth, and in many cases in the early part of the nineteenth century people did not know their exact birth date so ages could change drastically from decade to decade. A family secret might have caused your relatives to deliberately give incorrect information on the census return, perhaps describing an illegitimate grandchild as the son of the head of the household to cover up a daughter's indiscretion. Bigamy (and other forms of criminality) provides a reason for people to slightly change their biographical details for fear of being caught by the authorities.

Alternatively you might not be able to find your ancestor's family because they chose not to fill out their schedule. The Women's Freedom League organised a boycott of the 1911 census as a peaceful protest in the fight for suffrage – one woman wrote on her schedule: 'I fill up this form under protest, for if I am intelligent enough so to do, I am surely capable of putting my cross on a Parliamentary ballot paper.' Others avoided completing forms for fear of giving too much information to a 'Nanny' State, although they could have faced fines for not complying.

If no record can be found for your ancestor or any of their relatives using the online indexes, check to make sure whether all the census returns for the area in which you think they were living have survived. Ancestry and Find My Past have lists of the missing enumeration district returns. If they all seem to survive, then you can browse the pages for the relevant enumeration districts, going street-by-street to see if you can spot a likely entry that may have been mistranscribed or not located using a database search engine.

Census Returns for Scotland

Census returns of the Scottish population also survive for the period 1841 to 1901, though the 1911 census for Scotland has not yet been released. The enumerators' books are organised in much the same way as in England and Wales, and the originals are held at the GRO in Edinburgh. Regional microfilmed copies of the returns are available at local Scottish record offices, but digitised images can be searched online using the subscription website www.scotlandspeople.gov.uk, and transcriptions can also be found at www.ancestry.co.uk.

Census Returns for Ireland

The only complete census returns that survive for the whole of Ireland are the 1901 and 1911 censuses. The 1911 census was opened early to aid genealogists because a large majority of the earlier censuses were destroyed by fire in 1922. The censuses, and any substitute land records for earlier periods, such as Griffiths' Valuation, are available to search at the Public Record Office of Northern Ireland (PRONI) in Belfast and The National Archives of Ireland in Dublin. Parts of the digitised 1911 census can be searched for free at www.census.nationalarchives.ie, and the subscription website www.origins.net contains records of some surviving earlier census returns, such as the 1851 Dublin census, as well as a selection of less detailed census substitutes that can be used in place of the missing returns.

Probate Records

Finding a will is often like hitting a genealogical jackpot, providing a treasure trove of information about your ancestor, giving a unique glimpse into their personality and family life. Some wills contain information on immediate family members, relatives from the extended family, and even the deceased's circle of friends and colleagues. They can give details about a family burial plot where the deceased wished to be buried, describe the contents of their house and give you the name of the property so you can track down further records about it. The amount of property and the value of their estate will give you an indication of how wealthy they were and their social status. An eccentric relative may have left some surprises in their will – perhaps naming illegitimate children, or leaving scathing remarks about an individual who they did not want to have a share of their estate, thus giving you details of a family feud. Last testaments and wills may have been dictated to a solicitor and be interspersed with legal jargon, but they are written in the words of our ancestors and give an insight into that ancestor's personality.

We're lucky in England and Wales that a record of most probate records has survived in some form right from the medieval period up to the present day, though people tracing poor, working-class roots are unlikely to find that their ancestors left wills. We can access even the most recent wills, so they're a fantastic source for speeding up your research for the twentieth century where census returns are not yet available. Wills can provide the names of spouses, children, parents and extended family members, but these details should still be checked with civil registration certificates to ensure they're accurate.

There are a few things to bear in mind about the history of probate records when considering searching for wills left by your family. During the medieval period any land belonging to a family automatically passed to the eldest son upon the death of his father. The rest of the estate, such as money, jewellery, furniture and other household goods, may have been divided among the rest of the family by a last testament. In 1540 the Statute of Wills decreed that land could be divided and left to people other than the eldest son in a will, so from then onwards the number of wills increased, and wills and last testaments were normally amalgamated. Early wills were sometimes written in Latin, but the majority of wills from the 1600s onwards are in English, although some background research in palaeontology may be needed to decipher the words! Any man over the age of 14 could write a will, in which he would be referred to as the testator. Women over the age of 12 who owned property could also write wills, and they were known as the testatrix; however, until the Married Women's Property Act of 1882 a married woman could not legally own any property, so the majority of testatrixes up to that year were spinsters and widows. In 1837 the Wills Act increased the legal age for testators and testatrixes to 21. Prisoners, the insane, and anybody excommunicated from the Church of England were not permitted to write a will, although Roman Catholics and non-conformists were allowed to write wills, which had to be proved in the Established Church's ecclesiastical courts up until 1858.

People who died without a will are known as 'intestates'. A will may not have been drawn up if the death was unexpected and the deceased was young, or they simply hadn't got round to organising one. Families were entitled to settle things privately between themselves if there was no concern that other members of the family would challenge the way in which the estate was divided. In these instances no public record has been created, though you may find the original will deposited in a local record office with family or solicitors' papers. In cases where a dispute might arise, if there was a large estate or no immediate family existed, a court could grant letters of administration either to the next of kin or to a creditor if debts were owed. Letters of administration are not as detailed as wills, but still provide the name of the person granted administration and usually their relationship to the deceased. The deceased's date and place of death will also be given, and the value of their estate.

Finding probate records pre-1858

Up until 1858, wills were 'proved' in one of the many ecclesiastical courts of the Church of England, which would grant permission to the executor or executrix appointed in the will to go ahead with administering the estate, once the will had been proven to be genuine. The judicial process created registers, and a copy of the will was made and kept with the records of the court. Between 1530 and 1782 the ecclesiastical courts insisted on also seeing an inventory of the deceased's goods compiled by appraisers, usually family or friends, who went from room to room in the house and wrote a list of everything in each room. These give a wonderful insight into the fashions of the day, your ancestor's interests, and how wealthy they were. Inventories are usually kept with the original wills or the will registers kept by the ecclesiastical court.

The main issue with locating a will prior to 1858 is working out in which court the will, if it exists, could have been proved and when. It's obviously useful to have an idea of when your ancestor died, but it's also helpful to know where and how much property they owned, as these factors decided which court processed the will or letters of administration, as well as where they lived, as most of the ecclesiastical courts covered a particular geographical region relating to their jurisdiction. In 1796 death duty was introduced as a tax on estates worth over a certain amount of money, and Death Duty Registers were compiled detailing in which court the wills were proved. Not everyone was liable to pay the tax, but the registers cover the period 1796 to 1906 and provide a useful index to discovering the location of some wills. The Death Duty Registers are at The National Archives, but the subscription website Find My Past has an online index and digitised pages of the entire collection at www.findmypast.com, though a full subscription is needed to use these records. Alternatively The National Archives has a free online index to some of the names in the registers between 1796 and 1811 at www.nationalarchives.gov.uk/documentsonline. Images of the original index pages can be downloaded for a small fee at home, or for free when using computers at TNA. To access the entire collection of Death Duty Registers and Indexes free of charge you need to visit The National Archives. The collections are stored in series IR 26 and IR 27, and it's worth checking the registers for additional information even if you already know where the will was proved, because they list the date of death, the value of the estate, the amount of death duty paid and details of the administration of the estate.

There were over 300 ecclesiastical courts in England and Wales. The smallest of these were Archdeaconry Courts, which proved the wills of people who owned property in the parishes within their jurisdiction. If your ancestor owned property that was situated within the jurisdiction of more than one Archdeaconry Court, but all within the same diocese, then their will may have been proved in the bishop's Consistory Court. The majority of Archdeaconry and Consistory Court wills and registers are deposited at the local County Record Office or Diocesan Record Office, and most are indexed by name. The Society of Genealogists has various name indexes compiled from the records of ecclesiastical courts around the country. The indexes can be accessed at the Society's library in London, though a small fee is charged for non-membership day passes.

Some record offices have put indexes to their collection of wills online via the archive website, such as the Gloucester County Council Genealogical Database where wills proved in Gloucester between 1541 and 1858 can be searched at www.gloucestershire.gov.uk/genealogy, and the Cheshire Wills Database Online where wills proved at Chester between 1492 and 1940 can be searched at www.cheshire.gov.uk/Recordoffice/Wills and copies can be ordered online for a fee. Check the record office website for the areas where your ancestors lived to see if they have similar indexes. The subscription website Origins Network has indexed over 28,000 wills held by the London Metropolitan Archives and proved in Surrey and South London between 1470 and 1856 at www.origins.net. Origins also has a separate index to wills proved by the Archdeaconry Court of London between 1750 and 1800. If your ancestor's will is likely to have been proved in an Archdeaconry or Consistory Court and it cannot be found in an online index, check Gibson's *Probate Jurisdictions: Where to look for wills* (2002) to work out which archive you should visit.

In unusual circumstances, some parishes were administered by a different archdeaconry to the one within which they lay, and these were known as Peculiar Parishes. People whose property all fell within the boundary of a peculiar parish would have their will proved in a small, independent court. If they had property in a peculiar parish and an ordinary parish, then the Archdeaconry or Consistory Court covering the ordinary parish would grant probate. The Origins Network has an online index to wills proved in the fifty-four peculiar courts in the Province of York between 1383 and 1883. It also has another index to the Bank of England Will Extracts between 1717 and 1845 for people who left money in public funds and stockholders who went bankrupt or were declared lunatic.

If the deceased's property lay within the jurisdiction of more than one Consistory Court, or if the value of the estate was more than £5, or £10 in London, the will would need to be proved in one of the archbishop's ecclesiastical courts. For those with property just in the North of England, the will should have been proved either in the Prerogative Court of York (PCY), the Consistory Court of York or the Exchequer Court. Records of probate granted in these courts between 1389 and 1858 are held at the Borthwick Institute of Historical Research, part of the University of York, though few wills have survived from before 1630. The Origins Network has an online index to the wills granted and proven in the PCY and Exchequer Court between 1267 and 1500, and from May 1731 to January 1858. The period 1500–1731 will eventually be made available online too. If you find the will you're looking for in the indexes using an Origins subscription, you can choose to pay for a copy of the will to be retrieved from the archive.

If your ancestor had property in the southern part of the country, or in both the north and south, then the Prerogative Court of Canterbury (PCC) would have proved the will. The PCC was considered to be more prestigious, so people who should really have gone to the PCY sometimes went to the PCC instead. It also proved the wills of Britons who had property overseas. The entire collection of PCC Will Registers from 1384 to 12 January 1858, including copies of the wills, can be searched and downloaded online via The National Archives website at <u>www.nationalarchives.gov.uk/documents</u>

online. The database is completely free to use when visiting TNA, otherwise it's free to search the indexes but a fee is charged to download scanned copies of wills at home. The Origins Network offers a name index to PCC wills proved between 1750 and 1800 as part of its subscription package, and a copying service for the wills via the Society of Genealogists.

Finding probate records post-1858

The Probate Act of 1858 simplified the system of granting probate by transferring responsibility from the various ecclesiastical courts to civil Courts of Probate set up around the country, which were all centrally responsible to the Principal Probate Registry in London. After a will was proved in a regional court, a copy was sent to the Probate Registry in London, so all wills proved after 12 January 1858 can be found in one place.

The Principal Probate Registry is in Holborn, London, and has a search room where members of the public can search annual alphabetical indexes for the surname of the deceased. The registers contain a description of where the deceased lived, their occupation (or marital status in the case of women), when and where they died, whether a will or letters of administration were granted, where they were granted, the names of the executors and solicitors and the value of the estate. Duplicates of the register between 1858 and 1943, known as the National Probate Calendar, can be found at The National Archives and at many local record offices. If you find an entry in the annual registers, you can order a copy of the papers, including the will if it exists, from the enquiry desk at the Probate Registry in Holborn. An hourly service costs £5 per will (or letter of administration).

Some regional Courts of Probate may still have copies of the wills proved there, so if it's too difficult to make the trip to London it's worth contacting the court local to where the deceased lived to find out whether they can supply you with a copy. Alternatively, these records may have been passed to the County Record Office if they were proved more than fifty years ago.

Irish Probate Records

The early Irish probate system followed the same ecclesiastical court process as in England and Wales, the highest court being the Prerogative Court of Armagh. A civil court system was also introduced in 1858, when the Principal Registry in Dublin became responsible for eleven district registries. However, copies of probate documents kept in Dublin were destroyed by fire in 1922, so the district registries should be consulted when searching for wills between 1858 and 1922. Some pre-1922 wills donated by solicitors and families, along with probate indexes compiled from various sources and all wills proved after 1922, have been deposited at The National Archives of Ireland in Dublin or the Public Record Office of Northern Ireland in Belfast, depending on where the testator lived.

Scottish Probate Records

In Scotland the law until 1868 dictated that land must pass to the eldest son or to the eldest daughter if there were no sons. Testaments were used to bequeath all other moveable property to other family members and friends. A testament dative, the Scottish form of letters of administration, was drawn up if a person died intestate. Scottish church courts dealt with probate until 1560, when commissariat courts became responsible for probate cases. The commissariat court boundaries roughly covered the area of a diocese, and were administered centrally by the Principal Commissariat Court in Edinburgh until 1824 when Sheriff Courts took over the responsibility for all matters of probate.

The National Archives of Scotland hold Scottish probate records dating before 1824 and some early probate cases dealt with by the Sheriff Courts, but the majority of these are still held by the appropriate Sheriff Court for the county where the testator lived. The Scotland's People website at www.scotlandspeople.gov.uk has a free index where probate records can be searched between 1513 and 1901. The name of the testator, date probate was granted and the court in which it was granted are provided by the free index, but images of the original documents can be downloaded for a fee.

Parish Records

The final set of records that will be used to work back to earlier generations on your family tree are the ecclesiastical records created by parish churches and other religious bodies documenting your ancestors' baptisms, marriages and burials. Church of England parish registers were introduced in the mid-1500s and with a little determination can be used as an alternative to civil registration records prior to 1837. Religious records are a fruitful source of information before and after the onset of civil registration and census-taking – monumental inscriptions may give vital details for a whole clan buried in a family grave, providing the plot number so you can visit the tomb. Parish records provide the key to potentially tracing your heritage back to the sixteenth century, though they're not as easy to find as some of the other basic sources. Let's look at the various records created by parishes, how to use them, where you can locate them, and what to do if your ancestors did not belong to the Established Church.

Britain, as a Christian country, was divided into dioceses, each of which was under the administration of a bishop. The dioceses were split into lots of parishes, which served local communities. In the countryside a parish may cover several small villages, but large towns were divided into more than one parish to reduce the workload of the clergy there. Church of England parish clergy were obliged to keep registers of all the baptisms, marriages and burials that occurred in their church from 1538, and this is still the case today, so these registers can be used continuously for a 400-year period. Since the vast majority of people belonged to the Established Church, the registers chronicle the vital details of a large proportion of the population. Most parish registers dating back to around 1611 have survived, when bound books were first introduced to keep the records in better order. However, the very early registers were sometimes written in Latin, and can be difficult to read because the ink has faded and the paper has worn away. Not every single parish register entry has survived, so you should be aware that the record you need may simply not exist any longer, though the vast majority of parish records have survived and are freely open to the public.

Interpreting parish registers

The baptism, marriage and burial registers kept by parish clergy vary in content from parish to parish, because there was no set way of writing them. The information they contain varies depending on how diligent the clerk who wrote them was and how old the records are. The pre-1813 registers are usually less detailed than the nineteenth- and twentieth-century registers, when printed forms were provided for clergymen to fill in. The sentences used to record each event before 1813 were fairly formulaic, however, so if you're using early Latin registers it's possible to translate the months and Latin version of the names using a Latin dictionary, which should be available at the local studies centre.

If you're lucky enough to trace your heritage back past the nineteenth century, you need to be aware that England and Wales did not officially adopt the modern Gregorian calendar until 1752. Up until this date the

English New Year had begun on 25 March as opposed to 1 January. Therefore, years recorded in parish registers prior to 1752 may be slightly inaccurate according to the modern Gregorian calendar. It means that, for example, the day after 31 December 1679 was 1 January 1679 in the old calendar, and there was a difference in the year according to the old Julian calendar and the modern Gregorian calendar between 1 January and 24 March. Historians refer to a date before the year 1752 using both the old Julian Calendar year and the Gregorian Calendar year – therefore, to describe the old date 1 January 1679 you should write '1 January 1679/80' to indicate that it would've been 1680 if it was a modern date. Scotland adopted the Gregorian calendar in 1600, and evidence from Samuel Pepys's diary shows that in England the New Year was commonly celebrated on 1 January in the seventeenth century as well, so it's worth checking whether the registers you use change year in January or March before you begin a search in this period.

Generally, the baptism, marriage and burial registers for the church were kept in separate volumes in chronological order, and the details of each event were written in sentences and recorded in a list, so in most cases you'll have to search through at least a few pages to find the name you're looking for. Some registers amalgamated all the baptisms, marriages and burials for each year, so you should establish the clergyman's form of filing before beginning the search of a book to make sure you don't accidentally miss out a relevant page. Remember that the parish registers are recorded chronologically by the date of the religious ceremony (i.e. not the date of birth or death), and not everyone was baptised as a baby, so you may have to widen the parameters of your search.

Baptisms

Most baptisms were communal affairs held as an integral part of Sunday mass, and it was common for many children to be baptised together. The clerk would normally make a note of any private baptisms, which would indicate that there might have been some special circumstances. The bare minimum that's provided on a baptism entry is the child's name, the father's name and the date of the baptism. If the child was illegitimate, the baptism entry usually describes the child as 'the base child of ...' or 'the natural child of ...' followed by the mother's name; the father's name is rarely given in these cases. A detailed baptism register may provide some (though rarely all) of the information below:

- Christian name given to the child at baptism
- whether the child was a son or daughter (and in some cases whether they were the second, third, fourth or fifth child)
- both parents' names and address
- mother's maiden name (though this is quite rare)
- father's occupation or status
- when the child was born
- when the child was baptised
- the signature of the clergyman who performed the ceremony.

Marriages

Parish register marriage entries are not as detailed as civil registration marriage certificates because they don't give ages or the fathers' names, making it more difficult to cross-reference these with the baptism registers. Early marriage registers might just give the names of the bride and groom, their marital status, which parish they were from and when they married, but most marriage registers contain all of the following information:

- names of the bride and groom
- date of the marriage
- marital status of the bride and groom (whether they were widowed or unmarried)
- the parish they were from
- signatures of the bride, groom and two witnesses
- whether the ceremony was performed after the reading of banns or with a licence
- the signature of the clergyman who performed the ceremony.

The majority of people married after the reading out of banns in the parish church on three consecutive Sundays before the wedding, to ensure nobody had cause to object to the match. Marriage registers also record the three dates on which banns were read out in the church for each couple, though these do not provide any biographical information. People might apply for a marriage licence if they wanted to marry in a parish to which neither the bride nor groom belonged, or if they wanted to avoid the public nature of banns being read out. If the couple were married by licence instead of banns then details of the licence can be tracked down, which may provide ages and in some cases will give parents' names, particularly if one party was under 21. The original marriage licence is unlikely to survive, but marriage allegations stating the couple's intention to marry, or details of marriage bonds guaranteeing that the information provided about the bride and groom was correct may still survive. Allegations and bonds for marriage licences often supply additional information to the marriage entry in the parish register. Marriage licences, allegations and bonds are kept with the records of the bishop rather than the parish church, but should be found at the local record office. Many have been transcribed and indexed into bound volumes, and the Origins website at www.origins.net has online indexes to Marriage Licence Allegations granted by the Vicar General (the Archbishop of Canterbury) between 1694 and 1850, as well as those granted by the Faculty Office at Lambeth Palace, 1701–1850.

Burials

Basic burial registers just give the name of the deceased and the date they were buried. Most will state the deceased's age, which is helpful for locating a baptism record, and in some cases will provide their occupation and address as well as the date of death. In the case of infant deaths the parents' names may be given, and a married or widowed woman's husband's name was sometimes recorded, as was the marital status of spinsters who died unmarried. Once you've found an individual's burial record you can then search for a will, which may provide other biographical clues.

Unfortunately it's very rare to be able to work out where a person was buried just from their burial entry in the parish register. However, as church graveyards became overcrowded, large municipal cemeteries were built to accommodate the ever-increasing urban communities in industrialised Britain, and plans and indexes were created to keep track of the plots sold and the space available. Some of these are deposited at local record offices, while some cemetery offices have an index to the names of people buried there, so once you've found out which cemeteries served the parish church at the time your relative died, you can contact the cemetery office and ask the staff there to check the indexes to find out where the grave is. Poor families could rarely afford to pay for a headstone for their loved ones, who were often buried in an unmarked grave with other poor parishioners, but even so, the staff at the cemetery should know roughly where this was. If any other family members were buried in the grave, either before or after your ancestor died, the cemetery office will also have a record of this. The local archive will be able to tell you which cemeteries catered for the parish church you're interested in, and most cemetery office contact details can be found online by doing a web search.

Monumental Inscriptions

Many local family history societies have undertaken the arduous task of visiting graveyards and transcribing the monumental inscriptions inside the church and the memorials written on headstones. This important work has preserved loving messages written by close family and friends to the departed, which are being lost to erosion and neglect. Plaques inside churches and headstones in graveyards can contain a wealth of biographical information about the deceased, from their date of death and age, to the names of their parents, spouse, children, and any other relatives who may have been buried with them. Most local archives have a record of the churches that have been covered by family history societies in their region, some of which have published the monumental inscriptions in pamphlets. Many memorial inscription publications contain a plan of the graveyard and should indicate where each memorial was found. Copies of the transcribed inscriptions can be found in local studies libraries and archives. Some have been put online, including memorial inscriptions from over 600 graveyards in Norfolk and Bedfordshire that can be searched for a fee at www.memorialinscriptions.org.uk. If the burial ground where your ancestors were interred has not been covered already, then pay a visit and spend some time reading the inscriptions in and around the church to see if anything can be found for your family. The earliest inscriptions will be found inside the church, while wealthy parishioners may have paid for a large tomb or donated a decorative brass panel to commemorate their loved ones.

Finding parish registers

The biggest obstacle faced by genealogists when tracing a family tree back past the 1840s without the aid of civil registration indexes and census returns is trying to work out which parish a family came from, because parish records are not indexed nationwide in the way civil registration records are. The parish system was adopted in the sixth century, and by the time civil registration began there were around 11,000 parish churches. Each church was responsible for keeping its own records, though from 1597 the clergy were instructed to forward an annual copy of the registers to the bishop of the diocese. These copies are now known as Bishops' Transcripts and form a partial index to the parish registers, but in most cases do not contain as much information as the original records and contain inaccuracies. It also helps to know which diocese your ancestors belonged to before deciding which set of Bishops' Transcripts to search, as there is no combined index for all of these. Bishops' Transcripts can be found at the local record office, as can copies of the original parish registers. You should always double-check information found among the Bishops' Transcripts, or any other index, against the original record; firstly to make sure the index was accurate, but mostly because the original may contain additional information.

The Bishops' Transcripts do not provide a record of all parish register entries, and as they are known to contain errors you may need to turn to the original records to find what you need. In most cases you'll start looking for parish registers once you've got as far back as you can using the 1841 census and the earliest civil registration certificates, which should tell you the parish, or at least the village or town, where your ancestors lived. *The Phillimore Atlas and Index of Parish Registers*, available in local studies libraries, is useful for establishing parish boundaries and working out which places were covered by a particular parish church. If you're unable to locate any records for your family among the parish registers where they were last known to live, then you should use *The Phillimore Atlas* to work out which were the surrounding parishes and search those parish registers as well. It was customary for a couple to marry in the bride's parish, so if you know where the bride was from it can help to narrow down a search. If you are still unable to trace the line, and with no other leads suggesting where the family may have come from, there's the risk that you might not be able to get any further back with your family tree. However, over the years indexes have been compiled to cover wide areas of the country, and these may help to resurrect your research.

The main concern with parish register name indexes is that they are not comprehensive, and it's very easy to believe you've found the right person simply because the record you're really looking for has not been indexed and is not where you'd expect to look for it, or has not survived in any form. The other problem encountered with tracing your family history back past the Victorian period using parish registers is that they often contain less information than civil registration certificates, and so there's less data to cross-reference with other sources. Nevertheless, the following indexes are a great aid to locating parish register entries that may not otherwise have been found. You should look for each record using as many of the indexes below as possible, because they cover different regions and dates, though the coverage overlaps in places. Any records found using indexes should be double-checked against the original parish register, as the transcriptions are subject to human error and the originals will often contain extra information. All of the following name indexes provide the date and name of the parish where the original record should be found.

International Genealogical Index (IGI)
www.familysearch.org.uk

The International Genealogical Index was created by the Mormons (members of the Church of Latter-Day Saints) and contains millions of parish register transcriptions from around the country. The collection is not complete and mostly covers baptisms pre-1885. County Record Offices can advise to what extent their parish records are covered by the IGI, which can be accessed on microfiche at most archives. *The Phillimore Atlas and Index of Parish Registers* also has an index to the parishes covered by the IGI. The IGI can be searched online by name at the Mormons www.familysearch.org.uk website, and the database also provides results from records uploaded by other researchers in the form of Ancestral Files, Pedigree Resource Files and transcriptions of the 1881 British census. The LDS Church has set up Family History Centres around the world where the IGI can be searched. They also have duplicate microfilm copies of many parish registers from around England and Wales, which can be delivered to any Family History Centre. Details of your nearest centre can be found on the Family Search website.

British Vital Records Index
The Mormons have also published CDs containing even more baptisms and marriages than the IGI, taken from parish registers dating between the 1500s and 1800s, though this is not a complete index. The British Vital Records Index CDs can be accessed at most County Record Offices for free, or copies can be purchased by contacting your nearest LDS Family History Centre (details at www.familysearch.org.uk).

The National Burial Index (NBI)
The Federation of Family History Societies (FFHS) has arranged for millions of burial records from around the country to be indexed to complement the IGI, which mainly contains baptisms and marriages. The project aims to

cover burials in Anglican and non-conformist parishes as well as those found on cemetery registers between 1538 and the twenty-first century, though the majority of records so far date between 1813 and the 1850s. Details of county coverage can be found on the FFHS website at www.ffhs.org.uk/projects/nbi/nbi-coverage.php. The latest edition of the NBI was released in 2004 and contains 13.2 million records on four CDs. Many local archives provide free access to the NBI, or the CDs can be purchased from www.genfair.co.uk. Records found on the NBI have also been included on the www.findmypast.com subscription website's Parish Records collection (see below).

Deceased Online

A new project has been introduced to create a central Internet database for burial and cremation records in the UK, based on local authority files for cemeteries, burial sites and crematoria. The website www.deceasedonline.com has started to transcribe and upload these records, and their database allows a free search by name. If you find your ancestor listed, you can then purchase access to the actual registers, as well as associated material such as books of remembrance, memorial photos and cemetery maps showing grave locations.

Pallot's Baptism and Marriage Index

The majority of baptisms and marriages between c.1780 and 1837 in City of London parish registers, as well as a large number from Middlesex and surrounding counties, have been recorded in Pallot's Baptism and Marriage Index. The marriage index can be cross-referenced for the spouse's name, and both indexes can be searched separately using the subscription website www.ancestry.co.uk.

Boyd's Marriage Index

Percival Boyd and a team of researchers have transcribed and cross-referenced the names of brides and grooms contained in marriage records from across the country dating from 1538 to 1837. These include names taken from Bishops' Transcripts and marriage licences. The 7 million records can be searched for a fee at www.origins.net, otherwise most record offices provide free access to the index. Origins also has a separate index to marriages in St. Andrew's parish in Holborn between 1754 and 1812, which does not feature in Boyd's Marriage Index or the IGI, though it was one of the largest parishes in London. St. Andrew's, Holborn was also indexed in

Pallot's Marriage Index between 1780 and 1837, though this index is not as detailed as the Origins collection.

FreeReg
www.freereg.org.uk

FreeReg is a companion project to Free BMD run by volunteers, indexing millions of baptisms, marriages and burials from Anglican and non-conformist parish registers between the 1500s and early 1900s so they can be accessed completely free of charge. It is a huge undertaking and is far from complete, but the website has a breakdown of all the parishes and years indexed so far. Names can be searched on the website by county and results provide a full transcription of the entry.

Find My Past
www.findmypast.com

The Find My Past Parish Records collection covers the period 1538 to 2005 and includes indexes created by family history societies around the country under the umbrella of the FFHS, including the National Burial Index, a variety of regional baptism, marriage and burial indexes, London Docklands baptisms and City of London burials. The subscription website, which can be searched for a fee, has a list of the counties and parishes it covers as well as the date ranges. The records at Find My Past were formerly kept on the Family History Online website, which is no longer in use.

Non-conformists

Not everyone in England and Wales was Anglican, so if you can't locate any of your family members in the parish registers where you'd expect to find them this may be because they belonged to another religious group. Non-conformists included Catholics, Jews, Quakers and Protestant Dissenters, who all kept their own set of records. Up until the nineteenth century some of these dissident groups were unable to practise their religion openly for fear of persecution, so the records they kept can be patchy. You may find that your ancestors are listed in both the registers of the parish church and a non-conformist chapel, because only Anglican baptism certificates were legally recognised until 1742, and under Hardwicke's Marriage Act everyone other than Jews and Quakers had to marry in an Anglican church between 1753 and 1837. Non-conformist churches were also not allowed to have their own formally recognised premises with burial grounds until the Toleration Act of 1691, after which time separate burial grounds were established. A large number of non-conformist records have been deposited in County Record Offices, though some may not have survived at all and others are still held by the relevant religious body. Some of the indexes to parish records that have already been mentioned include non-conformist records as well as Anglican parish registers. Further information about immigrant communities from different religious backgrounds, including Jews and Huguenots, can be found at the end of Section One.

Protestant Dissenter records

In 1837 and 1857 Parliamentary Commissioners collected duplicates of the Protestant Dissenter registers from around the country, including those of the Methodists, Congregationalists, Presbyterians, Baptists and Huguenots. The registers were kept at the General Register Office and have now been deposited at The National Archives (TNA) in series RG 4 and RG 8. The holdings can be searched by the name of the chapel or the place name using the online Catalogue at www.nationalarchives.gov.uk/catalogue, and typing 'RG' into the series code search field. You can then visit TNA to find the document reference on microfilm. The records generally cover the period 1567 to 1970, but coverage varies greatly from one group to another.

Non-conformists were allowed to register their baptisms from 1742 in the General Register of Births of Children of Protestant Dissenters at Dr. William's Library in London. The certificates produced can be searched on microfilm at TNA in series RG 5, and cover records from around 1716 to 1837. If your ancestors were Wesleyan Methodists, then their baptisms may have been recorded with the Wesleyan Methodist Metropolitan Registry of Births founded in 1818, whose records are also deposited at TNA in series RG 4 and RG 5 and cover the period from around 1773 to 1838.

Anyone with Quaker ancestors is in luck, because the Society of Friends (as they are otherwise known) kept detailed birth, marriage and death records, which have been deposited at the Religious Society of Friends' Library in Euston, London. Duplicate copies of the Quaker registers, which date from 1650, can be found in local record offices and at The National Archives in series RG 6.

An index to the non-parochial sources deposited at TNA has been made available via the subscription website www.bmdregisters.co.uk, where the records kept in series RG 4 to RG 8 can be searched by name and original images of the pages can be downloaded for a fee. These include both the Protestant Dissenter records and Quaker registers, and also the overseas births, marriages, deaths and burials recorded by English churches and missions, kept at TNA in series RG 33.

Roman Catholics

Roman Catholic ancestry is less easy to trace, mainly owing to the fall-out after Henry VIII's break with Rome in the sixteenth century. Elizabeth I's Acts of Supremacy and Uniformity illegalised the practice of Catholicism in 1559, until the Catholic Relief Act was passed in 1778. Catholic parish registers are therefore particularly patchy between the sixteenth and eighteenth centuries, though Catholic ancestors may be found among criminal or taxation records at The National Archives and local record offices if they were caught practising their beliefs. The Catholic National Library in Farnborough, Hampshire, holds transcripts of Mission Registers dating back to 1694, and there is a list of the parishes and dates covered on the CNL website at www.catholic-library.org.uk/registers.html. Irish immigration in the nineteenth century created a surge in Catholicism in England and Wales, and the registers from this period onwards are more complete. Some were deposited with the Registrar General and are kept with those of the Protestant Dissenters at TNA in series RG 4, while others can be found either at the local record office or the local Catholic Church.

Parish records for Scotland

Surviving Scottish parish registers, which were first introduced in 1553, are held by the General Register Office for Scotland and can be searched for a fee online at www.scotlandspeople.gov.uk. The original images dating from 1553 to 1854 can be downloaded, but unfortunately the records' coverage of the population is limited because many registers prior to the seventeenth and even eighteenth centuries have not survived, and some of the smaller parishes only started keeping records in the nineteenth century. In addition to these limitations, there was no requirement to keep burial records so these are very sparse, and some people chose not to register events at the church owing to the cost, particularly non-conformists who preferred to be baptised or married at their own chapel. It's worth bearing in mind that Roman Catholicism was the official state religion until 1560. After this time, Presbyterianism became increasingly popular and was the official religion of the Established Church in Scotland by 1690. Non-conformist records can be found at The National Archives of Scotland, or at the local register office.

Parish registers for Ireland

The Protestant Church of Ireland was the official established church until 1869, and it was compulsory to keep parish registers from 1634 onwards. However, few were kept until the mid-eighteenth century, and many that did survive were destroyed by fire at the Public Record Office in Dublin in 1922. The remaining records can be searched at the National Library of Ireland in Dublin, and Northern Irish records from 1922 onwards can be consulted at the Public Record Office of Northern Ireland in Belfast. The Representative Church Body Library in Dublin also holds copies of parish registers for the Church of Ireland. Although the majority of the Irish population was Catholic, a series of anti-Catholic laws passed in the eighteenth century effectively illegalised the practice of Catholicism until 1829. Therefore, few parish registers were kept for Catholic Churches before this time, but those that were may be found in local archives and some copies have also been deposited at the National Library of Ireland in Dublin.

Chapter Five

FLESHING OUT THE FAMILY TREE

The basic sources used to build your family tree will only scrape the surface of your personal heritage. Census returns, civil registration certificates, wills and parish records provide the names and dates you need to trace your lineage further back in time, but also give snippets of detail about your ancestors' lives leading to a whole host of other sources. Occupations, places of birth and addresses found on certificates and census returns provide clues so you can flesh out your family tree and delve deeper into each ancestor's life.

A family tree should not just be a diagram of names without faces. While you'll be unable to find pictures of the vast majority of people in your lineage, you can conjure up an image of them in your mind using occupational records, military service records, paperwork generated by local authorities such as workhouse and hospital records, and emigration or immigration documents if they travelled around. Use the electoral register to find out if your great-grandmother took advantage of her right to vote after the Suffragists' long battle, and look at bomb census maps to see how close your grandparents' house was to being bombed during the Second World War. Some of these sources are explored in more detail in later sections, but we'll take a closer look at occupational and emigration sources here.

In addition, there are likely to be 'family secrets' that start to appear the more you investigate, particularly if you have heard one or two stories about distant ancestors during your initial research within the family. This chapter also offers some advice about tackling these sensitive areas, with particular reference to the 'standard' family secrets that surround illegitimacy, bigamy, divorce and adoption that tend to be covered up. And – whisper it quietly – you may even find evidence of criminal activity within the ranks of your ancestors!

The basic sources will be all that can be found for some people in your tree, but you can make up for any gaps in your primary evidence by investigating the history of the areas where they lived and the events they experienced using secondary sources. Famous moments in history can be brought to life when they're seen through your ancestors' eyes. How many men from their village were conscripted into the Army when the First World War broke out, and how many returned? Might the Lancashire Cotton Famine have affected your ancestors found working in Stalybridge mills on the 1861 census? A huge insight into your own personal heritage, the experiences that have made up the fabric of your family's history, can be gained by digging a bit deeper using both original documents and secondary sources.

Following Occupation Clues

The National Archives

A surprising amount of material survives from both the public and private sectors to help us investigate our ancestors' careers going back hundreds of years. Some companies have their own archives that contain information on past employees, though companies that have ceased trading may have deposited their records at the County Record Office. However, The National Archives holds a wealth of documentation for people who worked on the railways, men and women in the Armed Forces and Coastguard, staff of the Metropolitan Police and Royal Irish Constabulary, civil servants, customs and excise officials, tax collectors, merchant seamen, files for dissolved companies and bankrupts. Additionally the Postal Archives in London have records of people who worked for Royal Mail, and many other specialist archives across the country have supplementary records. Therefore the chances are high that a member of your family will have worked in a profession which generated employment records that were maintained or preserved by the state.

Records for staff employed in various sectors come in the form of joining papers, personnel files, pay ledgers, discharge papers and pension records. Employment records at Kew are not complete for every sector and time period, but The National Archives has published research guides on its website at www.nationalarchives.gov.uk/catalogue/researchguidesindex.asp detailing what records survive for each subject and where you need to look depending on the period your ancestor was employed. Some material is helpfully arranged alphabetically by name, while others filed are in numerical order by staff number, although some are not indexed at all. These include many of the railway company records that have been deposited at The National Archives after the nationalisation of the railways, despite the fact that most of the records are actually generated by private companies and therefore, as with coal mines and factories, should have been deposited in county archives or specialist institutions, if indeed they were preserved at all. Most employment records at The National Archives provide the ages of employees, sometimes their place of birth, and occasionally the names of next of kin, so it's possible to verify these details against what you already know of your ancestor.

It's important to look for clues that show what rank your ancestor attained in their profession, as many of the employment records at TNA are arranged this way: for example, the attestation papers of officers and other ranks in the Army that are kept in separate War Office series. Other records are arranged by region, such as the records of the nineteenth-century railway companies. You can build a fragmentary picture of your ancestor's career using the clues given on census returns and certificates before beginning a search of the employment records. The more information you have to go on, the easier it will be to locate personnel records. Write a timeline detailing where your ancestor was living and what their job description was given as on different sources, so you can take this into the archives as a reminder when you look for their service records. You may have found your great-great-grandfather was listed as a fireman living in Cardiff on the 1861 census, but on his daughter's birth certificate in 1869 he was described as an engine driver living in Merthyr Tydfil, so that's a clue that he was promoted sometime between 1861 and 1869 and may have changed railway companies when the family moved. Sometimes the initials of the railway company a person worked for will be given on census returns; for example, GWR stands for the Great Western Railway.

Once you've put together a summary of your ancestor's career from the details that can be gleaned from basic sources, check The National Archives subject research guides to find out what records exist for the period they were employed, and how to find them. The majority relate to military service, since the State paid the wages of the Army, Navy and Royal Air Force, and collected vast archives of material through the administration of the armed forces; you can also use the records at The National Archives to track other civil servants and government employees, such as customs and excise men mentioned above. Also included are records relating to some 'external' trades such as the Merchant Navy, because a Government department – in this case the Board of Trade and its successors – presided over a registration system for individuals that enlisted or took part in the sector. Don't forget, you will have to look in local archives for records of other large employers, such as factory and mill owners and coal mines. In addition, there are some resources outside The National Archives that will help you find out more about your ancestors, such as proofs of age for civil servants which are now stored at the Society of Genealogists, rather than with The National Archives.

Many of these occupations are described in detail in Section Three, where I'll be exploring some aspects of life that your ancestors will have encountered during their lives. So if you want to find out more about military and Merchant Navy ancestors, turn to Chapter 13 on War and Peace; or, to trace your railway ancestors, head to Chapter 14, Transport and Communications.

Research beyond The National Archives

If your ancestor worked on a family estate, for a private firm or for a local authority, then there may be a record of their employment at the local County Record Office or in a smaller, specialist repository. Even if you have found a record of your ancestor's career at The National Archives, it's worth checking the archive local to where they lived and worked to see if additional background information can be discovered about their living conditions. There are centralised finding aids to help you establish the location of the records you need, and these finding aids can also be used for tracing descriptions of all kinds of documents held in archives across the country, not just employment records. This is particularly important when you're looking for someone who worked in one of the mass-employment industries from the Industrial Revolution period, such as a cotton factory or a coal mine; these are described in more detail in Section Three in Chapter 12, Trade and Industry.

In the meantime, here's a brief summary of the ways you can find out more about your ancestors in record offices outside The National Archives.

Finding Aids and Catalogues
Every archive has its own unique cataloguing system, but centralised indexes combining catalogues for archives across the country are being compiled to make it easier to discover in which archive a document is stored. The online catalogues can usually be searched in a variety of ways, but most vitally the

document descriptions have been transcribed and can be searched by keyword. However, online catalogues are not comprehensive, do not cover every archive, and some of the more complicated indexes do still need to be consulted at the archives. It's advisable to speak to the archives that cover the area where your ancestor lived and worked to find out how much of their collection is indexed online. In addition to this not all documents have a full online description, so a keyword search will not always find every relevant document. Conduct searches under a few different keywords or variants to obtain the most results.

National Register of Archives
www.nationalarchives.gov.uk/nra

The National Register of Archives is a database containing information on the location and nature of manuscripts and historical records held by both private and public archives in the United Kingdom and overseas. The NRA contains a brief description of surviving records relating to around 46,000 individuals, 9,000 families, 29,000 businesses and 75,000 organisations, which can be searched by Corporate Name, Personal Name, Family Name and Place Name. These four search engines provide the location and a brief description of the historical records deposited by companies, family estates and prominent individuals. A breakdown of the document descriptions within each collection is not provided, but it is a good starting point for finding out whether a company archive still exists, or the various archives that hold the papers of a prominent family, and what time frame the records cover. A link to the ARCHON directory is provided on the results page giving the archive's contact details, so you can speak to the archivist to find out more detail about the collection.

Access to Archives
www.a2a.org.uk

Access to Archives (A2A) is an online database containing catalogue descriptions of documents held in local record offices, archives, museums, universities and libraries around England and Wales. The website aims to increase public awareness of and access to collections held in smaller archives, but it does not contain full transcriptions of documents or digital copies. The database currently includes descriptions of around 10 million documents from over 400 repositories that preserve records not available at The National Archives. These records can be searched by keyword, repository, area and date range. Don't forget to also find out if the archives local to your ancestor's place of work have an online Catalogue on their website.

Scottish Archive Network
www.scan.org.uk

The SCAN online Catalogue provides document descriptions for more than 20,000 records held in over fifty archives across Scotland. The collections can be searched by keyword and the results are arranged either by the name of the person or company to which the documents originally belonged, or can be viewed as catalogue results listing the title of the holdings and a general description of the documents contained therein. Covering dates and the name of the repository are also provided.

Emigration and Immigration

You may have heard a family rumour that your great-grandparents immigrated to Britain during the war, or perhaps you'll find out from a census return that your ancestors were born in foreign parts. Records of your family living in other parts of the world will be deposited in the archives of the country where they lived, but the UK does have information on people leaving and arriving in UK ports and applying for naturalisation certificates to remain in the UK as British citizens. Thousands of convicts were forcibly transported to the New World in the eighteenth century and later to Australia. The National Archives has detailed records concerning convicts sentenced to transportation, but additional material will probably be located in overseas archives as well. Some records kept in archives across the world are now available online, so it's possible to conduct research remotely.

Immigrants to the UK

The United Kingdom has over the centuries been a safe haven to many different immigrant communities fleeing their homelands during times of war and persecution. Thousands of French-Protestant Huguenots settled in London during the sixteenth and seventeenth centuries, and Eastern

European Jews followed suit in the nineteenth and twentieth centuries. The mid-twentieth century witnessed a huge influx of people from a wide range of nationalities as the British Empire finally collapsed and displaced communities seeking refuge after the World Wars arrived looking for work and stability. Immigrants from Commonwealth countries such as the West Indies and the Indian sub-continent, as well as countries closer to home like Ireland, were encouraged to settle in Britain to meet the demand for labour at the end of the Second World War. There were no restrictions on immigrant numbers between 1948 and 1962 and citizens of former colonies were entitled to British nationality upon arrival. Restrictions began to be introduced from 1963, although this did not stop people from across the world flocking to the UK in the 1960s and 70s.

Religious Refugees

French Protestants were forced to flee to England and Ireland during the sixteenth and seventeenth centuries after thousands were killed during the St. Bartholomew's Day Massacre in 1572 and when the Edict of Nantes, which was designed to ensure religious toleration of Protestants in Catholic France, was revoked in 1685. TNA holds lists of immigrants and applications for British citizenship among the State Papers in series SP and the Court of Exchequer Rolls in series E. The Huguenot Society of Great Britain has transcribed indexes to these records and registers, which are available to search at the society library in London. The Registrar General received Non-Parochial Registers for French, Swiss, German and Dutch churches for refugees in England, which have been deposited at The National Archives in series RG 4 and can be searched at www.bmdregisters.co.uk. The National Archives has a detailed online research guide entitled 'Refugees and Minorities' to advise how to locate original records for religious and political refugees who came to Britain from all over Europe, inside and outside the Commonwealth, and the Middle East.

Home Office Records

In 1793 the Home Office became responsible for regulating aliens, as foreign nationals were known. The Home Office issued Certificates of Arrival to some immigrants arriving in English and Scottish ports, which have survived between 1836 and 1852 and are kept at The National Archives in series HO 2, arranged by the port of arrival, with an index in HO 5/25–32. The Home Office issued letters patent of denization or certificates of naturalisation to those aliens who applied for British citizenship. Duplicate certificates of naturalisation, which were issued from 1844, can be found at The National Archives and detail the names, addresses, ages, places of birth, parents' names, next of kin and trades of many immigrants who settled in Britain throughout the nineteenth and twentieth centuries. Denizations enrolled in the Patent Rolls as far back as 1509 can be traced in series C 66 and C 67, to which there is an index. There are also typescript indexes in the Open Reading Room at The National Archives to denizations and naturalisations covering the period 1801 to 1948, which provide references to documents found in HO 1, HO 44, HO 45 and HO 144. Many of the names in the indexes are of Eastern European and Jewish origin owing to the large numbers of those communities displaced by persecution throughout the late nineteenth and early twentieth centuries. Some files can be searched by name using the online Catalogue and restricting the series code to 'HO', but if you don't find the name you're looking for, you should then consult the paper indexes.

The Aliens Registration Office, run by the Metropolitan Police, kept a collection of record cards for aliens living around London from 1914, though the covering dates for the cards are 1876–1991. A sample of the cards has been kept at The National Archives in MEPO 35, which contains a large concentration of records for Germans and Eastern Europeans fleeing the Nazis during the Second World War. Most of the cards and Home Office records are closed until the person has died or would have been 100 years old if their date of death is unknown, but applications to view a closed record can be made to The National Archives under the Freedom of Information Act. The National Archives has detailed online research guides to tracing immigrant ancestors under the titles Immigrants, Naturalisation and Citizenship, and Internees of the First and Second World Wars.

Moving Here
www.movinghere.org.uk

A good place to start tracing records for immigrant communities who arrived in England in the nineteenth and twentieth centuries, but particularly for Caribbean, Jewish, South Asian and Irish immigrants, is the www.moving here.org.uk website. The site is free to use and explores the history of migration to England through stories, a gallery, migration histories and guides to tracing your roots. Hundreds of oral histories have been collected and any visitor to the website can record their own experience of migration.

There are detailed migration histories of Caribbean, Irish, Jewish and South Asian ethnic communities, exploring the reasons behind migration from the home country, the actual journey to the UK, people's experiences when they settled in England, what connections remained with the home country, and a timeline of important events in the history of each community. The 'tracing your roots' guides for the four main immigrant communities describe the principal documents that can be used and what they'll tell you, where the records can be found, any other useful websites and organisations that may be able to help, and a case study to show you how the research is done.

Incoming Passenger Lists

The Board of Trade inwards passenger lists for ships arriving from destinations outside of Europe contain the names of thousands of immigrants to Britain. Some ships stopped off in European ports and collected more passengers en route to the UK, and these will also be found in the lists along with those people who had come from outside of Europe. Passenger lists often give useful genealogical data such as age, occupation, length of intended stay and residence. The inwards passenger lists survive for the years 1878–88 and 1890–1960 and are deposited at The National Archives in series BT 26. To search the original records you formerly needed to know which ship your ancestor arrived on, what date they arrived and the port they arrived at, but luckily the lists have recently been indexed by passenger name and digitised. The indexes at www.ancestry.co.uk enable you to quickly search for your ancestor by name and download a digitised copy of the passenger list if you have a subscription, but the Ancestry records can be downloaded for free using TNA on-site computers. The Moving Here website also contains some digitised immigration records from The National Archives collection that are free to download, including incoming passenger lists for Indian and Caribbean migrants who arrived between March 1948 and October 1960.

Emigration from the UK

British citizens seeking to start a new life in more exotic climes or those who had to follow their chosen career around the globe can be traced using a variety of sources at The National Archives and in the archives of the destination country. Brits who emigrated to countries within the British Empire can be found in records created by the British administration overseas. The number of emigrants from British shores reached its highest level in the nineteenth century, and records for this period are correspondingly the most voluminous. The principal destinations for nineteenth-century emigrants were the United States, Canada, Australia, India and other countries belonging to the British Empire where jobs could be found in civil engineering projects. Former soldiers and sailors were granted land at the end of their period of service if they agreed to settle in the new colonies. Here you'll find an overview of a variety of records that can be used for tracing ancestors who emigrated to different countries, but The National Archives also has an online research guide entitled 'Emigrants' giving detailed advice on how to use the vast array of original records deposited there.

Passengers leaving the UK

Board of Trade outbound passenger lists kept at The National Archives in series BT 27 record each individual who boarded a ship in a UK port headed for a destination outside of the Mediterranean and Europe, although these ships sometimes dropped passengers off in Europe en route to their final destination. Unfortunately the lists have not survived in their entirety, but can be searched for the years 1890 to 1960. Series BT 27 has been indexed by name, digitised and made available on the subscription website www.ancestorsonboard.com. Free access to the website is provided when using The National Archives computers. The lists provide most passengers' names, ages, the port at which they boarded and their destination port, as well as other passengers travelling on the same voyage, so it's possible to find a whole family emigrating together.

British travellers did not require a passport until 1914, though people could apply for passports from 1846. The majority of people travelled abroad without a passport. Most of those who applied for a passport were merchants and diplomats, though the pass was only valid for a single journey and needed to be countersigned by an official on the way home to be valid for a return journey. There are incomplete indexes to passport applications from 1851–62 and 1874–1916 at The National Archives in series FO 611. These indexes record the name, the number of the passport and the date of issue, but the passports themselves would obviously have been retained by the individuals. The index in FO 611 has been digitised for the years 1851–62 and 1874–1903 and made available online at www.findmypast.com. Additional guidance to locate applications to the monarch or Foreign Office to leave the country prior to the 1850s can be found among The National Archives online research guides for Passport Records.

Finding your ancestors abroad

If your ancestors settled in one of the countries of the British Empire you may be able to find a record of them among the Colonial Office records for the relevant country at The National Archives in series CO. There may be an entry book among the records of the embassy, consulate or colony detailing the names of new British settlers. The hard copy of the Catalogue is on open access in the First Floor Reading Room, and there is a country index at the front of the CO series on the shelves. If your ancestors lived in India, information about them should be found at the British Library (see below).

Anyone researching family members who emigrated to America should search the Ellis Island website at www.ellisislandrecords.org, which is completely free to use and contains records of passengers arriving at the Ellis Island immigration centre for the port of New York, which opened in 1890, digitised ships' manifests, as well as photos of the ships that brought people looking for a new life to the Big Apple. The National Archives of America has also digitised some of its genealogical records, which are free to access online at www.archives.gov/genealogy. The website includes guides on tracing US immigration records, naturalisation records and passport records.

The subscription website www.ancestry.co.uk has a wide range of immigration and emigration records dating back to the 1600s and covering destinations all over the world, from Pennsylvania to Poland and Israel. The collections include digitised published lists of emigrants pulled together from many sources, passenger lists and immigration cards. The bulk of the material relates to emigrants to America, though records can also be found for many different communities (Jewish, Quakers, Italians, Irish) who settled all over the world.

The Church of Jesus Christ of Latter-Day Saints (LDS) collects genealogical records from across the world and so its collections can be useful for tracing your ancestors in the countries where they settled. The website at www.familysearch.org contains the International Genealogical Index (IGI), transcriptions of US and Canadian census returns from the 1880s and the US Social Security Death Index. The website's Record Search pilot provides access to overseas records, including more census returns for America, Canada, Mexico and Argentina, civil registration indexes for America,

Jamaica, Peru, Brazil, the Netherlands and Ireland, and church records for many of the same countries as well as the Czech Republic, Norway, Germany, Spain, Hungary, France, Italy, Costa Rica, Russia and the Philippines. Regional Family History Centres run by the LDS contain microfilm copies of even more overseas genealogical records.

British India

India was the heart of Imperial Britain between 1600 and 1947. Thousands of people went there as merchants or traders, while serving a military career, or as Government officials and around 4 million Britons were born, married or died there. The East India Company conquered the country between 1600 and 1858, at which point the British Government assumed direct responsibility for India, governing through the India Office until 1947. The British Library is the central repository for records of the India Office and the East India Company.

Birth, marriage and death records, similar to those found in UK parish registers, were kept by both the East India Company and the India Office. Chaplains began compiling records from the late seventeenth century as Christian churches became established in India. The records are split according to region – the three main ones being Bengal, Madras and Bombay – and cover mainly European and Anglo-Indian Christians. The British Library holds sets of the registers, some of which have been transcribed and can be searched for free on the India Office Family History Search at http://indiafamily.bl.uk. Those records that are not yet online need to be searched using the British Library's microfilm copies.

The Families in British India Society (FIBIS) website at www.fibis.org provides free online access to records of families who lived or served in the Indian sub-continent from 1600 to 1947. This is an ongoing project and its database of transcriptions taken mainly from British Library India Office sources is not complete. The transcriptions have been taken from military and maritime records, wills, photos, personal papers and directories. To locate detailed research guides regarding civil, military and other occupational records, click on the Fibiwiki link.

Records of the India Office range from the private papers of the Viceroys of India to directories and genealogical records for thousands of British citizens who lived and worked in India when it was part of the British Empire. The East India Company recorded a vast amount of information about its activities and staff, which included merchants, traders, mariners and soldiers. Annual Army lists were compiled, detailing both native regiments and those commanded and staffed by Europeans. The Access to Archives (A2A) Catalogue at www.nationalarchives.gov.uk/a2a contains descriptions of part of the British Library's indexes to people entering into Indian military service between 1775 and 1939, which can be searched by surname and by restricting the search to 'British Library Asia, Pacific and Africa Collections' from the repository list. The Find My Past subscription website at www.findmypast.com also has indexes to Indian records in its migration database, including the 1793–1833 East India Company's Commercial Marine Service Pensions List, the 1855 East India Register & Army List, the 1869 Bengal Civil Service Gradation List, the 1873 Indian Army & Civil Service List and the 1933 India Office List.

Australian Immigrants

Thousands of Britons emigrated to Australia from the eighteenth century onwards. Some of the nation's founding fathers were convicts, forcibly transported; others were free settlers who chose to emigrate in search of land, work and the chance of a better life. Generally, the best place to find information about an ancestor who emigrated to Australia is from the State or Territory archive local to where they settled; however, the National Archives of Australia (NAA) holds some useful information and there is a wealth of records held at The National Archives (TNA) in England regarding convicts who were transported to Australia between 1787 and 1868. If your ancestors remained in Australia it's possible to locate and order birth, marriage and death certificates for them online.

Many convicts sentenced to death were granted clemency and had their sentence commuted to transportation. Petitions for clemency and judges' reports can provide interesting biographical detail about a prisoner, sometimes describing how respectable the individual was in a plea to show them some leniency. Petitions for clemency are indexed at The National Archives in HO 19, and the petitions can be found in HO 18 and HO 19 for 1819 to 1854. Judges' reports and circuit letters are in HO 47 (1784–1829) and HO 6 (1816–40). Reports of the actual trial may be found either at The National Archives or the County Record Office local to where the trial took place. Criminal records are explored in more detail in the following pages for investigating 'family secrets'.

If your criminal ancestor was sentenced to transportation then you can use records at TNA to find them listed on a transportation register in series HO

11 (1787–1867), detailing the ship they sailed on, when they left the UK and the term of their sentence. The transportation registers are being digitised on the subscription website www.ancestry.co.uk so they can be searched by convict's name. The ancestry website also has indexes provided by Australian archives and societies to lists of convicts created when ships arrived in New South Wales. More detailed descriptions of the holdings for transported convicts at TNA can be found in the research guide for 'Australia, 1787–1868, Transportation' on The National Archives website.

If your ancestor emigrated to Australia in search of a better life, then the best place to find out further information about them is from the place where they arrived and settled. The National Archives of Australia (NAA) website at www.naa.gov.au provides an overview of records held in Australian repositories, and has a free online Catalogue containing descriptions of around 6 million documents, photographs, maps and sound recordings that can be searched by keyword, name and date. On the general search page you'll find links to a name search, passenger index and photo search. While the NAA mainly has records relating to migration in the twentieth century, including passenger lists from 1924 onwards, the majority of records relating to immigration during the nineteenth century are held at the various State archives where immigrants settled. In addition to convict records, colonial migration documents, land settlement and land titles, civil registration records are also located in State and Territory record offices.

New South Wales is Australia's most populous state, founded in 1788. During the nineteenth century New South Wales was carved up to accommodate the British colonies of Tasmania in 1825, South Australia in 1836, Victoria in 1851 and Queensland in 1859, though many early immigrants passed through New South Wales before moving on to other territories. The NSW Registry of Births, Marriages and Deaths holds early church records from 1788 to 1855 and civil registrations from 1856 to the present day. The www.bdm.nsw.gov.au website's Family History pages have a Historical Indexes search engine, which locates births between 1788 and 1908, marriages between 1788 and 1958 and deaths between 1788 and 1978. If you find a likely entry this can be ordered online and the certificate sent to your home. The State Records NSW website at www.records.nsw.gov.au has online indexes to some census returns, convict, court, police and prison records, deceased estate records, immigration, naturalisation and land records among many other indexes searchable by name and keyword.

The Queensland State Archives has online indexes at www.archives. qld.gov.au to various genealogy resources held there, including registers of immigrants between 1864 and 1878, assisted immigration passenger lists between 1848 and 1912, land selections between 1868 and 1884, wills proved from 1857 to 1900 and many more useful sources. The Department of Justice and Attorney-General for Queensland have online indexes to births that occurred in Queensland between 1829 and 1914, and for marriages and deaths between 1829 and 1929 at www.justice.qld.gov.au.

Family Secrets

The closer you look at your family's past, the more likely you are to uncover some of the secrets and taboos that were never talked about. It can be exciting to uncover a skeleton in the closet of a distant relative who died long before your time, but there are often secrets kept within families even now that come as a surprise to a generation that is far more open than its predecessors. Your discoveries may change your perception of some family members, and you may need to tread carefully when you come to share your findings with the rest of the family. Some people may be fascinated to discover a convict in the family, while others may be shocked to find out about the birth of a child out of wedlock. Below are some tips to spotting secretive clues hidden in everyday documents, from illegitimacy, adoption and divorce to bigamy and criminality, and how to investigate those skeletons rumoured to be lurking in your family tree.

Illegitimacy and adoption

The birth of an illegitimate child is easy enough to identify from birth and marriage certificates as the father's name is usually left blank. In these cases the child usually took their mother's surname. While the birth of a child out of wedlock is nothing out of the ordinary in today's open society, not so long ago it could be the cause of pain and stigma for many years. Families sometimes went to great lengths to cover up a daughter's indiscretion, and you may find that the child was brought up by grandparents and described as one of their own children on census returns. If there is a large age gap between the two youngest children of the family on a census, this may be cause for investigation. Ordering the birth certificate of the youngest child would say for certain who the mother was. In more extreme circumstances illegitimate babies were given up for adoption. Prior to 1927 there was no official adoption procedure, and most adoptions were arranged privately or through religious organisations. The Adopted Children's Register was kept from 1927 and adoptions were arranged through the courts. The register provides an index to the adoption certificates produced, and can be found on microfiche at The National Archives. However, the index can only be searched by the child's adopted name.

Divorce

Divorce was hard to come by until the 1960s when regional divorce courts were set up and legal aid was provided for people on average incomes. Divorce was available through the civil courts from 1858, but it was expensive to pursue and would only be granted on certain strict criteria. The majority of divorce case files for the years 1858–1937 have survived and are kept in series J 77 at The National Archives. These can be searched by name using the online Catalogue, which provides a document description and full reference so the original papers can be ordered at TNA. Case files describe the reasons why the petitioner wanted a divorce, giving the name of the third party if adultery had been committed, and give the names and ages of any children of the marriage and who would receive custody of the children. Unfortunately the majority of case files since 1938 have been destroyed, but a record of the divorce may be found at the court where it was granted or in the local press.

Bigamy

Bigamy was a considerable problem before divorce became widely available. An unhappy spouse could potentially desert their partner, move away to an area where nobody knew about their past life, and marry again. Bigamists were not always caught by the authorities and brought to justice, so the evidence for a bigamous marriage may be purely circumstantial. If you suspect an ancestor was a bigamist then you should be able to order both their marriages from the General Register Office if they took place during civil registration. The key clues to look for when researching a potential bigamous marriage that was never pursued through the courts are the marital status of the bigamist on their second marriage certificate, and the death of their first spouse. Some bigamists claimed to be widowed, but if you cannot find a death certificate for the first spouse and are able to locate a strong possibility for the spouse on a later census return, then foul play may be suspected. If your bigamous ancestor was caught and prosecuted then you can trace the trial through criminal records.

Criminal ancestors

The National Archives holds many records relating to the trials, imprisonment and transportation of criminals. Records of Assize trials for each county are kept at TNA, though Quarter Sessions and Petty Sessions records are kept in the County Record Office. To locate a trial record you need to know where and when the trial took place. Criminal Registers are kept in TNA series HO 26 and HO 27 covering the dates 1791 to 1892, which record the names of prisoners, the dates of their trial, the place they were tried and the sentence. The proceedings of London's Central Criminal Court at the Old Bailey, the records for which are held at the London Metropolitan Archive, have been put online for the period 1674 to 1913 and can be searched by name at www.oldbaileyonline.org. Local newspaper reports of trials are useful for finding out trial dates and whether the trial was held at the Assizes or Quarter Sessions, and also for finding a detailed description of the evidence given in court, which doesn't always survive among the court records. The British Library has started to digitise its local newspaper collections for the seventeenth to nineteenth centuries and *The Times* has been digitised for the period 1785–1985, which makes it much quicker to find names in articles. The newspaper databases can be accessed for free using computer terminals in the British Library reading rooms. The National Archives online research guide entitled 'Tracing 19th and 20th Century Criminals' provides a county key to finding Calendars of Criminals, and the research guide for 'Assizes: Criminal Trials, 1559–1971' explains how to locate a record of a trial once you know where and when it took place.

Section Two

TRACING YOUR ANCESTRAL HOME

Introduction

One of the most important aspects of your personal heritage is the trail of houses that you are linked to, through family ties spanning decades and generations – these are the dwellings that our ancestors called home, where many of them were born or died, and that reveal so much about your personal background and origins. They will reflect a particular period of history, in a particular location or community – and therefore will form an integral part of your story.

This section will show you how to trace the history of a house, whether it's a property that your great-grandparents owned and lived in (and perhaps no longer stands today), or you have a general curiosity about the property you live in today – and want to pass on a record for future generations of your family.

From finding the first clues from your existing family tree, and using maps and plans to track when a house was built, and how the community changed over time; to more detailed searches concerning house ownership and occupancy – I'll introduce you to some new sources that will place your family in a physical setting.

Chapter Six

INTRODUCTION TO HOUSE HISTORY

There's something amazing about discovering all the addresses where your ancestors once lived – even more so if the houses are still standing, and you can visit in person. History begins to come alive when it transfers from being simply a paper trail, to a physical journey to real places and locations. The houses you will find out about become more than just bricks and mortar – they contain the rooms where your family members, in the distant past, used to prepare their meals, eat their dinner, play games and celebrate birthdays, tell family stories around the fire and rest their weary heads after a long day's work. This chapter will explain how you can interrogate your family tree to obtain addresses, and then start to draw upon new sources to find out more about the history of each one.

Examining the Family Tree for Information

Most of the documents that you've already used to compile your family tree will also provide you with information about where these people lived. For example, a birth certificate will state not only the name of the child, its parents and father's occupation, but also the address where the birth took place – for most families this would have been at home – or, if the birth took place in a hospital or other such institution, then the address of the informant, which was usually one or other (or indeed both!) of the parents and therefore equated to the family home. Similar information can be found on marriage certificates for both parties, which is handy if you want to work out where the couple were living prior to marriage (and you'll be surprised how many times that it turns out to be the same address for bride and groom – cohabiting wasn't such a modern phenomenon as you may have imagined), and death certificates.

Equally, census returns are a great way of finding out about the house and community in which your family lived, since they were essentially a head count based on property occupancy in the first place! Beware, though, that many addresses stated in census returns may have changed over time, particularly with reference to house numbering that was subject to frequent change. Equally, you may find that the house doesn't have a number or name at all, or that it's simply referred to as 'village' for smaller communities. Advice about tracking houses on census returns is given below.

Indeed, any of the main building block sources will provide information on property residency – wills often give the address of the deceased or the next of kin, and later parish registers (after the introduction of Government-authorised pre-printed volumes with standardised entries in 1813) will also provide data about residency.

Using Local Knowledge: Locating the House

It may sound faintly ridiculous, but make sure you know where the house that you're looking for actually is. It's easy enough to do with modern houses, but many of the properties you will be tracing are likely to have been demolished with the passing of time – some deliberately, as a result of slum clearances, new housing schemes and compulsory purchases; others through fate and the impact of historical events, literally so in the case of the Blitz during the Second World War. You will need to use a variety of historic maps and plans (described in the next chapter) to pinpoint these lost properties in the past, and then compare the old maps to modern equivalents to see what's standing there today, so at least you can see how time has marched by and the modern world has encroached on the old one.

In addition to finding the houses on a variety of maps, you should also spend some time investigating the administrative districts in which they stood. These should include the parish – civil and ecclesiastical; the parliamentary constituency; the Poor Law Union; and, more obscurely, the county division and manor or estate in which it was built. All of these administrative areas will generate records in which the house you are researching may appear, alongside information about its occupants and owners (many of whom will be your relatives). The golden rule is to never take anything for granted; there have been many boundary changes over the years, and you may even find that the houses you are tracing switched between counties over time!

Some of these districts can be found on Ordnance Survey maps, but if you are in any doubt – particularly concerning some of the older administrative units – then you should consult various historical secondary sources and local history guides, which can be found in most good libraries. In particular, you should visit your local study centre, where in addition to original material and collected research notes, you are likely to find important books such as the *Victoria County History*, which over the last century or so have produced detailed reference works tracing the history of each county, and the principal towns, villages and hamlets within. As well as providing an overview of the overlapping jurisdictions, you will also find detailed information about manors, local landowners and the main houses in the area – mainly linked via footnotes to the sources, and archives where the sources are stored, so you can follow up on any particular points of interest yourself. One top tip is to take a modern map of the house you're looking for (or a copy of an old map, if the house no longer stands) and mark on it the various districts in which it was placed over time, as a handy reference tool when you visit an archive.

If you are looking at the history of a house that hasn't been in the family that long, mainly because it was a 'modern' twentieth-century build, it's still important to trace the history of the plot of land back in time as well. Just because the house you are investigating isn't that old, this doesn't mean that the land on which it stands doesn't have a story to tell. Indeed, the history of the community's expansion to include new building plots on the outskirts will reveal a great deal about the area, and will naturally form an important part of your work in establishing key events that your ancestors would have witnessed. The coming of the railways, for example, in the nineteenth century transformed the face of Britain, as did the Industrial Revolution that drove the railway networks across the country. Both were accompanied by a massive house-building programme as factory owners built or created a demand for working-class accommodation in the emerging towns and cities, while railway workers were often given houses to live in alongside or near the stations and depots where they worked. These topics are considered in more detail in Section Three. However, it is important to consider the impact of historical events on the way our ancestors lived, and the houses that were created as a result.

First Research Steps

In many ways, the local study or municipal record office (if the house was within a large town or city) is the best place to start. Many archives have card indexes relating to miscellanea collected over time, based on street names. Material can be pretty diverse, from photographs to newspaper clippings. Indeed, it's worth scanning through the photograph catalogue to see if you can find any snaps of the local area. Not only might they contain the ancestral home, but you may well find an evocative picture of life from a bygone age – horse-drawn carts and carriages, gas lamps, children playing in the street, unfamiliar dress and local shops for local people. Indeed, these photos may be the last record of a house before demolition or destruction, and could even contain some of your family. Alongside photograph collections, see if there's a local or regional moving image archive. Films are an amazing resource, where they survive, and once again can provide some evocative context to your research, aside from the document trail that I'll be discussing throughout the remainder of this section.

There will be a natural temptation to visit the house that you're targeting in your work, but you have to exercise diplomacy or tact when trying to visit the house of a stranger – try to avoid 'doorstepping' at all costs, and instead consider writing a letter in advance, outlining your quest and finding a mutually convenient time to visit. Having done this for my own family, and visited a property in West Beckham where my grandmother spent her early childhood during the First World War, I found that the occupants were fascinated to find someone whose relative lived in the house, and could provide memories from ninety years ago to sit alongside their current experience of dwelling there. The trick is to not outstay your welcome, and realise that your family might not be as interesting to others as they are to you.

That said, you can draw upon local knowledge within the community to help you with your detective work. There might be a local history group that has conducted research into the area, or people who remember former occupants (including your family, perhaps) who can share their stories with you. If possible, take some pictures of the house for your records – and always with the permission of the owners! It might be an idea to leave a photo on the notice board of the nearest archive or study centre with an appeal for information: you never know, it might jog someone's memory into revealing some useful data about the house.

There may also be clues about the history of the house in its name, or indeed the name of the street or district. There's every chance that Miller's Cottage was once owned or lived in by a miller; The Rectory was once owned by the Church and housed the parish incumbent; or Garrick Villa was in the possession of someone who had that name. Many houses were simply referred to by their occupant in this way. Similarly, street names would reflect local owners, or people of influence in the area – and might also indicate a former use of the site on which more modern houses have been built, that can lead you to a particular set of documents or period of time. As with Miller's Cottage, houses were not always solely domestic dwellings, and many would have found a former use as a public house, coaching inn, shop or even place of manufacture. Many of the houses in Spitalfields, East London, were home to legions of silk weavers, working away in the garret rooms at the top; nowadays, they have been converted into sought-after residential properties.

You should not forget the house and its surrounds either. Properties were built in different styles according to the geographical region in which they stood, based on raw building materials and the techniques and fashion of the time and therefore every house will have its own architectural fingerprint that you can learn to read for clues. Regional building styles, often the signature of older houses, are described as having 'vernacular' architecture and would conform to a set pattern within that area. By the seventeenth century, 'polite' architecture was growing in popularity, which means that all fashionable, and aspiring to be fashionable, houses that were built in a particular era often followed the same design plan, and are often described by the period in which they were built – Georgian, Regency, Victorian, Edwardian, Art Deco, Modernist, Gothic Revival. These 'period properties' can therefore be assigned a rough construction date according to the architectural clues they contain, not just outside but within as well – again, provided you've secured access first! The way a house was furnished and constructed can be instrumental in telling you when it was built, or re-fashioned for a particular event. Weddings often resulted in a redecorating programme, particularly if the married couple were to move in. Some of the wallpaper samples or flakes of paint might have survived, and can be dated – further advice is provided in Chapter 10 about 'Occupancy' if you want to investigate the way your ancestors would have lived in a period property.

It's not just the bricks and mortar that have a story to tell. You may find important clues hidden in the fabric of the building – old trunks full of newspapers, photographs, personal possessions and correspondence might appear to be junk to a disinterested bystander, but in the hands of a researcher they can tell you about the lives of former occupants. The places to look for these are in cellars and attics (often the oldest spaces of the house, by coincidence) and they may be in a poor condition. But thousands of personal documents will have been thrown away over the years, so you will be lucky to find something left behind, unless your ancestors and their successors in the property were compulsive hoarders. One of the first things people do on the death of a relative, or moving into a new house, is to throw away piles of 'rubbish'. You may also find clues in the very fabric of the property – because older documents were often written on parchment (stretched sheepskin) they were often quite good at providing insulation against cold and damp, and have been found in the thatched roofs of old buildings!

Some material, though, might have escaped the various purges over time, particularly if buried in the back garden, as was the fate of many broken or disused domestic items. In particular, fragments of earthenware and pottery, clay pipes, internal fixtures and fittings, scraps of clothing and glass bottles can show you the sorts of items that our ancestors used, or surrounded themselves with inside their homes. It's all part of the story of your personal heritage, and takes you back to a time when electricity was unheard of and 'mod cons' probably consisted of a mangle to dry clothes. Again, you can become your own backyard archaeologist if you live in an inherited family home, but I'm not suggesting you turn up at a former residence and start digging! Many items found in the local area are likely to have been collected and displayed in a local museum, where in any case you can find out about the lifestyle of your ancestors from days gone by through exhibitions on clothing, design and décor, sport and leisure, religion and work – topics covered in Section Three.

Pitfalls

You will need to keep an eye out for a range of potential pitfalls when researching your ancestral homes. Probably the most common error is tracing the history of the wrong house because the number or street name has changed, especially if you're looking for a house in an urban area where re-numbering exercises were common in the late nineteenth and early twentieth centuries. Fortunately, there are a number of ways of checking for these changes, such as examining rate books or street directories, which continued to display the former and new names and numbers simultaneously for several editions, or the changes are marked on a contemporary map, such as the 1910 Valuation Office survey which is described in the next chapter.

Equally you have to beware of the changing use of plots of land, and that the present incarnation of a house might hide earlier properties that have been rebuilt on the same site. Sometimes rebuilds are constructed in a style that mimics an early type of architecture, suggesting that the fabric of the house was built at an earlier date than it actually was, so you have to beware of retrospective builds and use documents as much as possible to support or indeed challenge the architectural evidence. Many properties will incorporate the fabric of former buildings within them – the core of a medieval hall house might still be in evidence in a much later rebuild, for example, while the roof of an earlier property could have been hoisted onto the walls of a new construct underneath to save the owner some money.

Useful tips

In summary, here are a few useful tips to get you started in researching the history of your house:

- Construct a timeline for each ancestor you are interested in, focusing on birth, marriage and death plus key dates from census and other records (birth of children for example); and then assign an address for each one from the relevant source (certificate, census, etc.).
- Obtain a copy of a map, or series of maps, that show where all these houses were. Ordnance Survey maps are the best sources to use, and can be found at your local study centre or archive where copying rules and regulations can be explained.
- Try to ascertain from modern maps whether these houses still stand, and if so arrange a site visit, having contacted the current occupier first.
- With permission, take a photograph and see if you can post it in the local study centre or archive with a request for stories, documents, names of former owners/occupiers or even its history.
- Use secondary sources from the relevant local study centre or archive to determine the historical boundaries within which your houses fell, and mark them in the margin of the map copies for reference purposes.

Chapter Seven

USING MAPS AND PLANS

Introduction

B earing in mind you are going to be tracking a range of houses over time, you will almost certainly need to pinpoint them on a variety of maps. Luckily, there are several national sets of records that you can use, as well as assorted local maps that will have been created for many reasons, and are now likely to be stored in local archives and record offices. There is an added bonus when working with maps, because they are highly visual and therefore relatively easy to interpret; furthermore, because you can look at maps covering a wide range of periods, you might be able to see when your house first appears – or indeed disappears on a later map as part of a programme of slum clearance or an urban regeneration project.

There are four main sets of records that provide a fairly comprehensive mapping record for most properties that were built, or were standing, from the middle of the nineteenth century onwards – the same period when civil registration and census returns can be used to compile your family tree, and the places where the main events occurred. Ordnance Survey (OS) maps provide an overview of Britain from the start of the nineteenth century, although detailed series of maps were introduced from the mid-1800s and updated at regular intervals. However, they won't tell you who lived in a house, or perhaps owned it; luckily there are three nationwide sources that can give you this data at key moments in time – the National Farm Survey for farms and rural property, dated 1943; the Valuation Office survey, initiated in 1910 and conducted for several years thereafter; and the Tithe Apportionments from 1836 onwards, covering any parish which still paid tithes in kind to the church prior to that date. The last two sets of records are particularly important if you are moving from family tree to family house, since they correspond fairly well with census returns in key years.

Where to find maps and plans

The National Archives holds these three national sets of records, but also has an estimated 1 million other maps and plans among its holdings, many of which can be used to trace house history. In addition, there is a substantial although incomplete collection of OS sheets from various periods, although one of the best places to go for a full national set of OS maps is the British Library's Map Library (which also holds an impressive collection of local maps), while the National Library of Scotland and the National Library of Wales also hold full sets for their territories. Map sheets can now be downloaded from a variety of commercial dataset providers such as Cassini Maps (www.cassinimaps.co.uk) and Old Maps (www.old-maps.co.uk), or indeed direct from the OS website www.ordnancesurvey.co.uk. Nevertheless, the golden rule remains that if you want local information, you should go to a local archive where the majority of map data for the area in question will be held – estate maps, local authority maps, planning applications, sale details and county maps to name but a few.

Ordnance Survey maps

OS maps are considered a standard reference source for family and local historians, mainly because they are a national dataset that spans a wide period, with regular updates so that you can see how the landscape changed over time. However, our modern research requirements from historic and contemporary OS maps rather masks the fact that they originated in the Board of Ordnance section of the War Office in the mid-eighteenth century, when they were given a remit to produce a military map of the Highlands of Scotland – an aftermath of the Jacobite rebellions, and the subsequent network of roads and fortifications that were put in place to stop further insurrection and revolt. The role and scope of the Board of Ordnance expanded to include a general map as part of a Trigonometrical Survey in 1791, resulting in the publication of the first official civilian map in 1801 at the scale of 1 inch to the mile. The idea caught on and demand for professional maps grew, so much so that in 1841 the Ordnance Survey Act was passed to set up the OS as a separate institution outside the control of the military, with a wide remit of work; aside from periodical publications of national sets of maps arranged by county, the work of the OS included commissions to ascertain and record boundary changes.

OS County Maps

By far the most important set of maps produced by the OS, county sheets were published at various intervals from the start of the nineteenth century onwards, often using various scales, for each county. The British Library is a registered place of deposit, which means it is obliged to keep a copy of each OS map produced. However, regional and local archives will usually hold a pretty full set for the area they cover, while The National Archives holds stand-alone sets of OS maps, as well as OS material incorporated into a wide variety of Government departments because maps formed an important part of their work.

The earliest series of published OS maps dates from 1801, as previously mentioned, and are drawn at the scale of 1 inch to the mile. This does not give a particularly good level of detail for property in towns or cities; however, you might be able to spot rural properties and farms, or houses of sufficient size and importance – if your ancestors were of such social standing! The main use of this early series of OS maps is to provide an overview of an area, and therefore show parts of the country before the Industrial Revolution really took hold – in many ways, showing you a disappearing world.

The first set of comprehensive OS county maps dates from the 1850s after the Ordnance Survey Act of 1841, when 6 inch to the mile county maps were drawn up and published (with 5 inch to the mile mapping for London). This First Edition set of maps was completed by the 1880s, after which a revised Second Edition was published 1896–1904, giving even greater levels of detail for inner city areas at a range of scales – many of which are considered in the next section relating to the Valuation Office survey of 1910, which used many of these maps. A Third Edition followed shortly after, though many of the Second Edition maps were revised at about the same time, with the process continuing into the 1920s, 1930s and even 1940s. A full summary of what's available at the 6-inch scale, county by county, can be found on the British Library website www.bl.uk/reshelp where you can follow the directions to the map collection, and onwards to the OS section.

As mentioned above, you can obtain digital copies of many of these historic maps from commercial companies, based on postcode submissions, for a fee. Some maps can be downloaded, others posted as a gift pack – it's up to you to find a company and package that suits both your needs and your budget, so shop around. You can make copies (for research purposes only) from most record offices and libraries, and in most instances this will be your first port of call to save you travelling to London to examine the British Library's collections – unless of course you are tracing houses in more than one county.

Valuation Office survey

The Valuation Office survey, often referred to as the Lloyd George Domesday, was created by the 1909–10 Finance Act – a piece of legislation in which the Government (through the Valuation Office) would assess the value of land and property, and then raise money from tax based on this assessment. It is a little-used source, mainly because the records are predominantly stored in The National Archives, London and can be somewhat difficult to access. As a result, it is necessary to explain in some detail what records were created by the survey, and how you can find the right ones for your property. There is a useful research guide online at The National Archives website www.nationalarchives.gov.uk, while a useful chapter on the subject can be found in G. Beech and R. Mitchell, *Maps for Family and Local History*.

When looking at the records of the Valuation Office survey, your knowledge of the local area and the various administrative districts sourced through secondary literature will come in very handy. During the assessment, England and Wales were divided into fourteen valuation regions (later reduced to thirteen) and further sub-divided into 118 valuation districts, so you will need to know a bit about the geographical region in which the house stands. Surveyors used two sets of OS maps, of varying dates, for each region to detail all land or property that formed part of the survey. Each land unit – which varied in size from individual houses to large fields – was then assigned a hereditament or assessment number, which was usually marked on the map in red, with the boundary for that property marked in red (or sometimes green depending on district or region). If the property had associated fields attached, they are likely to be 'colour-washed' in the same colour and linked with red brackets (if separated by a road, river or other fields) to show they formed part of the same assessment.

The official 'record' maps were deposited in TNA, and can now be accessed in record series IR 121 and IR 124–35. The remaining working copies, where they survive, were usually placed in the County Record Office, but survival is patchy and so your best bet is to access the record maps, even if it does mean a trip to Kew. However, the maps were only one half of the assessment; the financial data that the inspectors and surveyors collected during the course of their work was recorded in Field Books, deposited at TNA in record series IR 58. A second set of records, known as Revenue Books or 'Domesday books', were created at the same time but are of less use to someone wishing to trace occupancy or ownership details, as they contain less information about individual properties and are more concerned with the financial data – perhaps unsurprising, since the whole purpose was to raise money from taxation!

Before looking at means of access for the records, it's important to flag up some of the parameters of this survey. While there's pretty much full national coverage, certain parts of the country are missing either maps or field books due to bomb damage caused by enemy action in the Second World War. Furthermore, the process of surveying the country was interrupted by the First World War, with the result that the records for some areas are more detailed than others given the need to wrap up proceedings rather speedily. Nevertheless, most of the records cover the period 1912–15, though some districts started the process earlier. This makes the Valuation Office survey a particularly good point of comparison if you've found your ancestors in the 1911 census, as you will be able to move pretty much from the census details and address to the Valuation Office survey records without worrying too much that the property details have changed. It should also make it easier to work back in time to the 1901 census as well, having obtained a copy of the map and recorded the names of neighbours (or indeed the whole street) for context.

Finding the maps at TNA

Since you need to find the heriditament number before you can access the relevant Field Book, the starting point for an investigation of the Valuation Office survey has to be with the maps. This means finding and ordering the correct Valuation Office survey map – which can sound easier than it actually is!

To help you identify the right map, there are some finding aids available at Kew – for instance, there is a key sheet (known as the County Diagram) for each county that shows its full extent, with the relevant OS maps overlaid for reference. There are two County Diagram folders for England, arranged alphabetically (noting that Hampshire is filed under S for Southampton, and to use the 'Old Series' sheet for Essex unless your property is in the SW corner of the county, in which case you use the 'New Series' sheet), and a third one for Wales. You will find that each key sheet is divided into a series of numbered grids with a large number printed in the middle, which in turn are sub-divided into sixteen smaller unnumbered rectangles, with each rectangle representing a map at the OS scale 1:2500 (or 25 inches to the mile). Ultimately, you will have to identify which of the smaller rectangles your property falls within, which can be a difficult process given the very small scale the key sheets are drawn at – particularly in built-up areas. Luckily, help is at hand.

First, make a note of the number in the large rectangle. You can use this to search the 6-inch OS county maps that are on open access in the Map and Large Document Room, as they contain individual maps that have exactly the same grid numbers, but at a scale that should allow you to locate your property with ease. It is then a case of comparing the OS sheet with the key sheet and judging which smaller rectangle is most appropriate – and, of course, it helps if you've already made a copy of the right OS sheet when you first visited the county or local record office for precisely this sort of situation!

The reason that it is so important to identify which of the sixteen grids is relevant is because each one is a separate map that you'll need to order out. Therefore if you still aren't sure which exact smaller rectangle your house is in, you may well need to order out both maps. The way of identifying the correct map in the Catalogue is to firstly convert the number from the County Diagram from arabic to roman numerals (thus map 10 becomes X, 26 becomes XXVI and 94 becomes XCIV for example) and then add the smaller rectangle number in arabic numerals. To obtain the smaller rectangle number, you'll see that the grids are arranged in blocks of four; simply count from left to right, assigning a number to each one. Top left becomes 1, top right will be 4, bottom left is 13, while bottom right is 16.

Having done this, you will need to find the equivalent map in TNA's Catalogue. You can run a quick keyword search via the Catalogue, including the county and both numbers; but it's best to stick with the old-fashioned way and use the paper series lists available in the Map and Large Document Room, since they show at a glance how each region was sub-divided into separate districts, with each district assigned a TNA sub-series number. The name that has been given to each district roughly equates to a geographical area, but they are quite broad in scope and so you may have to search several districts before you find your map – or indeed find the right map listed in more than one district where boundaries overlap, which means you will have to order both to make sure you've found the one that covers the property. Where there are gaps in the collection of record maps at TNA, you might want to check the County Record Office in case the working copy has survived.

The maps you will be working from are usually at the scale 1:2500, though to provide detailed coverage for towns and cities the surveyors filled out additional maps at the scales of 1:1250 and 1:500. There are four 1:1250 maps for each 1:2500 map, representing the north-west, north-east, south-east and south-west quadrants, while the 1:500 maps are even more detailed, with twenty-five for each 1:2500 map arranged in five rows of five using a similar series of row by row numbering to the sixteen grid system. Where more detailed maps have been created, their existence is marked on the 1:2500 map and they are usually listed separately in the series lists.

Once you've found the map and noted its reference, you can order it out and examine it for clues. You'll see that each property has been given a hereditament number, marked in red – make a note of this – and you may also see reference to an income tax parish (ITP) usually on the edge of the map. ITPs were created to group together small ecclesiastical or civil parishes, and are vital in locating the relevant Field Book in which your property is described. Boundaries between one or more ITP are usually coloured in yellow on the maps.

If you have found an ancestral property in either London or Westminster, or indeed one of the surrounding suburbs, you have to follow a slightly different procedure to locate your map. There are separate key sheets for the London area that divide large grids into 100 smaller rectangles, rather than the usual sixteen. The key sheet folder on open access also contains larger scale inserts to allow you to identify your property in more detail. A good knowledge of London geography helps, but there are various reference books (such as the A–Z series) that allow you identify the modern location and compare it to the older key sheets. Thereafter, the procedure for locating and ordering a map is exactly the same as for other parts of the country – you should make a note of which grid and rectangle is most appropriate to your property, and look for the maps in record series IR 121, which is sub-divided into nineteen districts, each with its own TNA sub-series number. As well as the caveats listed above about duplicate maps, there is an added complication in the sense that the London region contained maps for property located in the neighbouring counties, which means that you may need to search the relevant county key sheets as well as the London key sheet to find the correct map references. London maps are at the OS scale 1:1056, while county maps are at the usual 1:2500 scale.

Finding the Field Books at TNA

The key to locating your property in the relevant Field Book is to correctly locate it on the map, and make a note of the hereditament number assigned to your property – and where possible, the ITP in which the property falls. Every Field Book contains the information for exactly one hundred hereditaments in numbered blocks, for example 1–100, 101–200, 201–300 and so forth, and each hereditament will have been assigned four pages in the book. Every entry contains crucial information about the property and its owner or occupier. Although the details will vary, you should at least find out the names of the owner and the occupier, plus the full street address, which you can use to corroborate the information found in the 1911 census. You may also find a description of the property – which is often rather unflattering – as well as the occasional sketch maps or inserts, descriptions of outbuildings and even the dates of previous sales or construction dates.

The Field Books are arranged in valuation districts, a bit like the maps; however, it is not as simple to identify which region to look within because the descriptions are quite vague and the ITPs often don't correspond to actual places – or rather, smaller places may be amalgamated into an ITP. If you are lucky, the ITP will be marked on the map – with boundaries with other ITPs usually marked in yellow either on the main map, or on the edge. However, if these are not marked – and in many cases they are not – you will need to use several place name-based finding aids in the Map and Large Document Reading Room to help you find the correct ITP and valuation district. The place name index should provide you with the valuation district (to be found under the 'Valuation' column) so that you can search the IR 58 series list which is thereafter arranged alphabetically by the names of the ITPs within that valuation district; there are separate indexes for London that are arranged by street name which then assign a valuation district and ITP.

If you can't find the place you are looking for, you can check the Board of Inland Revenue's *Alphabetical List of Parishes and Places in England and Wales*, which is also on open access in two volumes. This will list all the small parishes, hamlets and townships that were grouped into a single ITP, and you will find their records incorporated under the new ITP. Another problem can be linked to finding the correct valuation district, as the place name index

The Fleckney family, photographed in 1905, had five generations alive at the same time which was most unusual for the period.

A good place to start your research is collecting together any old letters and family photographs that may have been kept.

findmypast.co.uk and ancestry.co.uk will both prove invaluable in your research.

CERTIFIED COPY OF AN ENTRY OF MARRIAGE   GIVEN AT THE GENERAL REGISTER OFFICE

Application Number R003994/A.

1880 Marriage solemnized at *The Parish Church* in the *Parish*
of *Christ Church Spitalfields* in the County of *London*

No.	When Married.	Name and Surname.	Age.	Condition.	Rank or Profession.	Residence at the time of Marriage.	Father's Name and Surname.	Rank or Profession of Father.
387	February 23 1880	Henry Ernest Hillier	23	Bachelor	Butcher	9 Pelham St	Henry Ernest Hillier	Tailor
		Emma Hervey Taylor	19	Spinster	—	9 Pelham St	William Taylor	Hawker

Married in the *Parish Church* according to the Rites and Ceremonies of the *Established Church* by or after *Banns* by me,

This marriage was solemnized between us, *Henry Ernest Hillier* *Emma Harvey Taylor* in the presence of us, *Charles Small* *Lydia Small +*   A. L. Hunt Curate

CERTIFIED to be a true copy of an entry in the certified copy of a register of Marriages in the Registration District of *Whitechapel*
Given at the GENERAL REGISTER OFFICE, under the Seal of the said Office, the 13th day of February 19 98

MXA 219296

This certificate is issued in pursuance of section 65 of the Marriage Act 1949. Sub-section 3 of that section provides that any certified copy of an entry purporting to be sealed or stamped with the seal of the General Register Office shall be received as evidence of the marriage to which it relates without any further or other proof of the entry, and no certified copy purporting to have been given in the said Office shall be of any force or effect unless it is sealed or stamped as aforesaid.

CAUTION.—It is an offence to falsify a certificate or to make or knowingly use a false certificate or a copy of a false certificate intending it to be accepted as genuine to the prejudice of any person, or to possess a certificate knowing it to be false without lawful authority.

WARNING: THIS CERTIFICATE IS NOT EVIDENCE OF THE IDENTITY OF THE PERSON PRESENTING IT.

Form A513MX

Form MXA   Dd &413990   100M   7/97   Mor(IL0088)

Marriage and death certificates can provide clues to your ancestors' lives.

IA 853777

CERTIFIED COPY of an ENTRY OF DEATH
Pursuant to the Births and Deaths Registration Act, 1953

(Printed by authority of the Reg

ory fee for this certificate is 3s. 9d. search is necessary to find the entry, fee is payable in addition.

Registration District

1963. Death in the Sub-district of in the

When and where died	Name and surname	Sex	Age	Occupation	Cause of death	Signature, description, and residence of informant	When registered	Signature of registrar
Twenty eighth November 1963. 6. Manor Close Henfield	Gertrude Louise Chater	Female	75 years	Wife of Frank Chater a Fitter (Retired)	1a Bronchopneumonia b. Bilateral hemiplegia c. Carotid insufficiency and generalised arteriosclerosis II Diabetes mellitus certified by Paul Wellings MB	G. K. Chater Son Y. Morrison House High Street Feltham	Twenty ninth November 1963.	J. R. Mayes. Registrar.

I, *Reginald Mayes*, Registrar of Births and Deaths for the Sub-district of , in the County
do hereby certify that this is a true copy of Entry No. 54 in the Register Book of Deaths for the said Sub-district, and that such Register is now legally in my custody.

WITNESS MY HAND this 29th day of November, 1963.

J. R. Mayes Registrar of Births and Deaths.

N.—Any person who (1) falsifies any of the particulars on this certificate,) uses a falsified certificate as true, knowing it to be false, is liable to

The 1911 census can provide information about where your ancestors lived and with whom.

A will, pre-1858. Often wills from this period would include instructions for the disposal of the body, sometimes giving details for the location of the burial.

The National Archives website, www.nationalarchives.gov.uk, contains the Access to Archives (A2A) database. This can be used to find archives held locally in England and Wales.

War memorials such as this can be found in most villages and towns across the UK.
They list men from the area who fought and lost their lives.

Chances are that some of your ancestors will have worked in a profession that generated employment records, such as coal mining.

RUTHERHAM MAIN COLLIERY, CANKLOW.

Unveiling of the war memorial in
Dodworth, Barnsley on 13 May 1923.

A page from the service record of Horace Sydney Dickens, providing details of the surviving members of his family. The form was completed by his widow Louisa in July 1919.

You can search and download over 600,000 service records for those who joined the Royal Navy between 1853 and 1923.

Service records of RAF Officers that served prior to 1922 and Airmen that served prior to 1924 are held at The National Archives. Service records for Officers and Airmen that served after these dates are retained by the Royal Air Force.

Schoolchildren photographed in the late 1920s.

From left to right: Distinguished Service Order (DSO), the 1914-15 Star, the British War Medal, the Allied Victory Medal, Second World War Medal, the Coronation Medal, Légion d'Honneur.

A workhouse for the poor, 1906.

A northern town in around 1900.

Gibson Mill, Hebdon Bridge. A typical cotton mill from the nineteenth century.

Railway station staff in the early 1930s.

Typical street scenes from a working class area.

doesn't always tally with the correct ITP. You will have to use local knowledge where possible to estimate the valuation district. Alternatively, the Catalogue permits a keyword search (which you can restrict solely to series IR 58), and this may help you locate your ITP and associated valuation district if you are having problems – and indeed, should be your first port of call, although you should always use the paper lists to avoid locating an incorrect ITP that happens to have the same name, but is in a different valuation district.

If all else fails and you are still unable to locate the ITP in the IR 58 series list, then you could perhaps check the relevant Revenue Book in the County Record Office. They contain a list of all the parishes that made up an ITP, as well as listing the full range of hereditament numbers that were allocated to each parish – a handy guide. This will be of particular use in certain areas where the Field Books were destroyed by enemy action in the Second World War – Southampton, Winchester, Portsmouth and Coventry, as well as parts of Chichester and Chelmsford. The Revenue Books for the City of London and Westminster (Paddington district) are also held at TNA.

Similar Valuation Office records for Scotland are at the National Archives of Scotland, while some material is available for Northern Ireland at the Public Record Office of Northern Ireland. An earlier land survey, known as the Griffiths Valuation (covering 1848–64) is also held there, which is accessible online from www.origins.net via their Irish collections.

Tithe apportionments

If the Valuation Office survey of the early twentieth century is a good marker that connects with the 1911 and 1901 census returns, then there's an equally important land survey from the other end of the chronological period that can be linked to the 1841 and 1851 censuses – the tithe apportionments that were created from 1836. Tithes were payments in kind of a tenth of the annual produce of land assessed on crops and animals cultivated there, and were payable to either the parson of the parish, or an entitled lay person, or both. Payment of tithes had been made for centuries, but over time many individual arrangements had been made to commute the payment to a fixed sum of money, or in some cases a grant of land, for ease of payment and to secure a guaranteed income for the incumbent. Enclosures of common land along with changes to estate and land management hastened this process, in particular the Enclosure Acts of the eighteenth and nineteenth centuries, of which more information is provided a bit later.

By the 1830s, tithes had become highly unpopular among rural landowners because the sums of money or value of crops did not accurately reflect the changing social and economic conditions of the dawning industrial age, when increasing urban wealth was being generated in areas where no tithes were payable, or in areas of economic activity that were exempt from paying tithes. Under the Tithe Commutation Act of 1836 (6 & 7 Will. IV, c.71), remaining payments in kind were to be commuted into fixed monetary sums based on a seven-year average of the price of wheat, barley and oats taken across the country. Naturally, this affected many rural parishes as well as places that had not yet begun to be industrialised; in some cases, the process was handled between church and landowners by negotiation, but a Tithe Commission was set up to help parties reach agreement and arbitrate in disputed cases, in which case an award was produced. Either way, whether negotiated or arbitrated, the end product of the commutation process was a tithe apportionment that formalised the agreement or award.

The resultant tithe apportionment consisted of a map, created by surveyors (but not the Ordnance Survey, whose creation was influenced by the work generated by the process) that showed all properties that were liable to tithes; and an associated apportionment schedule based on the agreement or award that set out the financial liabilities for each landowner concerned. An official apportionment and two copies were made, with the original retained by the Tithe Commission (and now deposited at TNA in two series IR 30 for maps and IR 29 for the associated apportionment schedule). One copy was sent to the parish church and the other to the relevant register of the diocese, and where these copies have survived they are usually found in the County Record Office, or possibly the Diocesan Record Office.

The process of creating the maps continued until the mid 1850s, although the vast majority of agreements and awards had been concluded by the mid 1840s. Although many communities would have been unrecognisable to their modern incarnation, you can still work back from later OS maps to find the plot of land where your ancestral home would have been built, or indeed had already been constructed, as well as get a sense of the size of the local community in the middle of the nineteenth century. The tithe maps should allow you to find the equivalent entry in the schedule where you'll find out information about ownership, occupancy and the size of the plot of land. Coverage is not complete for England and Wales, as no apportionments were created for areas where agreements had previously been reached through other means. As a result, tithe apportionments will also be of limited use for properties in towns and cities, as most historic urban areas would either have commuted to money payments centuries earlier, or had a different system of paying its clerics; although where tithes were still payable you will find detailed maps and assessments that provide an invaluable source. Tithes remained a complicated issue and further legislation followed, including the 1936 Tithe Act, which produced further related documents including District Record Maps in TNA series IR 90. These maps were compiled from more recent OS maps and – where they survive – provide a useful point of comparison between the historic tithe maps in IR 30 and the modern landscape.

Finding the records

The best place to start looking for tithe maps and awards will be the relevant County Record Office, as in theory, they should have at least one of the deposited copies in their holdings. This potentially provides you with a choice of maps if one is of poor quality. Furthermore, later amendments that affected the value of the apportionment, such as the subsequent use of land for building railways and canals, were attached to the apportionment; these are not always to be found on the copies at TNA.

However, if you are planning to undertake a range of property searches across the country, using a range of national land survey sources described in this chapter, or you can't find a serviceable copy at the county archives, then the best place to start your work will be TNA, which holds approximately 11,800 maps and apportionment schedules. There are combined series lists for IR 29 and IR 30, as the maps and apportionment schedules share the same piece number for each parish. The lists are arranged alphabetically by county, and thereafter by parish. Each county has been assigned a number, as has each parish, and these numbers combine to form your piece number, prefixed by IR 30 if you wish to locate the map, or IR 29 for the apportionment schedule. Alternatively, you can undertake a search of the Catalogue using the parish name as the keyword and restricting your search to IR 29 or IR 30 (either series should work). There is also a very useful publication in the Reading Room, Kain and Oliver's *The Tithe Maps and Apportionments of England and Wales* which provides a similar county and parish listing, assigning piece numbers to each parish with an accompanying brief description of the documents you will be accessing, such as the date of the map, features depicted, the scale of the map, the name of the surveyor (if known) and the date of the apportionment. Furthermore, there is an introduction for each county that provides a detailed description of tithe liability, with a map of the county that shows a general overview of how many parishes were liable to tithes and therefore produced documents as part of the survey.

Checking tithe liability is a popular line of research and is widely used for genealogical purposes. To help conserve these fragile documents, all agreements/awards at TNA have been copied and are now produced on microfilm, whereas the tithe maps for English counties, running alphabetically from Bedfordshire to Middlesex, are available only on fiche; thereafter, from Norfolk to Yorkshire and for all Welsh counties, you will need to order the original maps.

Using the records

As with the Valuation Office survey, you have to take a variety of steps before you can access the records. Step one is to view the tithe map for the parish in which the house stands, having identified the correct historic ecclesiastical parish from the secondary research you conducted earlier! The maps may appear unfamiliar, so you will need to compare them with OS maps, or indeed the equivalent map from series IR 90 (if one survives) which often note the plot numbers on modern OS maps. You'll also see that the maps vary in terms of scale, scope, content and quality from parish to parish: if you're tracking more than one property, you may have to adjust to different surveying techniques and annotations, or inconclusive information about individual properties.

As with the Valuation Office survey, each plot of land was assigned a number on the map that corresponds to an equivalent numerical entry in the apportionment schedule in IR 29. You can skip the legal jargon at the start of the schedule, which describes the process by which the apportionment was agreed and assessed; the relevant content lies in the apportionment schedule, when each plot was described. Although the purpose of the documentation was to apportion cash rent-charges for each plot of land, the columned entries are of great interest to a house historian as they cover the names of the landowner and occupier; plot number that corresponds to the plot numbers on the map; the name and description of the land and premises; the state of cultivation; quantities in statute measure (acres, rods and perches); the names of tithe-owners and relevant other remarks. The schedules are usually arranged alphabetically by the name of individual landowners, rather than by plot number, but there is a key at the front of each apportionment book where you can find the page number on which each plot appears. The first three columns are the ones to focus on, since they will provide the name of the owner or occupier and a description of the property, be it a cottage, house, outhouse, inn or shop.

The tithe apportionment process generated a whole range of other records, many of which are stored at TNA and can be investigated via the Catalogue and Research Guides. Many simply won't be of any use if you are specifically researching the history of a house; however, they are worth reading if you are looking for colour about the history of the local area, and this particular piece of social history that would have affected the lives of many of your ancestors and their neighbours. In particular, you can have a look at the tithe files in series IR 18, which contain papers and correspondence to and from the tithe commissioners working in the local area, particularly concerning disputed payments; and associated boundary awards in series TITH 1 that were created where the commissioners were forced to make judgments; there are further papers with schedules and plans, many of which contain information about owners and tenants. Furthermore, many of the original apportionments had to be updated in the years after 1836, either through subsequent building plans or the intervention of projects such as railways. Some amendments to the original apportionments were filed with the main schedules in IR 29, but others were incorporated as Orders for Apportionment in series IR 94 (linked to equivalent maps in IR 90).

The 1943 National Farm Survey

This set of documents is only going to be of use if your ancestors owned, rented, lived on or worked at a farm – but that will be a surprisingly large number of people. Although many of our ancestors moved away from Britain's rural communities in the nineteenth century to find work in the emerging industrial towns and cities, they tended to be among the poorest elements of society who were seasonal agricultural labourers; land owners or farm tenants tended to remain wedded to agriculture for much longer. Many were fairly small tenant farmers, living in a modest farmhouse that can be traced today, working from the tithe apportionments and Valuation Office survey and using the field patterns to follow the boundaries of the property as they changed over time. There is one additional set of records that can take your research into the middle of the twentieth century, which has fairly good national coverage – the National Farm Survey.

In an attempt to assist the war effort, the Ministry of Agriculture and Fisheries (MAF) set up County War Agricultural Committees to increase food productivity and ensure that there were sufficient supplies to feed the country. As part of this initiative, in 1940 a survey was commissioned, covering all working farms in England and Wales, to identify the productive state of the land, assigning 'A', 'B' and 'C' grades. A second and far more detailed survey was conducted between 1941–43, listing information on conditions of tenure, occupation, the state of the farm, fertility of the land, equipment, livestock, water and electricity supplies, weeds and general management. A plan of the farm, depicting boundaries and fields, was also produced as part of the process.

These records have been deposited at TNA and will be a particularly good source if you are tracing rural property, or suspect that your ancestor's house once formed part of a farm. Not only will you obtain the name of the owner and address of the farm, but also details of the number of employees and the nature of the farm's output (dairy, arable), and this can provide background information on the way people lived. The survey can also be helpful if you are investigating the social history of an area that changed from farmland to housing after the Second World War.

Accessing the records

There are two main sets of documents for the 1941–43 survey; the maps are in series MAF 73, and are arranged alphabetically by county. To find the relevant map that covers your ancestor's farm, you will first need to consult a key sheet that is available on open access in the Map and Large Document Reading Room at TNA. Each county was assigned a number, which forms part of the document reference, and this is stamped on the corner of the relevant county key sheet. Thereafter, each county map is sub-divided into numbered grids; you will need to locate the grid in which your property falls, and make a note of this number alongside the county number. Together, these numbers form the final part of the reference required to order the maps that fall within this grid.

Once you have obtained your maps, you will need to find the one that relates to your property. You'll receive a folder containing all the maps within the grid, which will either be sixteen maps at the scale 1:2500, which adopt the same numbered grid system as employed on the county key sheets for the valuation survey (i.e. 1 to 4 across the top row, 5 to 8 on the second, 9 to 12 on the third and 13 to 16 along the bottom), or with four maps at the 1:1056 scale (north-east, south-east, south-west and north-west quadrants). Once you have located your farm on one of the maps, you will see that the extent of its holdings is marked using a colour wash, and has been assigned a reference; this usually consists of the abbreviated county code (a series of letters), the relevant parish number (the first number) and the farm number (the second number).

The next step is to order the individual farm record that accompanies the map. The records are contained in TNA series MAF 32 and are also arranged by county, and then alphabetically by parish (as ever – make sure you've done the background reading!). You should consult the series list, which contains an index that tells you where to find the records for each county. Work down the alphabetical list of parishes until you find the relevant one, and note the corresponding piece number in the left hand column. Also note the code that has been assigned to the parish, as this also forms part of the document reference. You will be provided with an envelope containing the records for all farms that lie within the requested parish, and your farm can be identified by the reference numbers assigned to it from the map.

The individual farm record consisted of four parts. The first was completed by the farmer, and contained details of small fruit, vegetables and stocks of hay and straw; animals are also listed. The second surveyed agricultural land, also completed by the farmer, while the third was a similar survey completed by inspection and interview. The final part is the most useful for house historians, as it contains details of utility services, farm labour motive power (i.e. number of employees and farm hands), rent and length of occupancy. It also bears the final grade assigned to the farm. All documents contain the address of the farm and the farmer's name, and taken as a whole can provide a great insight into the extent of farming communities in the mid-twentieth century. While your ancestor may not be named in the documents if they were a labourer, you can at least obtain a sense of their work and duties, and the size of the workforce in which they operated. There are some further associated records, such as minutes of the various County War Agricultural Executive Committees in TNA series MAF 80 and these may contain detailed indexes that include farm names; and parish lists for June 1941 in TNA series MAF 65 that provide the names and full postal addresses for the occupiers of all agricultural holdings in each parish. These records are closed for 100 years, so you would have to approach the MAF using a Freedom of

Information Act request for permission to view them. Details of this procedure can be obtained from TNA staff.

Enclosure maps and awards

The enclosure movement is a complicated topic, and subject of much debate among historians. It relates to the way land has been managed and cultivated in England and Wales through the centuries, in particular the way its management has changed from time to time. One of the most important methods of change was the enclosure movement. The term 'enclosure' is employed by social and economic historians to describe a variety of mechanisms of change, whereby smaller plots of land were consolidated into larger, often compact and usually more efficient units. The phrase also covered the change of land that was previously in communal use – in particular common land that was used to graze cattle and sheep – to private use, often for the benefit of a single owner.

Since there was no single mechanism for early change, the process of enclosure was slow and patchy across the country, although it started to gain momentum from the sixteenth century onwards. Most early enclosures were conducted by private agreements between landowners and tenants, and rarely leave a formal record outside private collections or deposited title deeds; although in the case of contested or disputed agreements, the individuals concerned might have taken the case to court to settle the issue, or initiated a special commission of inquiry to look into the matter if Crown rights were involved. Many of these 'official' records where dispute or commission was used to settle matters can be found in TNA in equity court records.

Records of enclosure awards

Formal enclosure awards were drawn up as legal documents, and record the subsequent ownership of land so that proof of title was created in the event of future sale or inheritance; these records were commonly enrolled by the decree of one of the equity courts, in particular Chancery, Exchequer or Court of Requests, or another court of law to provide a legal basis for the award.

From the mid-eighteenth century an increasing number of enclosures were instigated by private Acts of Parliament, and many of these awards are now stored at the House of Lords Record Office, with duplicates also deposited at some of the relevant County Record Offices. The increasing popularity of landowners wishing to enclose common land prompted General Enclosure Acts to be passed in 1836, 1840 and 1845 so that the process could be monitored and formalised, to protect the interests of all parties involved in an attempt to reduce the number of potential disputes. Enclosure Commissioners oversaw this process, and their records from 1845 survive in TNA series MAF 1 – an interesting insight into the working of local landholding in the shires at a time of great change, bearing in mind that tithe apportionments were taking place during this same period. Many of the Parliamentary enclosure awards were also enrolled and in official Government series, and are now located in a variety of places such as TNA (where there's a Research Guide available to lead you through all the various possibilities), although the best place to find the majority of enclosure awards and maps will be the relevant County Record Office. One of the best places to start looking for a relevant enclosure award is in W.E. Tate's *A Domesday of Enclosure Acts and Awards*.

Using enclosure awards

In general, enclosure maps and awards will be more useful when you are trying to find out about the local area in which your ancestors used to live, since it is rare – but not unknown – to find an individual property marked or listed in the documentation. Instead, they provide a visual snapshot of the local area at a given time, as well as information on the names of local landowners involved in the process and the land they owned.

Although there is no such thing as a 'standard' enclosure award, they usually include a description of the boundaries of land that formed part of the Enclosure Act, followed by a list of any changes to ancient manorial or other rights (if applicable), and a description of the allotments of land made to various landowners made under the terms of the Act, distinguishing between copyhold and freehold tenure (a tricky legal subject that has great importance if you are tracing the history of a house further back in time; they are tackled in the next chapter). This piece of information can in its own right be of great use if you wish to search manorial documents for further data on the house, or land on which it once stood. There is usually a detailed schedule listing the owners, and this provides a number for each plot – therefore acting as a means of reference to any surviving map.

Although enclosure awards are scattered across a range of archives and in a variety of sources, Tate's *A Domesday of Enclosure Acts and Awards* summarises the details for the most common places where you will need to go if you want to track down a surviving enclosure award and associated map. The volume is arranged in county order and lists the type of award and the date it was granted, alongside a list of where the documents can be found. The vast majority of all enclosure awards listed are now stored at the relevant County Record Office or local archive, with duplicates and official enrolments filed at TNA (which can be accessed via a series of supplementary lists of awards that provide document references). Furthermore, a large number of enclosure maps are separately listed in TNA's extracted map catalogue, with links to the parent awards from which they were originally taken. You can also try searching the Catalogue by keyword, using the place or parish to locate suitable records.

Apportionment of rent-charge

The term 'rent-charge' refers to rent that was charged on a particular piece or unit of land, and the need for apportionment of rent-charge arose when large land units were sub-divided into smaller units, usually a consequence of the enclosures of the eighteenth and nineteenth centuries. Under the terms of the Enclosure Act 1854, Law of Property Act 1925 and Landlord and Tenant Act 1927, it fell upon various Government departments to equitably distribute the rent-charge between the new plots of land. The records generated by these apportionments are stored at TNA, and can provide information about how the charge was divided in a particular area; many of them will give details of individual streets and properties. There are three main types of record: orders (MAF 17 for the period 1854–1965, HLG 61 for 1965–67), certificates (MAF 19 for the period 1854–1965, HLG 62 for 1965–67), and certificates of redemption of rent-charge (MAF 21 for the period 1843–1965, HLG 63 for 1965–67). The records are fairly easy to access, and are arranged by the street or district that was affected. You should be able to obtain an idea of the individual who made the application for an apportionment, plus the person or persons who held the lease of the land.

Maps and plans for public schemes

Government surveys form the most useful areas in which to search for cartographic material relevant to your ancestral homes and the surrounding localities because they have a pretty good national coverage. However, there are a range of sources relating to regional and specific local planning movements and schemes in which individual property details can be found. Some of the more important ones are listed here.

Railways

One of the most dramatic changes to the British landscape occurred in the nineteenth century, when a network of railway lines, owned and run by private companies, began to be constructed. From the outset, the requirement to compulsorily purchase private land, usually backed up by an Act of Parliament, created the need to map and assess the value of the land in question for compensation purposes; while many landowners were happy to hand over their property in exchange for money, others protested, generating further records. The main period of railway expansion outside regional lines came from the 1830s onwards, with many local communities undergoing dramatic change as stations and associated dwellings to house the construction teams and subsequent railway employees started to appear, coupled with the destruction of older properties that were either in the way of the new routes, or needed to be cleared in town centres to make way for the new infrastructure.

Many of these changes are depicted on maps that formed part of individual railway company archives, and are now deposited at TNA as part of the former holdings of the British Transport Historical Records section (BTHR). For the pre-nationalisation period the records are arranged by local railway company, so you will need to identify which company operated along the line nearest to the house you're researching (there's a research guide available to help you do this). Most of the railway archives relating to maps and plans can be found in TNA series RAIL 1029–37 and 1071, plus some in MT 54. Photographs of railways are contained in AN 14 and 31, and RAIL 1057 and 1157. Other material will be located with the administrative papers of the individual railway companies, including papers on accommodation and other related property that may have eventually found its way into private hands.

A large collection of maps and plans, along with the associated Parliamentary Acts, can be viewed at the House of Lords Record Office, while some specialist railway archives are deposited at the National Railway Museum, York. Of course, you can also have a look in the County Record Office or municipal archive for stray maps and other contextual material.

Roads

In a similar manner, road-building over time has necessitated the creation of maps, plans and a variety of associated documentation. One of the earliest methods of road management was to set up legal bodies called turnpike trusts, which were locally administered and funded. Their remit was to ensure the maintenance and upkeep of the roads in their care. Records of the trusts will be found either at parochial level in the county archives, or possibly among quarter sessions papers whenever the trusts failed to adequately maintain the roads and were therefore liable to prosecution. Where such cases were recorded, you may well find that the area of road that required repair was linked to the property or properties outside which it ran, and the names of the owners are sometimes listed. Quarter sessions records are usually found at the relevant CRO.

Aside from local prosecutions, Royal Commissions were often appointed to enquire into the state of roads administered by the turnpike trusts, and the maps produced as a result of this process can depict property. Relevant material can also be found at TNA in Ministry of Transport files in the MT series where many useful maps can be found. After the dissolution of turnpike trusts, the responsibility for road-building and maintenance was passed to local authorities, and some road-building or improvement schemes can be found among the Ministry of Housing and Local Government files at TNA in the HLG series. However, in general the most likely place to find maps and plans relating to turnpike trusts and roads will be the relevant CRO, where local authority maps and plans for road improvement schemes will have been deposited.

Private roads and streets developed out of the turnpike trusts, and in addition to the maps and plans referred to above, you may wish to explore various files on their maintenance and development. Earlier records can be located with material on turnpike trusts at TNA in series MH 28, while more modern records are in HLG 51 and MT 149. Correspondence regarding conflicts of interest – i.e. the choice of routes – between private roads and railway companies can be found among the records of the individual railway companies, for example RAIL 1057. You will also find references to private roads in enclosure awards, although county archives will once again be the best place to begin searching.

Over time, topographical atlases that focused on roads and popular travel routes were published, especially from the eighteenth century onwards. Again, many of these have found their way into county archives, though the British Library map catalogue can be used to select key maps from a variety of dates. These may be of interest if your ancestral home was built on a busy highway or road, or perhaps was once used as a coaching inn.

Slum clearance and local authority building plans
Many of the public communications schemes described above had a profound effect on the built environment, not just because of the new buildings and structures that were created, but also by the need to clear space to make way for them. This often included slum clearance plans as part of local authority plans to improve the local area, and these records are particularly relevant if you are tracing an ancestral home from the nineteenth or twentieth centuries, since it might have been caught up in the changes. You will find most of the records at local level, but any public housing scheme or slum clearance required approval, so duplicate copies – often the fullest record – were retained by the relevant Government department and can now be found in The National Archives.

Housing policy before the Second World War
During the nineteenth century, the rapid growth of towns and cities created problems of overcrowding, which in turn impacted upon public health. From the 1840s, the spread of epidemics, such as cholera, prompted numerous Royal Commissions to investigate how to tackle the combined health and housing crises. Much of the work fell upon newly-created Poor Law Unions, which had responsibility for implementing Poor Law legislation. Some of the records and correspondence of the Poor Law Commission and subsequent Poor Law Board, which coordinated the work of the unions, are at The National Archives in MH 1 and 12, but rich though they are in terms of social history, these will give only background information rather than specific references to houses. You may have better luck looking through the collections at the county archive for more relevant material.

Of similar importance was the 1843 Royal Commission on the Health of Towns and Populous Places: measures were drafted to prevent the spread of infectious disease, and a Board of Health was established. There are many records that deal with the problems caused by housing and overcrowding in correspondence located in MH 13 and HLG 1 and 46, but – as with the records of the Poor Law Board – the records will provide only background information rather than specific property details. However, this will be important if you are serious about putting your ancestors' lives into context, as the issues raised in these files will have impacted upon their lives.

You will also find information on the housing conditions that were prevalent in the works of Charles Booth and Edwin Chadwick, great social reformers from the nineteenth century, who compiled reports based on specific houses in the urban slum areas. Much of their work was submitted to Parliamentary Commissions, many of which are now available on CD ROM. Equally important for social historical context on housing and sanitary conditions for the poor and working classes is *The Builder*, first published in 1842 and extensively developed under the editorship of George Godwin from 1844. It also focused on architecture and building debates of the age. Copies can be found at many main libraries, and there are annual indexes from 1842–79 and half-annual indexes from 1880 bound with the relevant volume.

Slum clearance, redevelopment and planning schemes
The establishment of the Local Government Board by Act of Parliament in 1871 created an institution with powers to tackle housing problems at a local level, and the Board inherited many of the responsibilities of the Poor Law Board. Early responsibility for housing fell to the Sanitary Department, but by 1910 a separate Housing and Town Planning Department had been formed. In an effort to address the problem of housing for the working classes, from 1875 local authorities were permitted to purchase areas that were considered to be slums under the terms of the Artisans' and Labourers' Dwellings Act and submit redevelopment schemes to the Board for approval.

After the First World War, the Ministry of Health inherited most of the housing work of the Local Government Board, and also developed an interest in building control in general. An important piece of legislation was the 1930 Housing Act, which enabled the Ministry of Health (Housing Department) to establish clearance and improvement areas, and to require the demolition of unfit houses while building new ones. In consequence, there are many useful records now deposited at The National Archives that relate to urban regeneration in the late nineteenth and early twentieth centuries, housing for working classes and the creation of local authority housing estates. To make searching easier, you should begin by identifying which local authority your property falls within. Maps created by the Ministry of Health and previous departments that depict the boundaries of some of the Poor Law Unions and district authorities can be found in HLG 6 for the period 1800–1900, with similar and related material in HLG 44. These will at least afford some assistance if you are unsure, and can include properties that were affected by boundary changes.

If you are trying to track down slum clearance and redevelopment plans in your area that commenced before the Second World War, the place to begin should be the county archive for the area, where many of the local authority files are kept. However, The National Archives contains registered files for the planning schemes themselves developed by local authorities that were referred to the Local Government Board and its successors for approval under the Town and Country Planning Acts 1909–32; these are to be found in series HLG 4. The records are arranged by the name of the local authority, and there is an introductory note in the series list to assist you. Alternatively, you can search for material in registers stored in HLG 95. Although a large amount of the contents will not be property specific, you will obtain a general overview of the planning schemes and their extent; and of particular relevance will be the extracted maps and plans that accompanied the schemes in HLG 5, with additional material bound with the paperwork in HLG 4.

Local authorities were required to seek the permission of the relevant Government department before they could start to proceed with their plans. Consequently, the department's legal branch gained responsibility for drawing up the housing instruments for the erection of houses and new streets. These records are stored in HLG 13 and contain maps, along with instruments and consents for land sales, leases and purchases, construction of new streets and sewers and general housing issues. Registers to the series exist in HLG 14 and are arranged by date and type of local authority; the indexes will lead you to an instrument number, which is listed in HLG 13. Similar material will also be found in HLG 95. Officially sealed orders made by the various institutions and departments that authorised permission for planning schemes to go ahead are to be found in HLG 26, with sealed plans in HLG 23; later post-war material is in HLG 111. The records can contain great detail, in some instances describing a property and listing the current or former occupiers, but the level of information will vary according to the type of order and the date.

Post-war reconstruction and development
The need for regeneration of urban areas was brought into sharp focus by the devastation to domestic property caused by bombing raids during the Blitz in the Second World War. Although planning for urban and rural redevelopment had long been a function of the various bodies described above, an Act of Parliament in 1943 established a separate Ministry of Town and Country Planning. Its remit was to regulate local authority wartime construction, and subsequently to redevelop areas that had been worst

affected by damage or blight caused by the war. The result of the department's work was the 1947 Town and Country Planning Act, which made fresh provision for planning development and use of land. It also gave additional powers to local authorities to develop land for planning.

A Central Land Board was established, and councils were directed to create development plans for their area of authority. From 1951, functions formerly under the Ministry of Health were added to create the Ministry of Local Government and Planning. All local authorities were required to survey their area and prepare a development plan, which was to be submitted to the Ministry of Town and Country Planning. Maps and written statements for each county are stored in series HLG 119, along with amendments to the plans made under later surveys. In addition, HLG 79 contains the detailed submission of the proposals and plans by local authorities. The records are listed by the local authority and cover a vast amount of material, such as housing programmes, war damage redevelopment, surveys, planning and reconstruction. Although the quality of information will vary from location to location, some records provide great detail, including maps and plans of the areas under consideration.

New towns
In addition to the work on redeveloping existing towns and rural areas, the Ministry of Town and Country Planning, and after 1951 the Ministry of Local Government and Planning, were responsible for developing new towns. The first piece of legislation to consider developing new urban areas was the New Town Act of 1946, which was based on the experiences of the 'garden' cities of Letchworth and Welwyn. New Town Development Corporations were established to project-manage the creation of new towns, covering the acquisition of land, development of all services required by the new towns and provision of adequate housing. Consequently, there are numerous records of use to the house historian who lives in one of the post-war new town developments. General correspondence and files relating to planning policy and development of new towns can be found in HLG 90, which lists several specific proposals. The records of the New Town Development Corporations are in HLG 91, and there is an index to the corporations in the series list. There are maps, plans and papers on the entire planning process required to create a community from scratch, including references to specific houses and streets.

Additional records maintained by local authorities

The records described above relate to official files maintained by the relevant Government departments and institutions in response to legislation regarding housing. This is only one side of the story, as the local authorities themselves created and maintained similar files that can provide even more detail on these topics, plus more specific information on council housing in general.

These records, as indicated above, are generally held in the County Record Office, municipal archive or registered place of deposit for local authority records. Most local authorities maintained departments with responsibility for housing, building contracts, architects, engineers and surveyors, and urban development. Of particular use will be applications for planning permission to build or extend properties, as the relevant department would have to consider each application in turn before delivering a verdict: this process would create paperwork that lists names of owners and occupiers, as well as plans that were submitted as part of the planning procedure.

Similarly, local authorities had responsibility for all aspects of town planning, and in addition to the files listed above you will find reams of paperwork on decisions reached at a local level, plus deposited plans for the various schemes. The everyday administration of local towns and villages generated records that feature property in a number of surprising places. Local authorities also inherited maps and plans that accompanied the work on public improvement works such as sewers, paving committees and other bodies responsible for public works.

Finally, the administration of council housing created under the various planning schemes and redevelopment plans listed above will contain a wealth of information on individual properties. Some archives will have a wider range of material than others, depending on what the individual authority both created and preserved, and there may be restrictions on access depending on how recent the records are. However, if you suspect that your property was once maintained or owned by the local council, then you could find the names of previous tenants, rebuilding works and repairs, and even a construction or purchase date – usually linked to maps showing which properties were owned by the authority.

Other Major Map Collections

It might be worth checking a range of other areas, in particular non-Government sources or records generated by a specific historic event. Here are a few areas that might be worth exploring.

Estate maps and plans

So far, the official records generated by Government surveys or Acts of Parliament have been considered. However, individuals who owned estates would also have required access to their own maps and plans over time to assist with the administration of their lands, often coupled with periodical surveys of their property, so that new estate management procedures could be introduced, for example. As with the Government surveys, maps were often linked to assessment books which, in turn, can often be linked to other forms of local administrative record such as manorial material. These miscellaneous and privately commissioned records, where they survive, provide an invaluable snapshot of landholding and property, and seem to occur most frequently when an estate changed hands. They can be found pretty much anywhere, but exist in the largest number among the personal records of the families that owned the estate, the accumulated paperwork of their land or estate agents, or solicitors, who were responsible for maintenance of legal documentation. It is important to remember that they are private files, and therefore may not exist – or have restricted access. The most likely place to find such material is at the relevant CRO, but TNA does have a collection of private estate maps that are listed in the various map catalogues. Make sure you've identified the main estates that owned land in the area where your ancestors lived, so that you can locate any surviving material.

In addition, it's worth remembering that the Crown owned (and still owns) vast swathes of property across Britain, and required a similar level of administrative material that has since aggregated to various Government departments. TNA is the logical place of deposit for maps, plans, rentals and surveys relating to Crown estates and property, plus areas of autonomous jurisdiction. These can be found among the papers of the Office of Land Revenue Records and Enrolments (LRRO series of records) and the Crown Estates Office (CRES series), with maps for the Duchy of Lancaster in DL 31.

Historic event maps

Aside from the main categories of maps described above, you are going to have to use your knowledge of the local area, and its history, to uncover cartographic material connected to subjects that, on the surface, appear to have nothing to do with house history. For example, one of the most amazing collections relates to a survey undertaken by the nineteenth-century social reformer Charles Booth, who was interested in the living conditions of the poorest ranks of society. In 1886 he began to survey areas of London, and produced colour-coded maps according to the level of poverty that he found in each area. Booth's maps and associated papers are stored at the University of London Library, and the Library of the London School of Economics and Political Science; however, they can be accessed online at http://booth. lse.ac.uk, where you can also purchase copies of the maps. Therefore you may find maps, plans, drawings and sketches that lift the lid on what life would have been like in your local community, even if your ancestral house was not directly featured; this is all part of the process of adding colour to your personal heritage.

Another collection linked to a specific moment in time is the Bomb Census maps from the Second World War, primarily linked to London but applicable to any area that suffered damage during the Blitz. There's a research guide available from TNA's website, as the main series of maps is located there in record series HO 193 and associated reports, focusing on damage and casualties, are in HO 198. Many local authorities kept their own series of incident reports and maps, and these can be found in the County Record Office or municipal/local authority archive, with a large collection of records for London stored at the London Metropolitan Archives appearing in print. This can be used with locally-held photographic archives, and checked against material held at places such as the Imperial War Museum for wider context.

Related organisations
You may also find some useful information from the records of the Geological Survey. Although their main work from 1835 was involved in geological science, many of the functions included survey work and map-making, and will be of use if your property is situated on a place of geological value. Indeed, many geological surveys were conducted before building commenced, and therefore the maps and associated documents can provide information about when a property was built. You can try looking for records at the British Geological Survey, while the Geologists' Association is also worth contacting.

Finally, useful mapping data can be found in the most unlikely places. Records of utility companies – gas, water and electricity, for example – often include plans to introduce services into an area, or conduct repairs and maintenance work. They are often linked to schedules and correspondence relating to the owners or occupiers of property that's affected by the work, giving you another link to the past. Take sewers, for example. Vitally important for the health of major towns and cities, and often set out to a pattern that exists today by the Victorians, the records generated by the planning and construction process have been described above. However, they were often paid for by rate books, which were assessed and written up by household and street. So there is a direct link between sewers and house history. They may not be the most exciting records ever created or preserved, but you can be certain that your ancestors would have been grateful for the benefits provided by the services they represent!

Chapter Eight

TRACKING OWNERSHIP OF THE ANCESTRAL HOME

One of the real thrills of tracking down your ancestors is the discovery that they actually owned a house – as opposed to renting one, as was the situation for the vast majority of people that you're likely to find on your family tree. The aim of this chapter is to introduce you to the key sources you'll need to examine. However, this also means that you'll need to know a bit about the mechanism by which property was bought and sold, as it was this process – called conveyancing – that generated many of the records you'll be hunting for. Therefore it's unavoidable that some of this chapter will cover some fairly advanced areas relating to land law: don't worry, you won't have to enrol for a law degree to understand what follows, but while some of the details may seem a bit arcane, it's well worth persevering with because you'll find the records easier to locate, understand and interpret if you've read up on the background first.

Land Law and Conveyancing

The ways in which property could be transferred from one party to the next took many forms over the centuries, and usually involved the creation of legal documentation at each step – many of which can be difficult for the beginner to understand or interpret. Collectively, these documents are known as 'title deeds', but before outlining the main sources and where to find them, it's important to sketch the basic ways in which land itself was held, as the type of tenure determined the method of transfer. There were basically two main groups of tenure – 'free' (freehold) and 'unfree' (copyhold) – and the notes that follow firstly cover the common ways in which freehold property was held and transferred.

Technically, land could be passed from one party to another in a variety of ways – as part of a marriage settlement, via inheritance from father to eldest son (primogeniture) or as a sale between two parties – but in general the process of transfer was known as 'conveyancing', which is strictly defined as the 'legal transfer of ownership of property from one party or parties to another'. The transfer of copyhold land was restricted by the regulations of the manorial system until the late nineteenth century, and is described in detail in Section Three when ways of investigating the history of your local area are examined.

In terms of record-keeping and the evolution of the variety of different ways in which conveyancing took place over time, the main cut-off date for the topics under consideration here end in 1925, when a series of Statutes were passed by Parliament to regulate land law and conveyancing – in particular elements of the Settled Land Act (1925 c.18), the Trustee Act (1925 c.19), the Law of Property Act (1925 c.20), the Land Registration Act (1925 c.21), the Land Charges Act (1925 c.22) and the Administration of Estates Act (1925 c.23). Although the impact of these pieces of legislation is not within the remit of this book, they have been described when relevant, with particular reference to the whereabouts of modern records and the restrictions imposed by the terms of these Acts, which are described later. Because of the legal nature of the records, reference is often made to 'land' or 'property' rather than specific houses, because in the eyes of the law the term 'land' included any buildings that were constructed upon it.

The feudal system

The origins of modern landholding, and consequently the ways in which land was transferred, lay in the establishment of the 'feudal' system in England and parts of Wales after the Norman Conquest in the eleventh century. As with land law in general, this can be a complicated subject and is much debated by historians; but a simple version states that the Crown technically held all land, but granted large portions to reward key followers, who held this land directly from the Crown as tenants-in-chief. In turn, the tenants-in-chief granted land to their supporters, who became their tenants, and thus the process continued down via a series of grants to create a pyramid structure of landholding. This method of linear land grant was known as 'subinfeudation', and with the exception of the Crown at the top, left everyone who held land as the tenant of an overlord.

The basic unit of land was known as the 'manor', and was probably based on an Anglo-Saxon system of land division. It is important to grasp the concept that manors were not distinct or compact land units with clear geographical boundaries, but were instead defined by the unifying bonds of allegiance to a single lord and were therefore more of a socio-economic unit that could sometimes stretch over several parishes, or be separated by lands of other manors. Indeed, confusion between parish and manorial boundaries is common: not only could a manor spill over several parish boundaries, but there may also be more than one manor contained within a single parish. One thing that quickly becomes clear when you start investigating these local administrative units – nothing is ever as simple as it might first appear!

Landholding in the manor was determined by its 'lord', who granted strips of land within the manor to his tenants in return for the performance of specific service, usually a combination of monetary rent, military obligation or physical labour on the lord's land. Any surplus land retained by the lord was known as his 'demesne' land. The terms by which tenants held land from the lord of the manor would vary from manor to manor, and was called the 'tenure'; this would determine whether the tenant was free or unfree. Free tenants could hold land by either military or socage tenure. In the case of the latter, free tenants were required to perform an agreed amount of work of a specific nature on the lord's demesne land each year. However, unfree tenants, or villeins, had only the amount of work set, and were instructed by the lord's representative as to the nature of the work when the time came.

Types of freehold land

Because of the strictures of the manorial system, technically no-one 'owned' land as the feudal pyramid meant that the ownership could be traced back to the top, and the original grants to the tenants-in-chief from the Crown. Nevertheless, the terms by which land was granted throughout the feudal chain were of vital importance in determining how it could be transferred in future, and this is where the complexities of land law reside. There were three main ways in which freehold land could be granted to an individual, known as 'estates' – referring to the technical period of time that the recipient could hold the land. In addition to the three freehold estates, a fourth type of estate developed, namely 'lease' or 'term of years'. As it was possible for leases to be made on copyhold land as well as freehold, it was deemed a non-freehold estate. There was a further important distinction between freehold land and lease. In legal terms, freehold land was deemed as real property, or 'realty', and could not be 'devised' (or bequeathed to another) by will until the Statute of Wills was passed in 1540, and more specifically after the Tenures Abolition Act of 1660. However, leases were considered to be personal property, or 'personal', and therefore could be included in a will; these are considered from the perspective of tracing the occupants of a property in the next chapter.

Fee simple

Land that was granted to an individual 'and his heirs' was deemed to be fee simple. In essence, this meant that on the death of the recipient it would pass to his immediate heir at law, unless the fee simple had already been granted (or 'alienated') to another by a previous agreement. When the line of heirs of the recipient finally died out, then the land would return to the original grantor or his heirs – the technical 'overlord'. Thus the word 'fee' indicates that the land was inheritable. However, as a fee simple was realty, it could not be devised by will to another until the law was changed in the sixteenth and seventeenth centuries.

Fee tail

Land granted in fee simple guaranteed only that it would be passed to the heirs of the recipient as long as it was not alienated. This was inconvenient to landowners who wished to keep their landed estates within the family for future generations. A solution was created by the 1285 Statute de Donis Conditionalibus, which stipulated that land granted to a recipient and 'the heirs of his body' would pass to all future issue of the recipient without the possibility of alienation. This was known as a fee tail, and only when all future issue had died out would the land revert to the original grantor or his heirs. This type of freehold became increasingly popular among dynasties who wanted to ensure that their land was not granted away by offspring or siblings.

Life interest

As the name suggests, the grant of a life interest in land would last only as long as the lifetime of the recipient, who became the 'life tenant'. This meant that the heirs of the recipient could not inherit the land. However, a recipient of a life estate could grant the land to others, but the new recipient was said to hold the property 'pour autre vie', or for the life of another. This meant that the interest of the new recipient could last only as long as the life of the original recipient, at which point it would revert to the original grantor.

Leases

If an individual wished to grant land to another for a limited period of time but did not want to grant a life interest, since the recipient could live for an uncertain length of time, he leased the land for a 'term of years' (or 'demised' it). The following are the most common forms of lease that you will probably encounter in documents, although you should bear in mind that it was possible to lease both freehold and copyhold land. This type of tenure was also referred to as fee-farm.

Fixed leases

Fixed leases were for a set period of time (for example, six months or ninety-nine years), and usually involved the payment of a fixed sum at the beginning. At the end of the agreed term the original lessor would either reclaim the land or renegotiate another lease with the tenant. The default position therefore was change, unless action was taken by either party.

Periodic leases

Periodic leases were also for fixed periods (for example, weekly, monthly or yearly), but would be automatically renewed for the duration of another period of time unless either party provided a period of notice. Rent was paid on a regular basis (for example, per week, per month or per year). The default position therefore was continuity, unless action was taken by either party.

Other forms of lease

In addition to these 'terms of years', other forms of lease were possible, based on individual circumstances and the varying nature of tenant-landlord relationships as land use developed over time:

- Tenants at will were created when an agreement was made between the lessor and the lessee that either party could determine, usually when a fixed or periodic lease expired. Although no rent was payable, the tenant was generally expected to pay some form of compensation to the lessor for the loss of revenue.

- Leases for life were tenable for the duration of the tenant's life, as were similar forms of specific leases that were curtailed by the marriage of the tenant, for example.
- Tenancies at sufferance came into being at the expiration of a lease when the tenant remained on the land without the lessor's permission. This was a form of legal squatting, and often resulted in legal action or court cases that you might be able to follow up.
- Renewable leases contained a clause that allowed the lessee to request the grant of a new lease on the same terms as the old, as long as the request was made within a stipulated period before the original lease expired. Perpetual renewable leases were possible before 1925.

Grants of freehold land

There was a variety of ways in which freehold land could be granted, and you will need to familiarise yourself with the main terms that crop up in the legal documents you'll uncover during your research, because in many ways they reveal what sort of property-owner your ancestor was – and their plans to keep land or houses in the family! Here are a few of the most important words and phrases that are used to describe land transfers.

Possession, reversion and remainder

When a landholder, A, made a grant of land that was held as 'fee simple' to a second individual, B, for life, B was deemed to be in 'possession' of the land. On B's death the land would eventually revert to A (or his heirs if he predeceased B), as the life interest in possession had thus ended. Therefore, during B's lifetime, A still held the fee simple 'in reversion', even though he did not actually possess the land. However, if A had specified that the land should pass to a further individual, C, for life at the death of B, then C was said to hold a life interest in the land 'in remainder'. At the death of B, then C would take on the life interest in possession. Therefore, the grant would be 'to B for life with remainder to C for life'.

Conditional and determinable grants

If a grantor wanted to specify various terms to a grant, he would make it either conditional or determinable. A grant of 'conditional fee simple' meant that there was a condition attached to the grant. You will find that phrases such as 'on the condition that', 'provided that' and 'but if' were commonly used to frame such a grant. There were two types of conditional grants – a precedent condition, which stipulated the grant could not be received *until* the condition was fulfilled, and a subsequent condition, which would *end* the grant if the circumstances described in the condition ever arose. Alternatively, a grant of 'determinable fee simple' meant that a limiting restriction was imposed, and this type of grant commonly contained the phrases 'until', 'during', 'while' and 'as long as'. Conditional and determinable grants could also apply to grants of life interest, but were not permissible for grants of fee tail. If a grant was not conditional or determinable, then it was called 'absolute'.

Various types of interest
A future interest in a grant is one that has yet to be enjoyed by the recipient. As we described above, the grant of land, held in fee simple by A, to B for life, with remainder to C for life only resulted in B taking immediate possession of the property. C could claim to have a future interest in the grant, as it was dependent on the death of B. A contingent interest was where a condition had yet to be fulfilled before the grant took effect, or when the identity of the recipient was still unknown. Contingent interests were most commonly associated with future heirs to a property, either because they had not attained the age of 21, or were not yet born (so that it was not possible to specify the identity of the intended recipient). If an interest was not contingent, then it was said to be vested, as no conditions had to be fulfilled before the grant could take effect, or when the identity of the recipient was already known. Therefore a grant of land, held as fee simple by A, to B for life, with remainder to C for life when he attained the age of 21, gave B a vested interest and C a future contingent interest.

Trusts
Trusts were originally designed to grant the legal possession of land to one individual while permitting another individual to enjoy the actual benefits of possession, such as any rents that were collected from the land. For this reason, you might also find such grants described as 'uses', because they were often established so that a third party could enjoy the 'use' of the property for a specific purpose on behalf of another. Usually two or more trustees were named in the original grant, and they were bound to hold and administer the land under the terms of the trust. Therefore, if A made a grant of land in fee simple to B and C 'for the use of D', then A would no longer be the legal possessor of the fee simple – it would now be the trustees, B and C.

D also had an interest in the estate, but not in the eyes of the common law. Instead the interest was deemed 'equitable', as the law of equity compelled the trustees to carry out the terms of the trust for the benefit of D. Hence, if trusts were disputed, cases would be heard in the courts of equity, whereas property transfers made solely under the principle of common law ought, in theory, to end up in one of the common law courts. Advice about tracking down such disputes in the law courts is provided below, and is a very rich source for someone tracing an ancestral property; it's amazing how often trustees failed to adhere to the original 'use' of the grant!

The trust would end only when the trustees transferred the legal fee simple to D. Trusts were normally set up that transferred the fee simple to the trustees, but in theory they could hold either life interests or fee tail. The trust would end only when the legal estate was transferred to the beneficiary of the trust, provided they were of full age and that their equitable fee was not conditional or determinable.

Settlements

A settlement was the term given to a land grant that involved the creation of a succession of interests in the land, either by direct grants or via trusts – often a very complicated legal chain that you will need to analyse and untangle to establish where descent was intended. Settlements became especially important in the nineteenth century when the owners of large landed estates created chains of inheritance that bound land to their families, known as 'strict settlements'. These are considered a bit later.

Methods of conveyancing freehold land

Having described various ways in which freehold land was held and could be granted, you can then start to look for the most likely method by which your ancestral property was transferred from one party to another in accordance with its estate. As a rough rule of thumb, the combined trail of historic documents that describe each conveyance – known as the title deeds, and described a bit later – will be deposited, if indeed they survive, according to who the principal landowner was, and how the land passed from family to family through time. Records of the transfer of land from or acquisition of land to the Crown are to be found at The National Archives, Kew. Private transfers of property may be deposited locally in the relevant county archive, or in the record office serving the county where the family that owned the land, or the estate in which it lay, held their main seat; with firms of solicitors that handled the conveyance process, or perhaps acted as land agents for a large estate owner; or maybe is still retained in private hands today. Many of the processes described here were specifically designed to create a paper trail, though, and consequently involved some form of official process, thus generating a record in a court. In short, there is no one single place to find these records, as you will see later when private title deeds – as opposed to the record of a single conveyance or land transfer – are discussed.

One final word – most of the documents described below will be in Latin, as they were often generated by legal processes which were written in that language until 1732. While this will be disconcerting at first, you will quickly learn to spot key phrases – indicated below – where details of your ancestors and their property will be hidden; you can focus on these, and use various dictionaries, phrase books and palaeographic aids to help you work out the important data amid quite a lot of legal repetition!

Feoffment

Enfeoffment was the technical term used to describe the conveyance of land held by fee simple from one party to the other within the confines of a manor. In medieval times, this was an actual transfer of land – the seller physically passed a sod of land taken from the property to the buyer, a process known as 'livery of seisin', to symbolically show that they had delivered ownership of the property. Once the transfer had been completed, the purchaser was then a tenant of the manor and subject to its rules and regulations. Although no written evidence of the transfer was legally required until the Statute of Frauds in 1677, both parties, as well as the lord of the manor, found it expedient to produce a record of the transaction. The result was a 'feoffment', known as a 'deed of gift', and was in effect a private charter (or legal statement) that described the transfer from one party to the other. You will find that the format of the document will vary from case to case, but most tend to give the names of the people or parties concerned and a description of the property involved, with a summary of the feudal terms and conditions under which the property was held from the lord of the manor. The grant was permanent, signified by the Latin clause *habendum* which in full usually reads *Habendum et tenendum … in perpetuum* ('to have and to hold … for ever'). The date of the transfer was usually provided at the foot of the text.

Feoffment originated in the eleventh century at the time of the Norman Conquest, but had lapsed as a form of conveyance by the mid-nineteenth century. No official enrolment in a court was required, and so most feoffments will turn up as part of title deeds; therefore the best place to begin your research will be at the relevant County Record Office, where you are likely to find a disparate collection of documents among the collected private papers and deposited archives of solicitors and estate agents, who historically acquired such material and held onto it for their clients. Many specialist institutions also hold feoffments, such as academic libraries and the British Library.

Deeds of lease

Documentation was also created when land was leased to individuals by one of the means described above. The *habendum* clause defined the period of the lease, and the rent is stipulated by a *redendum* clause ('yielding and paying'). Once again, any surviving records will probably be stored in the relevant County Record Office, academic libraries or even private hands. However, bearing in mind that leases could involve copyhold or 'unfree' land, you may well find deeds of lease for copyhold property enrolled on the official manorial court rolls, which are described in Section Three.

Of particular use will be leases that were used to convey building rights to a plot of freehold land. These allowed the builder to construct a property and then rent it out, while the freeholder enjoyed rent from the leaseholder. Building specifications can often be found in the terms of the lease, and may include a description of the intended property with measurements and proposed room layout, as well as the person or persons intending to carry out the construction.

Final Concord or 'Feet of Fine'

From the late twelfth century until 1833, one of the most popular methods of land transfer that generated a formal record of the process was the Final Concord, or Fine. The conveyance was achieved through a fictitious legal dispute between the purchaser, or querent (plaintiff), and vendor, or deforciant (defendant), which was usually resolved in the Court of Common Pleas – a medieval court with its roots in the Conquest. A final agreement, known as the concord or fine, was reached between the two parties as a form of restitution payment. The concord was written in triplicate on a sheet of parchment, two copies side by side and the third along the foot of the parchment. This was then split into three parts by means of an indented or wavy cut, giving rise to the legal or contractual use of the word 'Indenture' to signify more than one copy was made via this process. One copy was given to the vendor, another to the purchaser, while the court retained the final part, the 'foot'. This gave rise to the popular name by which surviving documents at The National Archives are known – the 'feet of fines'. The aim of this mechanism was to prevent fraud, because only the three legal sections could be fitted together perfectly when examined in one place, a measure designed to stop forgeries appearing when land ownership was in dispute.

From the fifteenth century, fines were commonly used to convey land that was held in fee tail, as the legal process partially broke (or 'barred') the entail; a 'base fee' was created that was similar to a fee simple, except that it lasted only as long as the original fee tail would have done. Thus the new possessor of the land would need to check whether the original entailed interest had expired, as that was when the land would revert to the original grantor, usually the lord of the manor in which the land was situated.

The text of each fine was formulaic, beginning with the phrase 'this is the final agreement', followed by the date of agreement and the names of the judges. The document then provides the names of the parties, identified by the word INTER (between), with the querent listed first, which was then followed by the name of the deforciant. A description of the land or property in question was then provided, although you will find that there is no great detail given. A 'purchase price' is usually recorded, although this was a standard sum as early as the fourteenth century and did not reflect the actual purchase price. The documents were written in Latin until 1733, with the exception of the Interregnum period 1649–60, and if you are unfamiliar with the language, this standard pattern by which the documents were written will allow you to identify enough key words and phrases to extract useful information about your property as indicated above.

Although the copies taken away by the querent and deforciant were incorporated into title deeds, and are therefore likely to be in county archives or private collections, feet of fines are held at The National Archives in record series CP 25/1 for the period 1195–1509 and CP 25/2 for the period 1509–1839. Many feet of fines for individual counties have been published by relevant record societies, so it might be worth checking a local study centre first. If you are looking for records at The National Archives, then the means of reference to feet of fines is through a series of contemporary indexes from 1509–1839 that are arranged by legal term and then by county or city in IND 1/7233–44 and IND1/17217–68. These will provide you with the names of the county, querent and deforciant, and the location of the property. There are other contemporary indexes available, with information about what they contain and how they can be used available from a Research Guide.

You will also find out about a range of supplementary material related to the feet of fines, such the notes of fine files, draft texts, annotations and background information on the agreements. Feet of fines for Wales are at the National Library of Wales.

Common recovery

The common recovery was developed in the fifteenth century as a permanent means of barring entailed property, as long as the tenant in tail was in possession of the land, or had obtained the permission of the tenant in possession. In effect, it was another fictitious legal dispute brought before the Crown in the Court of Common Pleas, designed to convert the fee tail to a fee simple. The potential purchaser brought an action against the tenant in tail, claiming that the land was his all along and that he wished to 'recover' it. The tenant in tail appointed a third party, known as the common vouchee, to effectively represent him in court. The common vouchee was therefore required to appear in court to defend the suit on behalf of the tenant in tail. However, he would default, thereby providing the justices with the opportunity to make a judgment against the tenant in tail in favour of the original plaintiff. The entail against the land was thus broken through legal judgment and the land passed to the plaintiff as fee simple. In reality, the land would have been sold before the court case on pre-agreed terms.

The documents can appear quite complicated, given the complex legal process involved in effecting the conveyance. However, as with feet of fines, you will find that they tend to follow a fairly common format, and are once again in Latin until 1733, with the exception of the period 1649–60. As it was a court judgment, the record begins with a royal greeting, followed by the names of the justices and the relevant county. You will find that the description of the property is fairly brief, but you will obtain the names of the two main parties. Usually the name or names of the common vouchee relate to court officials, who essentially stood in by proxy since there was no actual dispute between parties, but occasionally they can refer to people who genuinely had a vested interest in the case.

Until 1583 these judgments were originally recorded in the plea rolls of the Court of Common Pleas, which are stored at The National Archives in record series CP 40. Contemporary indexes exist in the form of docket books in CP 60, which will provide the names of the parties, the county and the relevant membrane number within the roll. The process proved to be so popular that from 1583 separate Recovery Rolls were kept to separate the fictitious lawsuits from the real cases brought before the Court, and these are now stored in series CP 43. Indexes for the period 1583–1835 once again provide the names of the parties, the county and the membrane number, along with varying amounts of information on the property itself, and are to be found in IND 1/17183–216.

Bargain and sale

One of the most important developments for conveyances and land transfers came with the Statute of Uses (27 Henry VIII c.10) in 1536, mainly because it revolutionised the way property could be passed from person to person within a family or via a will. As we have seen, realty could not be devised by will before this date. However, the tenant was able to set up a trust, or 'use', by making a grant of the land to trustees 'for the use and behoof' of himself for the duration of his lifetime, and then in trust to the use of whoever he designated in his will. This was possible because the trustees would be the legal possessors of the realty, while the tenant continued to enjoy the benefits and rents due from the land, which were considered personalty and thus could be devised – in other words, the descent of the land was taken out of the equation and the profits from the land could instead be passed on. Once the tenant died, the legal recipient of the land would then direct the trustees to dissolve the trust and transfer the legal fee simple to him. This arrangement benefited all except the lords of the manor in which the property was situated, as they were in danger of losing track of the rights and services due to them – the trustees legally owed these services to the lord, but as they were administering the land on behalf of another they did not enjoy the benefits, and so could not perform the services; whereas the tenant was no longer under legal obligation. The Crown was one of the biggest losers under this system, and the Statute of Uses was designed to rectify this by giving the beneficiary the legal estate of the land, thereby restoring the lord's ability to exact service from him. One of the most important consequences was that tenants with a life interest in the land were often created. In response, a device called the 'bargain and sale' was employed to convey uses from one party to the next.

In essence the bargain and sale was an indenture between two parties, whereby the first party bargained and sold property to the second. The first party remained the legal possessor of the fee simple, and conveyed the use of the land to the second party, who was liable to perform services to the lord of the manor under the terms of the Statute of Uses. To enable people to legally identify the correct person to perform these services, the Statute of Enrolments (27 Henry VIII c.16) was also passed in 1536, which required all bargains and sale of freehold property to be enrolled, either with the county Clerk of the Peace in the quarter sessions, or with one of the central courts at Westminster. Quarter session records are held in County Record Offices, so this would be the best place to start your research – though many of the earlier records are in a poor state, both of survival and quality. Another major source of enrolments is The National Archives among the Chancery close rolls, held in record series C 54, where they were written on the back, or 'endorsed', for a fee. These are described in more detail below. The documents usually contain the following information that will be of use. First, the date of the transaction and the names of the parties are given, followed by details of the financial transaction and, most importantly of all, a description of the property. The terms of the use are then defined, followed by the names of the witnesses. You may find that some enrolled bargains and sale contain recitals of earlier transactions, giving you a unique link to past transfers and the names of previous owners.

Lease and release
Most of the means of transfer discussed to date relate to much earlier forms of conveyancing, and were designed to break some of the conventions about freehold land transfer. From the seventeenth century onwards, a new form of conveyance was introduced that combined the principle of the 'bargain and sale' with some of the flexibility of the lease to create a means of conveyance, with the advantage to all parties that the need to enrol the transfer in one of the courts – a costly process – was removed. The vendor drew up a bargain and sale for a lease of the property to the purchaser, usually for a term of one year, with the rent on the land being a nominal amount, typically one peppercorn (hence the phrase 'peppercorn rent'). Under the Statute of Uses, the purchaser became vested in the lease without entering into possession, hence avoiding feudal dues. However, the lease was not enrolled, as only direct transfers of freehold property were subject to the Statute of Enrolment. The second part of the deed took place the following day and was a release that, on payment of a sum of money, removed the terms of the original lease and therefore vested the freehold interest with the purchaser.

This was a popular method of transfer in the land market and for private vendors, but very unpopular with the Crown, since the legal chicanery eroded their ability to keep track of their right to raise money from the feudal system. Furthermore, the requirement to enrol the transfer had been effectively bypassed, so there was no need to enrol the transfer in court – another line of revenue that was cut off. You would therefore need to start your search for surviving deeds by lease and release in the relevant County Record Office or personal estate records where the land was located.

Disentailing assurance

Further developments in the law evolved to make the process of transfer easier, including legislation such as the 1833 Fines and Recoveries Act which replaced the need to undertake a fictitious lawsuit to bar the entail to land – a source of great discontent among major landowners in the eighteenth and early nineteenth centuries – with a document known as a disentailing assurance. This permitted the holder of the fee tail to bar the entail as long as he was in possession of the land, or had the permission of the tenant who was in possession, which gave them much more freedom to dispose of the land in the way they wanted. However, it was a legal requirement to enrol these documents in Chancery, and examples can be found on the close rolls at The National Archives in record series C 54.

Strict settlements

By the nineteenth century, it is estimated that nearly half of all land was regulated by 'strict settlements'. To ensure that land was passed down and retained in the family, landholders had combined various forms of conveyance to establish a restricted or 'strict' settlement of their land so that certain named successors and 'the heirs of their body legally begotten' would inherit. At the heart of the settlement was a series of life interests for the current tenant and his son, followed by an entailed remainder to unborn future heirs, whose interests were known as 'contingent remainders'. Since it was possible for an existing life tenant to destroy a contingent interest at any point, from the mid-seventeenth century onwards trusts were used to protect any contingent remainders. This was made easier after 1660 when the law was changed so that realty (freehold land) could be devised by will. By the nineteenth century, the format of a typical strict settlement was as follows:

- The first clause was the premises of the deed, which set out the date and the names and occupations of the parties involved in the settlement.
- This was typically followed by recitals of previous transactions that related to the current deed, which will allow you to trace the title of the property; this clause began with 'WHEREAS'.
- The next section was the *testatum*, which outlined the purpose of the deed and began with 'WITNESSETH'. You will find out the reason why the deed was being created; a description of the property, introduced by the phrase 'ALL THAT'; and any exceptions to the property under settlement.
- The *habendum* clause, 'TO HAVE AND TO HOLD', set up the trusts contained in the deed, which related to the settler and often included an annuity for the heir until he inherited; pin-money to the settler's wife; jointures (money after the death of the husband) to his widow; and portions to any younger children. The property was then conveyed to the trustees for a term of years or in fee simple.
- The crucial section was the entail, which set up a series of life tenancies in the land for those already born, and a series of fee tail for those unborn. The trustees would be granted the fee simple, or a term of years, to protect the contingent remainders, and a final remainder was included to the settler and his heirs. This section would also include any conditions that might be attached to the grant to future heirs.
- The trustees were then given various powers that allowed them to administer the estate.
- Finally, the *testemonium* clause, 'IN WITNESS THEREOF', concluded the deed and stated that the parties had signed and sealed the deed in the presence of witnesses.

There were various rules and regulations governing the creation of a strict settlement: under the terms of the 1925 Settled Land Act, two documents were required – a vesting deed, which described the settled land, conveyed the legal estate to the tenant for life, and stated the names and powers of the trustees; and a trust settlement, which essentially described the trusts concerned in the settlement and appointed the trustees. Strict settlements were therefore complicated documents, and the above summary is only a very brief introduction to their format and potential use. If you find evidence of strict settlements for property your family owned in the past, you can find out more about the legal processes from specialist works.

Strict settlements are usually enrolled in one of the nascent local land registries that emerged at the end of the eighteenth century and are described below; or in an official court, which will necessitate a search of records at The National Archives or in a County Record Office. However, you are more likely to find evidence of a strict settlement among private family papers, and primarily among the landed gentry and aristocracy who had vast lands and sources of revenue to administer. Therefore you should be searching for collected title deeds, rather than single transactions – which is the topic considered below.

Copyhold property

Having examined the way freehold land could be conveyed, this section examines the way copyhold (or 'customary') tenants, who formed the majority of manorial tenants and held their land under the terms of the prevalent customs of the manor, were able to pass on or dispose of their property. According to the strictures of the feudal system, the customary tenant was required to work for a fixed number of days on the lord's land in return for holding land of their own within the manor. However, in contrast to freeholders, the nature of work was not fixed in advance, and would be decided by the lord's steward only when the appropriate moment arrived. The lord of the manor regulated the entry of tenants into copyhold land through the manorial court, which was a regular administrative and judicial session that produced a record of its business known as a court roll. This is where the origin of the name 'copyhold' lies, as the recipient of land was also given a copy of the relevant court roll entry as proof of title. The way in which land descended to the next tenant varied from manor to manor according to the unique local customs, but essentially there were two main types.

Land held by 'customary holders of inheritance' passed on the death of the tenant to an heir decided by the custom of the manor. There were various types of inheritance, such as primogeniture, partible inheritance or gavelkind (which was mainly found in Kent and parts of Wales).

Alternatively, land held by customary tenants for life received only a life interest in the property. On the expiration of the interest, the land reverted to the lord. He was free to re-grant it to anyone he liked, although it was often the heir of the original tenant. Some manors accepted tenants for succeeding lives, a typical example being successive life interests for the tenant, his wife and one of his children. Copyhold land could be sold, but until 1815 was not regarded as inheritable and so could not be devised by will.

Copyholders were also required to pay a heriot (a financial payment), plus an entry fine when entering into a property. Default of payment could, and often did, result in loss of land. Other causes for default include the failure to repair the property or keep it in a good state, and such entries in the court rolls can often provide the house historian with crucial evidence about the date of rebuilds or extensions to a property.

The manorial courts

There were essentially two types of manorial court. The 'view of frankpledge' and 'court leet' were held twice a year to try minor offences and inspect 'tithings', which were groups of ten men who had mutual responsibility for each others' good behaviour. However, the most important type of manorial court was the court baron. The court was held on a regular basis to conduct and regulate the routine business of the manor, and court rolls are the written record of this process. The business varied from session to session, but generally included financial punishments for offences against the manorial rules; issues relating to the administration of the manor; the deaths of tenants and changes of occupancy since the last court meeting; and surrenders of land and admission of new copyhold tenants according to the custom of the manor. The lord of the manor's appointed steward or deputy officiated at the sessions. All free tenants were required to attend, and usually acted as jurors for the court. Customary tenants were also required to attend, and were amerced (penalised) if they failed to do so without paying an essoin (excuse).

Copyhold transfers in court rolls

If your property was originally held as copyhold, then you can start your research within the manorial court rolls, which can be the most useful series of documents because they contain property transactions. Court rolls are the written record of the court baron, and usually follow a standard format. The heading of the court roll details the type of court held, the names of the manor, lord and steward in question, plus the date of the session in progress. The first section of the roll concerned presentments of all matters that the court would subsequently deal with. These were usually minor matters, such as disputes between tenants, but will occasionally feature repairs to property ordered by the lord of the manor, and references to property can be made in boundary disputes.

Admission and surrender

However, the most important section of the court rolls concerns the administration of the copyhold land. Land transactions concerning copyhold property were permissible only with the consent of the lord of the manor through the jurisdiction of the court. All new copyhold tenants were required to undergo a process of entry known as admission and surrender. First, the death of the old tenant would be announced in court and recorded in the court roll. Technically the land was 'surrendered' back to the lord, and the heir would then seek 'admission' to the property. A ceremony would be conducted in court whereby the tenant would grasp an official rod in the possession of the steward to mark his formal admittance to the property, and a record of the admittance would then be made in the court roll. A copy of the entry was provided to the tenant as proof of title. The entry usually contained a description of the property or piece of land in question, the name of the deceased tenant, the relationship with the new tenant, plus details of any longer terms of lives that might be involved. The property is usually referred to with reference to property on either side, or by the names of previous owners, although specific property names are occasionally provided.

Conditional surrender

Yet it is important to remember that the manorial tenant might not be the occupier of a property, merely the owner. Tenants often leased their property, but required the permission of the lord first, and a written record is provided in the court rolls. Sales of customary land grew increasingly common, and were also recorded in the roll as an admission and surrender, the only difference being that the tenant was still alive. Customary tenants increasingly followed the practice of freeholders by taking out mortgages on their property to raise loans, and these were entered into the court rolls. The practice was known as making a conditional surrender, as the tenant would surrender the property at court. The terms of the mortgage would then be entered onto the roll, so that if the mortgage was not repaid within the specified period the tenant would default the property to the mortgage provider, who would become the new tenant and therefore be admitted. However, if the mortgage was paid in full, then the payment was recorded on the roll and the conditional surrender would be declared void.

Surrender to the uses of a will
'Surrenders to the uses of a will' was a device used to bypass the descent of land through the customs of the manor. The land was surrendered to the court, and then the use, in this case defined by the terms of the tenant's will, was recorded in the court roll to be honoured on the death of the original tenant. This method of transfer became increasingly popular following a sale of copyhold land, to ensure that the purchaser retained the right to pass the land to his heirs without the restriction of the customs of the manor.

Means of access
Many court rolls contain internal alphabetical indexes to admissions and surrenders, which will be of use if you already know the name of a tenant who possessed your property. These become more common in later court rolls, and in addition separate index books, or even registers of admissions and surrenders, sometimes survive. Where they do, they can provide the date of the previous admission, and can often instigate a chain search back to the earliest surviving court roll or book. This can be lengthy, given that courts continued to regulate copyhold land until the beginning of the twentieth century, and could in theory stretch back to the Middle Ages.

Related records produced at the manorial court
In addition to the official court rolls, the steward who presided over the court also created subsidiary documents to assist him with his duties. Many of these sources can help you to trace an ancestor who was a manorial tenant, as well as possibly glean some more information about their house or property within the manor.

Minute books and draft court rolls usually contain notes taken during the court sessions, and provide details of admissions and surrender. As they were working documents, they were hastily written and contain many abbreviations, and as such they can be difficult to interpret. However, they serve as a useful substitute where official court rolls have not survived.

Estreat rolls contain records of amercements and fines made during the course of a court session. These can include financial penalties for not repairing houses, as well as details of entry fines for new tenants. You will usually find lists of names of the tenants who were due to pay, plus a note of the reason why they owed money.

Suit rolls and call books contain the names of all tenants who owed suit to the court, and in effect doubled up as court attendance registers. Although they will not contain details of property as such, they were amended and dated on the death of tenants and can serve as a useful means of reference to the court rolls themselves when trying to trace property descent.

Locating court rolls and manorial records

The majority of court rolls and related records will be found in the relevant local archive. The obvious place to start looking will be at the County Record Office for the shire in which the manor is located, but if the lord of the manor was not a local resident you will have to search for their principal family seat, and look at the archives there instead. To assist researchers to find court rolls, the Manorial Documents Register (MDR) was established from 1926 with the sole aim of listing the location of such records in the public domain and private hands. This is now part of The National Archives, Kew, and can be partially searched online from their website www.nationalarchives.gov.uk. Secondary sources such as the *VCH* may provide clues as to the whereabouts of manorial material, and often give detailed descents of manors that can help you to locate relevant archives or collections as well as helpful footnotes leading you to local and national collections of documents. You may also like to examine the records at The National Archives HMC 5/6–8 that provide lists of owners of manors in 1925, or try to track down the last known steward.

You will also find court rolls at The National Archives, with an index to collections in series SC 2; and another for the Duchy of Lancaster in DL 30. A third index relates to manors that remained within Crown hands, covering a range of series such as ADM 74; C 104–9, 111–16 and 171; CRES 5; DL 30/351– 587; E 140; F 14; J 90; PRO 30/26; TS 19; SC 2/252–350 and 2/506–92; LR 3 and 11; and MAF 5. In addition, you will find references to material in E 315; DURH 3; WARD 2; E 36; SP 2, 14, 16, 17, 23 and 28; LR 11; DL 42; SC 6 and 12; E 137; C 54; and E 106.

Enfranchisement of copyhold tenants

By the nineteenth century, the conversion of land tenure from copyhold to leasehold meant that less land was subject to the customs of the manor, making the process of admissions and surrender increasingly obsolete. Where the practice still existed, changing ways of life, increasing urbanisation and more tenants who resided many miles from the manor itself meant it was inconvenient to perform the ritual admission via a court and to attend sessions that were increasingly irrelevant. In consequence, the enfranchisement of copyhold land was introduced in 1841.

Enfranchisement is the term used to describe the legal conversion of copyhold land to freehold. The process was started at the request of either the lord or tenant, but once it had been initiated the other party was required to give his or her consent; compensation for loss of manorial income was granted to the lord, and where disputes arose, the Ministry of Agriculture and Fisheries became involved as an arbitrator. The 1922 and 1925 Law of Property Acts abolished all copyhold tenure, and all outstanding copyhold land was made freehold from 1 January 1926.

The records of enfranchisement are now stored at The National Archives in the collections of the Ministry of Agriculture and Fisheries. Voluntary agreements and awards for compulsory enfranchisement from 1841–1925 are in series MAF 9. The records are arranged in county order, and thereafter by the name of the manor, and you will obtain the date of the award and the name of the tenant, plus evidence of title supplied from the court rolls by the lords from 1900; earlier evidences are in series MAF 20. Correspondence and papers can be found in MAF 48, while registers to enfranchisement records relating to MAF 9 are in MAF 76. It will also be worth investigating the records in MAF 13 and 27, which contain agreements and certificates of compensation. Many of your ancestors will be contained in these files, along with information on their homes and houses.

Title deeds

The previous section has specified some of the main ways you can trace single property transfers or conveyances, but these tend to be linked to transactions made in isolation that required some formal method of enrolment. The vast majority of documents relating to the transfer of a house over time will form what is known as the title deeds, and the process of generating title deeds continues today – though as you will see, 1925 marks a key turning point in the way records were generated and stored. When you purchase a house the legal documentation affecting the purchase will be added to the existing title deeds for the property, and a solicitor will assist with the formal registration of the transaction with the Land Registry – a process which is done online these days. To finance the purchase, most people apply for a mortgage, and the title deeds for the property are then deposited with the mortgage provider or solicitor acting on their behalf as security against the loan until the mortgage is paid off, or the property is sold on.

However, there was no systematic registration of land or property transfers until a centralised Land Registry was created in 1862, and even then, registration remained a voluntary process for most areas outside inner London until late into the twentieth century. Before the existence of the Land Registry, transfers of property were often enrolled in courts of law; but as we have seen above, the rules, restrictions and regulations that governed land transactions and sales varied across the centuries, which means there will be many potential places in which to look for evidence. It is also important to stress that the very nature of the records can cause confusion, because the documents contain legal jargon and can be lengthy and repetitive. Furthermore, many records created before 1733 will be written in Latin, with the remainder in old-fashioned English or even French, as explained above – although it will not always be necessary to transcribe the material in full if it is only the names of the owners or parties that you are interested in.

While information to date has focused on the transfer of freehold land, title deeds were also created for copyhold and leasehold property, and therefore may contain details of bequests and devises in wills – so standard genealogical research for probate material may actually provide the first clue that there was an ancestral property in the family which can lead you to other sources in the local and national archives.

What are title deeds?
Defined in the strictest terms, a 'deed' is a legal document and title deeds (also referred to as muniments of title) are therefore a collection of legal documentation that relate to past transfers for a particular piece of land or property, and who 'owned' the title of that property; consequently they should perhaps be more accurately described as the 'deed package'. In effect, title deeds represent legal proof of ownership through previous transfers and were a vital record that would be handed over whenever the house or land was sold to a new person. As such, a variety of different types of document might be included in the deed package, depending on the type of property and the method of transfer, such as indentures, mortgages, wills, manorial records and court papers. In theory, title deeds can stretch back for many centuries, and until 1925 this was often the case. However, under the terms of the 1925 Law of Property Act, the requirement to prove descent of land as far back as possible was removed, with a new period of proof limited to only thirty years. This period was further reduced to fifteen years in 1970. In consequence, older title deeds became redundant, and often no longer

formed part of the deed package that was passed from one purchaser to the next – it is hard to believe, but thousands of these historic documents were simply thrown away by land agents, solicitors and even owners who didn't want the clutter!

Therefore, title deeds will differ from property to property, depending on how previous sales or transactions were conducted; this is the unique research trail that reflects the history of your house, and no other. You may find that there are no title deeds for your property more than fifteen years old, or you may strike it lucky and find deposited deeds that stretch back many years, if not centuries. Regardless of how far back they go, you can use these records to identify the names of the vendor and purchaser; a description of the property in question, along with its boundaries and abuttals (the properties that border it – where your ancestral neighbours would have lived!); the date of transfer; and the sums of money involved. Tenants and occupiers are also occasionally listed in the body of the text, important if your ancestors were renting a house; and you may also find that the dates of previous sales are recited too. If you are interested in the antiquity of an ancestral home, the date of construction might be specified, particularly if the original building lease for the plot of land is included.

Where are they to be found?

Trying to locate old title deeds can be time-consuming and rather frustrating, as there is no logical place of deposit, and no guarantee that historic title deeds actually survive. Modern title deeds are usually retained by the mortgage provider as security, therefore banks, building societies or solicitors acting on behalf of a mortgage provider are the logical place to begin your search – although you will find that most mortgage providers will charge a fee before they allow you to view the title deeds. Once the loan has been paid off, the need for this security ends, and you are entitled to claim your title deeds. This raises the problem that older title deeds may well be in the private hands of former owners, and consequently there is very little chance of tracking them down unless you can identify where the previous owners might now reside.

The alternative is that old title deeds have been deposited in the public domain. When the 1925 Law of Property Act was passed, many solicitors and mortgage providers took the opportunity to dispose of title deeds that had accumulated over many years, and presented them (or in recent years, posted them for a small fee) to current owners; others have been sent to the relevant municipal or County Record Office. Where they survive, the title deeds are usually listed either by place or by the name of the family or business collection within which they were deposited. However, a large proportion of old title deeds – probably the majority – were simply thrown away and ended up in skips or rubbish tips, shocking as this may seem. Nevertheless, it is still worth approaching solicitors that operate in your area on the off-chance that they still have old title deeds squirreled away in cupboards. It might also be worth talking to local estate agents, as they can often provide information about where and when previous sales occurred.

It is worth spending some time beginning your research online searching Access to Archives via The National Archives website www.nationalarchives. gov.uk/a2a where many title deeds are listed. Similarly, many County Record Offices and municipal archives have in-house card catalogues for these records, particularly if they are 'buried' within the holdings of solicitors or estate papers. Many topographical catalogues are also full of title deed references – the National Library of Wales has a huge collection, for example – while family and estate papers are another useful place to hunt around for information.

In addition to specific local collections, the main place to look for strays, enrolled deeds and records of Crown estates – a major landowner through time – will be The National Archives.

Title deeds in The National Archives
Title deeds have accumulated at The National Archives for a variety of reasons. Some properties had become part of the Crown estates through purchase or forfeiture, which meant that the legal proof of ownership was deposited with the relevant administrative body or Government department. Alternatively, property disputes that ended up in court often required the litigants to provide evidence of title; sometimes the documents were left behind and remained within the holdings of the court. However, there is no overall index to title deeds at The National Archives – the best place to start is with a speculative search of the online Catalogue, followed up by more specific searches in some of the most likely places of deposit, described below, as well as more obscure areas.

Private property
Large collections of title deeds relating to private properties fell into Crown hands for a variety of reasons, and are scattered across a wide range of record

series at The National Archives. The material will also include deeds for former monastic land and property that were seized by the Crown in the aftermath of the Dissolution of the monasteries. Most title deeds are described as Ancient or Modern, depending on their date: Ancient deeds usually pre-date the seventeenth century, whereas Modern deeds date from the seventeenth century to the early nineteenth century. Most are to be found in the archives of the two great medieval departments of state, the Chancery and the Exchequer. The main record series are C 146–9, E 40–44, E 132, E 210–14, E326–30 and E354–5, while some have been transcribed and indexed in *A Descriptive Catalogue of Ancient Deeds in the Public Record Office*, 6 volumes (HMSO, 1890–1906) which is available for consultation in the reading rooms. These deposited deeds will be of most use if your property once formed part of a large private estate, as the vast majority of the material relates to principal landowners or tenants-in-chief who fell foul of the Crown and escheated (lost possession of) their property. Most of the records will also be very early, so you will be highly unlikely to find title deeds to a specific modern property; most will relate to land on which houses were later built, rather than to the transfer of a building itself.

Crown lands

In addition to private property deeds, there are also areas where you can look for deeds to property that was formerly owned by the Crown, or was leased from the royal estates. Many of the key Government departments administering Crown lands held these records, and they are now to be found in record series CRES 38; LR 14–16; LRRO 13–18, LR 20, LR 25, LR 37 and LR 64; IR 10; TS 21; and WORK 7–8, 13 and WORK 24. Many of these series have registers or card indexes that can aid identification of people or places. As with private deeds, it is important to remember that it will be unusual to find references to individual properties, and you will find that much of your research will focus on prior usage of a site, rather than a later house that was to be built there.

Deposited deeds as evidence

In addition to title deeds that relate to private or Crown property, the records preserved by central law courts can prove to be a rich source for the house detective. In cases of disputed property ownership, litigants were required to provide evidence of title to support their case. Quite often the litigants failed to collect this evidence, and the courts retained these papers to form a wonderful archive that is rich with private records. This topic is covered in more detail below in relation to disputes over property ownership.

Enrolment of title deeds

The Land Registry

In 1862 the national Land Registry was established to provide a means of recording land transfers across England and Wales. As we have seen, certain types of land transaction were required by law to be enrolled in court, but there was no central body coordinating or checking the number and type of transactions. Even when the Land Registry was set up to fulfil this role, at first there was no legal requirement to enrol land transfers there until compulsory registration was introduced by the Land Transfer Act 1897 on only a gradual basis, county by county, with particular importance given to urban areas. It is astonishing to learn that, technically, compulsory registration for all counties has existed only since 1990, even though for most counties this has been the case since the 1970s.

The records maintained by the Land Registry will contain information on the sale, plus maps or plans that depict boundaries of the land or property in question. The register of a property contains details of the current ownership only, as well as details of any registered mortgage or deed affecting the land, which might contain references to previous sales. Anyone can order a copy of the register and most documents referred to in it, as well as a copy of the title plan, for a small fee via the Land Registry website http://www.landreg. gov.uk. Only records of the last legal transaction are registered and available for purchase, and the Land Registry states that it is not a place of deposit for title deeds, though some very limited historical records are available at the discretion of the regional Land Registry office concerned, and application should be made in writing, explaining why the records are needed. Again, a fee would be charged.

Local deed registries

Before the Land Registry was set up, registers of deeds were already in existence in some parts of England, set up by statute to prevent fraud, given that the possession of title deeds conferred legal ownership upon the holder of the documents – hence the expression that possession is nine-tenths of the law. The statutes also defined the type of transaction that was eligible for registration in the local registries. Usually these were leases over twenty-one years, freehold transfers, mortgages and wills. The local registers do not contain the actual deeds as such, since they would be retained by the property owner; however, they do contain a memorial or written record of the important sections of the deeds, and the date of enrolment in the register. The main registries were for Middlesex (c.1709–1940), with records held at the London Metropolitan Archives; the Bedford Level which included the surrounding counties (seventeenth century onwards) at the Cambridgeshire Record Office; and the North, East and West Riding registries of Yorkshire (eighteenth to late-twentieth century), held at Northallerton, Beverley and Wakefield respectively. In addition, registration of property or land transfers for the City of London appears on occasion on hustings rolls, which can be found at the Corporation of London Record Office at the Guildhall, Aldermanbury. Similar urban registration occurred in borough or municipal courts, with records usually deposited in the appropriate local archive. Some counties have collections of deeds enrolled under the Statute of Enrolments 1536. In addition, from 1715–91 Roman Catholics and non-juror Anglicans had to register their estates and changes of ownership, with records generated locally with some at The National Archives.

Official enrolment of deeds

Many of the relevant courts where conveyances were enrolled have been listed above in relation to the means of conveyance, but people were able to have their deeds enrolled in other Government departmental records for a fee, so that they had written evidence of title. Here is a quick summary of the main places you should look for enrolled title deeds at The National Archives:

(a) Chancery

One of the most accessible places for deed enrolment was in Chancery. For a fee, private individuals had memorials of property sales or land transfers copied onto the back of the close rolls, contained in record series C 54, particularly after it became compulsory to enrol conveyance by bargain and sale (see above). After the establishment of the central Land Registry, the close rolls were used less frequently as a place of enrolment. Close rolls are especially useful if the land was formerly owned under the terms of a charitable trust, often set up to create a place of worship which might subsequently have fallen into your ancestor's hands. There are separate indexes by place available in the reading rooms.

Grants of land made by the Crown were initially recorded in charter rolls in record series C 53. These tend to be quite early, focusing on the medieval period, so you might find that later grants were recorded on patent rolls in series C 66, and between 1483–1625 confirmations of previous grants were enrolled separately on confirmation rolls in series C 56. Patent rolls are of particular use in the Reformation period and beyond, when grants of land and property formerly belonging to monastic institutions were enrolled.

(b) Exchequer

Although primarily a financial institution, the Exchequer served as a court of common law and equity where deeds and land transactions were also enrolled, and you might find relevant records in one of three main areas. Memoranda rolls were kept in duplicate, known as the King's Remembrancer in series E 159 (1218–1994) and as the Lord Treasurer's Remembrancer in E 368 (1217–1835), where enrolments of legal business, fines and conveyances developed during the sixteenth century as part of the Exchequer's jurisdiction as an equity court (see below), and from 1927 separate enrolment books, recording conveyances and associated plans, can be found in E 159 alone. The plea rolls in E 13 (1236–1875) were, as the name suggests, enrolments of common law pleas and often related to land transfer cases brought by private litigants into the Exchequer of Pleas. Repertory rolls, which act as indexes, are in the series E 14 and cover the periods 1412–99, 1559–1669 and 1822–30. Finally, miscellaneous books of the Exchequer in E 315 (1100–1800) cover a disparate range of material bound up in the 527 surviving volumes. A huge amount of information relating to land transactions after the Reformation is stored in these documents, including enrolled deeds and leases that were gathered by the Augmentation Office.

(c) Court of King's Bench

The court of King's Bench heard civil pleas, as well as its main work dealing with criminal justice, and because copious records were kept it proved a popular way to register deeds or conveyances via lawsuits. There are a range of places you can look for information: coram rege (before the king) rolls exist from 1273–1702 in series KB 27; lists of deeds enrolled during the reigns of Edward I and Edward II, and for 1656–1702, are in KB 173/1; enrolled deeds from 1390 to 1595 and from 1649 to 1655 may be traced through the Docket Rolls or Docket Books in IND 1 (though are not indexed by place so can be pretty hard to use!), whereas after 1702 Judgment Rolls were maintained in series KB 122 for which a basic catalogue of enrolled deeds and wills down to 1805 is available.

(d) Court of Common Pleas

The Court of Common Pleas was one of the most popular courts where deeds and conveyances were enrolled, as we have already seen with Feet of Fines in CP 25/1 and CP 25/2. In addition, civil pleas were entered onto the plea rolls in series CP 40 (1273–1874), which became used so frequently to enrol the common recovery that a separate series of Recovery Rolls was created in 1583, in series CP 43 (1583–1838) which were also used to enrol deeds.

The plea rolls were composed of distinct sections, one of which was usually reserved for the enrolment of writs, deeds and charters. There are no indexes as such, but you can work out a rough rotulus (or roll number) from the docket rolls in CP 60 for the period 1509–1859. Many means of reference survive for the recovery rolls, mainly in series IND 1 which you can use to obtain the county, the names of the parties and the number of the rotulus on which the recovery is enrolled, although in some cases you may find additional details about the property involved in the case. A separate index to deeds enrolled in the recovery rolls between 1555 and 1629 is in CP 73/1, and from 1629 to 1836 in IND 1/16943–9.

(e) Crown lands

Enrolments of deeds relating to Crown lands are usually to be found among the records of the offices and Government departments responsible for managing the Crown estates. The most important record series in which to look will be LR 1 and LRRO 13–18, LRRO 20 and LRRO 25; series LRRO 64 and 66 act as indexes to enrolments.

Searching for sale or transfer particulars

It's a bit of a Catch 22 situation – unless you are in possession of title deeds that provide details of when a sale occurred, it can be difficult to track down how and when a property changed hands. However, without information about when a sale took place, it can be tricky to home in on enrolled title deeds! Luckily, there are various areas where you might start to look for property transfers, or even details of leases to tenants.

Local newspapers are probably one of the best places to begin searching for details, especially as you'll find that more and more papers survive from the eighteenth century onwards, which usually carry details or notices that advertise property for sale, rent or lease. Searching the papers may be a time-consuming task as there are no internal indexes, although many County Record Offices have compiled their own rudimentary indexes to names, events and places (though they are rarely complete and won't cover all local titles). However, where advertisements do survive, you are likely to find a detailed description of your house, plus the name of the sale agent or vendor. It is then possible to approximate a date of sale, and then search for evidence for the method of transfer. The best place to start your research should be the local studies centre nearest to the property in question – there are usually newspaper clippings alongside the main series of local newspapers – and failing that, head to the county or municipal archive. If you find that they are missing some of a particular series, you could also try the British Newspaper Library, Colindale, as they hold the largest national collection of newspapers in the UK, both national and local.

Alternatively, sale catalogues and estate agents' prospectuses can be discovered among the deposited business records of the relevant company, where they survive. These will also provide you with a rough date of the sale, and possibly information about the interior of the property. Many auctions were publicised on a regular basis, and produced pamphlets and brochures to help facilitate sales; many of these will have been deposited too. As with newspapers, the best place to start your research is at a local level, in all probability the relevant county or municipal archive. Don't forget that details of a late-nineteenth or early-twentieth century sale might be recorded in the valuation records of c.1910 via the Field Books, described in the previous chapter.

Title deeds for Scotland, Wales and Ireland

Although the main focus of this chapter has been on enrolled deeds and land transfers in England and Wales, there are different sources and methods of land transfer for Scotland and Northern Ireland as well. Furthermore, deeds for property in Wales can also be found at regional archives, and at the National Library of Wales, with many items now available for online searching via its integrated catalogue.

Land transfers and registration in Scotland was different to that in England, with a different set of documents created. A key means of transferring ownership of a piece of land or building was via sasines (summaries of the conveyance documentation). A register of sasines exists from 1617 onwards, arranged in counties and by royal burgh, and detailed transcripts known as abridgements begin in 1781. The records are stored at the National Archives of Scotland in Edinburgh, where you can obtain further information about the nature of the records and the evidence for house history that they contain. The NAS also holds registers for deeds in the various courts, such as the Register of Deeds in the Court of Sessions known as the Books of Council and Session (NAS series RD, from 1554), the Sheriff Courts (NAS series SC, generally from the nineteenth century onwards), Royal Burgh Courts (NAS series B for varying dates), Commissary Court (NAS series CC), and Local Courts (NAS series RH 11, before 1748).

The Irish Government passed an act setting up the Irish Registry of Deeds in 1708, now based at the National Archives in Dublin, with microfilm duplicates stored at the Public Record Office of Northern Ireland. The registry contains memorials that are much more detailed than those in England and usually comprise a complete copy or a fairly full abstract of a document. Copies of the memorials known as Transcript Books are also available on microfilm, from 1708–1929; indexes to these series also exist, which after 1832 provide details of the townland or street, the county, city or town, and the barony or parish in which the lands are situated.

Chapter Nine

CONTESTED OWNERSHIP:
LEGAL DISPUTES

As we've just seen in previous sections, a range of law courts were used to generate official documentation about property transfers, many of which were in the form of fictitious lawsuits. However, alongside these statutory requirements and voluntary initiatives to enrol title deeds, there were a massive number of legitimate suits brought before the courts relating to property disputes. Our ancestors did not always enjoy undisputed possession of their land or property! In many ways, looking at the records of the various courts where arguments over title, or convoluted claims to inheritance revolving around land or property, will show you just how important written evidence was to our forebears, and reveal the lengths they were prepared to go to in defence of their houses, estates and land.

The English legal system can be complicated at the best of times, and even more so when property or inheritance is concerned. Proof of ownership was vital if land was to be sold or passed on without challenge, and contested successions, sales or transfers were frequent, especially when families disagreed with the terms of an inheritance, settlement or will. Furthermore, there were many statutes in place that regulated and controlled the erection of new properties and the extension of an old one, and failure to comply often led to prosecution.

Fortunately for the modern house historian, if a little less fortunately for the contemporary house owner who was embroiled in legal action, disputes and prosecutions have left a trail for us to follow – indeed, the rigours of the law and the almost pedantic need for detailed record-keeping have resulted in a huge archive of material that you can trawl through for evidence of ancestral squabbles over houses and inheritance. However, a cautionary note should be sounded before you think about heading straight for legal records, because you need to know that a property dispute ended up in court, which court it ended up in, and usually a rough date in mind, plus the names of the parties concerned. Without this information, to find your property via a random search of the surviving records would require an enormous quantity of luck, or patience, or probably both.

Background: the English Legal System

It is worth taking a little while to sketch out the basic ways in which a case might come to court, as well as describing the various courts where litigants could bring their suits, otherwise it is easy to become confused! Before 1875 there were two main branches of civil litigation that you will need to consider.

Common law courts, such as King's Bench and the Court of Common Pleas, dispensed justice according to the 'common law' and ancient custom of the land, and as such awarded compensation or damages but were unable to enforce contracts that had been broken. This meant that they were less effective at solving property disputes that involved breach of trusts or wills. In comparison, the courts of equity, primarily Chancery and the Exchequer, were able to make judgments on the grounds of justice and conscience as opposed to 'law'. This meant that they were in a position to force remedial action to be taken, although they were not allowed to award damages.

Confusingly, some of the equity courts heard common law pleas as well. In 1875, all were abolished and a Supreme Court of Judicature was created with five divisions – Chancery, Common Pleas, Exchequer, King's (Queen's) Bench and Probate, Divorce and Admiralty. In 1881 the Common Pleas, King's (Queen's) Bench and Exchequer were amalgamated to form the King's (Queen's) Bench. Although cases could be heard in any division, and common law or equity rules applied whenever needed, the King's (Queen's) Bench heard most actions relating to contract, and Chancery usually dealt with land, trusts and mortgages.

Technically, a property dispute could end up in one of many places, and it was not unknown for a single dispute to move between courts during the course of the action, or indeed for a case to be started in more than one court. However, local newspapers can often provide clues as to which court heard a dispute, and you would be surprised by how much attention was focused upon contentious local disputes that ended up in court; while legal papers in private hands can also give an indication of where to begin your research. Furthermore, many of the indexes to the equity courts are available online and can be searched for names via the Catalogue.

Equity proceedings in Chancery

In terms of popularity, as well as survival of useable records (also for ease of access), the court of Chancery will be the best place to begin your quest for ancestors quarrelling over property. Thousands of equity cases were brought before the court of Chancery each year from the fourteenth century onwards to resolve disputes between individuals or parties, covering a wide range of topics such as disputed wills, legacies, estate administration and property transfers.

During the course of a court case, many different types of document were created, based on the equity principle of bill-pleading (explained below). However, it is important to remember that all documentation for a single case was not filed together but rather in separate series, now held at The National Archives, according to the type of document, making it difficult to accurately collate all material relating to a single case. Furthermore, documents were filed under the name of the first listed plaintiff, so it can be very difficult to locate multi-party cases where the principal name is unknown – though the expansion of the online Catalogue has partly rectified this, as document descriptions often include more than just the first-named individual. Party names also changed over time, especially in long cases where plaintiffs or defendants died and were succeeded by their relatives and descendants.

Another complication surrounds the fact that not all cases came to a judgment or recorded conclusion, as they were often initially brought into Chancery in an attempt to force the defendant to settle out of court. Consequently, it can be difficult to locate a definite outcome for many cases – which may leave more questions than answers if you're tackling a mystery in your ancestral background!

Here is a summary of the main records you will be consulting while tracing a property-related dispute in Chancery. All record series relate to material held at The National Archives.

Chancery Proceedings

Imagine a property dispute – the unlawful seizure of a house and its land under the terms of a disputed will, for example. The wronged party – the plaintiff – would instruct a lawyer to file an initial 'bill of complaint' with the Lord Chancellor, the official who technically presided over the court. The bill of complaint would state the charges that the plaintiff wanted the defendant to answer, as well as a justification for bringing an equity lawsuit as opposed to a case under common law. The bill of complaint would commonly include name, occupation and residence of the plaintiff at the start, while the main text would then provide specifics of the nature of the complaint, where you will find information about the property and possible reasons for the dispute.

Once a bill of complaint was filed, the defendant was required to provide a written 'answer' to the charges, explaining why they refuted the accusations and lay any counter-charges against the plaintiff. The plaintiff might counter with a replication, and the defendant with a rejoinder. In essence this process, known as bill-pleading, defined the limits of the case so that a recommendation could be made by one of the Masters of Chancery, who considered the case and reported back to the Lord Chancellor. Witness statements (depositions) were then taken and evidence (exhibits) brought into court to help the masters make a decision about the merits and legality of the case and pass this up to the Lord Chancellor. Once a verdict had been reached, a decree or order was issued settling the matter.

The size, scope and detail of the documents varied throughout time, but you will find that, apart from the very earliest, they were written in English and should be relatively legible – an advantage of working with equity records, as opposed to common law courts which recorded their business in Latin. However, you may find the original bill was lost and you are left with later papers that contain unfathomable references to earlier documents. Similarly, the bills and answers tend to get longer – much longer – as time progresses and can take some wading through; it's easy to get lost amidst the convoluted legal language at times.

The records are arranged chronologically and are located in several TNA series, partially reflecting the way Chancery operated its equity court; from the mid-seventeenth century there were six clerks working for the Masters, and proceedings for a single case could have been filed with any of them – or moved between the clerks. To ensure that you have not missed any paperwork, you should search for the case within all six divisions. A summary of TNA series can be found via the online Catalogue, which can be searched by the names of the parties involved – as well as place or case details for earlier records – while there are further cataloguing projects that will place key details of each case into a searchable database.

Early proceedings are in C 1–C 4 (up to about the mid-seventeenth century), with the Six Clerks series running chronologically in C 5–C 10 (to 1714), C 11 (1714–58), C 12 (1758–1800), C 13 (1800–42), C 14 (1841–52), C 15 (1853–60) and C 16 (1861–75) when the court was amalgamated into the Supreme Court of Judicature. Further information about on-site indexes and finding aids, and which series can be searched online, can be found on a research guide via The National Archives website www.nationalarchives.gov.uk.

Depositions and affidavits

Once the pleadings had produced a final case to be answered, the Masters of Chancery collected evidence so that they could make an equitable decision. Depositions and affidavits played an important part in this process and are a good source of evidence about the background of the case and, in cases of property disputes, include detailed descriptions of the nature of the case as well as eye-witness accounts from the local area – so not only do you get information about your family and their ancestral home, but also their friends (or enemies!) and neighbours.

Depositions were written statements taken from deponents, namely individuals with knowledge of a dispute who were selected by both parties. A list of pertinent questions was compiled, known as an interrogatory. Sworn, signed and dated statements were then made in answer to the interrogatories and were brought before the court to be used as evidence. In comparison, affidavits were voluntary statements made on oath during the case. Town Depositions were sworn in London, and are in series C 24 with some earlier material in C 1 and C 4, and later files in C 15 and C 16. Country Depositions were sworn elsewhere, and can be found in C 21 and C 22, with later material in C 11–C 14. Affidavits are in C 31 and C 41, while surviving interrogatories – mainly linked to Town Depositions – are in C 25.

Decree and Order Books

Despite the bill-pleading, and production of witness statements, it might have been necessary during the course of a case for the court to issue an order to one party or another; the conclusion of the case being via a final decision, it would then issue a decree in favour of the victorious party. Before 1544, decrees and orders were sometimes enrolled on the back of the bill of complaint; between 1544 and 1875, they were recorded in Decree and Order Entry Books, in series C 33, and thereafter in J 15. The indexes are on open access in the reading rooms – arranged by year, by legal term and alphabetically by plaintiff – and can be consulted to obtain the case reference so you can order the relevant book in C 33.

Decrees could be enrolled at extra cost, and are more likely to survive in cases involving property so that a permanent record was preserved. Decree rolls (1534–1903) are in C 78 with supplementary rolls in C 79; there are some indexes, mainly by name but a place name index survives as well. However, before starting a search of these records it is important to bear in mind that the majority of cases (approximately 90 per cent) never reached the stage where an order or decree might have been issued, and therefore the pleadings and depositions might be the only surviving evidence.

Equity cases in the Court of Exchequer

Another court where property disputes could end up was the Exchequer, which dealt with equity cases from the mid-sixteenth century until 1841, when all such actions were transferred to Chancery. The procedures were the same as in Chancery, namely bill-pleading. In theory, the plaintiff had to be a debtor of the Crown for their suit to be heard in the Exchequer, but this was usually a fiction designed to allow the action to be brought before the court.

Although the records of Exchequer equity cases are similar to those in Chancery, and are also stored at The National Archives, the means of reference are much harder to use. Fewer indexes exist, with far less material available online for keyword searching – particularly for the bill-pleadings. Therefore one of the main ways of gaining access to these records is via the Country Depositions in series E 134, which have been thoroughly listed and are readily available to search online as they contain not only names of the parties concerned, but also detailed descriptions of the case and mentions of any disputed property.

Exchequer Proceedings

There are two series of bills and answers. Record series E 111 mainly contains strays from other courts, and covers the reigns of Henry VII to Elizabeth I; but it is listed and available to search online. The main series of bills and answers is in series E 112, and covers cases brought before the court from Elizabeth's reign to the cessation of the court's business in 1841. The documents are arranged by the reign of the monarch in which the action was first filed, and thereafter grouped into counties, depending on where the subject of the dispute was located. There are some stray replications and rejoinders from E 112 in series E 193. The files are indexed by means of contemporary bill books, now stored in IND 1.

Depositions and affidavits
Exchequer depositions taken in London (the equivalent of Chancery Town Depositions) are stored in series E 133. There is an original calendar for the period 2 Elizabeth I to 45 Elizabeth I in E 501/10 and this is arranged in chronological order, providing the county, date and legal term where the deposition was made, the suit number, the names of the plaintiff and defendant, and most importantly the subject of the deposition. The period 1603–1841 is not so well served by indexes, though some material is available in the reading rooms at The National Archives as well as online via the Catalogue.

Exchequer Country Depositions are perhaps the most informative and easily accessible documents. These were taken by Exchequer commissioners, and are now stored in series E 134. Although there are topographical calendars available on open access, which provide the names of the plaintiff and defendant plus an outline of the case, the calendared entries are fully searchable online via the Catalogue. Equally, the commissions, which are in series E 178, are also contained in the same calendars and can be searched by keyword online; they provide the interrogatories on which the depositions were based. Once you have identified a case, the documents will provide a list of statements in answer to the interrogatories, and often provide detailed descriptions of property, property boundaries, owners and occupiers, local events that impacted upon property, and disputed trusts, wills and property transfers.

Affidavits can be found in series E 103 (1774–1841) and E 218 (1695–1822); partial indexes survive for the former, but none exist for the latter. You might find statements relating to surveys requested by either party, many of which relate to property or boundaries.

Decree and order books
At each stage of the case, an order was made so that the next stage could proceed. An order was entered in a minute book (E 161), written out (E 128 and 131) and registered (E 123–5 and 127). Sometimes the orders can provide

additional information about the case. Where a final judgment was reached, a decree was produced. As with orders, they were first entered in a minute book (E 162), written up (E 128 and 130) and registered (E 123–4 and 126).

Other equity-based courts

In addition to Chancery and the Exchequer, other courts developed that followed the principle of equity when reaching decisions – the Court of Requests and Court of Star Chamber were offshoots of the King's Council; the Court of Wards and Liveries may contain some information about contested administrations of the estates of Crown tenants-in-chief; and the short-lived Court of Augmentations dealt with a mass of property suits following the distribution and sale of former monastic land after the Dissolution of the Monasteries. All contained the same type of documentation described above – bill-pleadings, depositions and affidavits, decrees and orders. A brief summary of the lifespan of each court is provided below:

- Court of Requests – established in 1483 with the aim of providing the poor with access to justice; records end in 1642 on dissolution. Proceedings in REQ 2, all other material in REQ 1.
- Court of Star Chamber – established in 1485 and abolished in 1641, so-called because of the stars that decorated the ceiling of the room in which the court sat at Westminster. Proceedings in STAC 1–STAC 9, miscellaneous material in STAC 10.
- Court of Wards and Liveries – established in 1540 to settle issues relating to Crown sales of profits from wardship (when the heir of a tenant-in-chief inherited under age, and the right to control that revenue fell to the Crown), abolished 1660. Proceedings in WARD 13, WARD 22; depositions in WARD 3; decrees and orders in WARD 2; surveys of tenants' lands in WARD 5.
- Court of Augmentation – in existence 1536–54 to regulate disputes of former monastic possessions, with pleadings in E 321, E 315; all other material in E 315.

Equity court exhibits

In addition to the official records created to support each party's case – such as the depositions and affidavits described above – other evidence was often required, and was brought into court to help the officials reach a decision. In property disputes, this meant proof of title to land or evidence of prior legal agreements. However, at the conclusion of the case the litigants sometimes failed to retrieve this evidence, and the courts thus accumulated a vast collection of title deeds, legal papers, family trees, manorial records, maps, plans and other such material. These have been deposited at TNA and are an amazing source for the house historian. Furthermore, they can (in theory) be linked to the cases that generated them, providing even more information about the litigants concerned.

Chancery Masters exhibits and documents
Once the pleading process was complete, documentary evidence was presented to the Chancery Masters for consideration. During the eighteenth and nineteenth centuries the Masters preserved a vast amount of this private documentation, although the material itself dated from at least the twelfth century onwards. These are known collectively as the Chancery Masters Exhibits series and are stored in Chancery series C 103–14. Although there is a composite index to the parties in the C 103 series list, which can be linked to a particular suit or pleading, additional information such as place names, occupants or previous owners for property that was the subject of the case can be found via a keyword search of the Catalogue. There are some amazing collections; the Duchess of Norfolk's Deeds are in C 115, which include great detail about estate management covering a large number of properties, tenants' names and other miscellanea that tell you about life at that time. Similarly, manor court rolls extracted from C 103–14 have been deposited in a separate series, C 116. Exhibits from a later date collected by the Six Clerks are stored in C 171.

Chancery Masters Documents are similar to exhibits in terms of content, though they were collected and used in a different manner; these can be found in record series C 117–29. The records are arranged by the name of the Master who presided over the case, so you'll need to locate the relevant Master's name from an index in C 103 before you can search through the relevant file. Because they are not the easiest records to use, but are potentially as rich a resource for both the family and house historian as the exhibits, work is in progress to produce a fuller set of indexes which, including enhanced document descriptions, can be searched directly on the Catalogue. Later exhibits and documents can be found in J 90, which has its own indexes with the series list.

Exchequer exhibits

The Equity Court of Exchequer also collected evidence, and there are a few areas where you can look for surviving exhibits. The main records are in series E 140, which contains documents dating between 1319 and 1842; the series is well listed and searchable online, though there are various indexes and lists available on-site at The National Archives. Stray documents from Exchequer cases can be found in C 106, but you will also find other series such as E 219 (Clerks Papers, 1625–1841), E 163 (Miscellanea, 1154–1901); and E 167 (Papers of the Clerk to the Deputy Remembrancer, 1689–1877) contain exhibits and other useful material too.

Civil litigation in common law courts

Common law courts

So far, we've concentrated on the records of equity suits, mainly because more property disputes were brought before the courts – though the records are much easier to access as well! However, it is possible that a lawsuit might be prosecuted according to the common law; and before 1875, there were four main central common law courts where litigants could enter a case. Property disputes between individuals that were settled under common law were less frequent than in the equity courts, mainly because the plaintiff could only seek compensation for their loss, rather than restoration of land or enforcement of contract. As with equity courts, you may find that many suits were dropped or a private agreement was reached before a judgment could be made, because the initial stages of a case were sufficient to bring both parties to a negotiated settlement out of court. In these instances it will be difficult to extract much information about the process, as surviving records are difficult to use: the records of a single case can be scattered across many areas, and at present less cataloguing work has been done on common law records compared to those of the equity courts, making them harder to access.

As such, it is easier to focus research on the main series of documents that were generated – the plea rolls – and having found an entry, use their contents in an attempt to look in other areas, such as judgment books, for information. However, these tend to record the later stages of a case, and consequently many disputes that were dropped at an early stage will simply be impossible to locate. It is also important to remember that the common law courts were used to record fictitious legal disputes as part of a conveyance, and it is necessary to distinguish between a genuine dispute and an enrolled deed or land transfer. As described above, the growth of conveyance in the court of Common Pleas by 'common recovery' led to a separate series of records, the recovery rolls, being created in 1538.

In theory, cases relating to property disputes might appear in any one of the four main courts – Common Pleas, King's Bench, Exchequer and Chancery (the last two having common law functions as well as equity); however, you are more likely to find pleas of cases between private individuals entered in the courts of Common Pleas or King's Bench. The Exchequer of Pleas was usually reserved for revenue cases, especially those that impinged on royal revenue-generating rights, although many land disputes found their way into this court. Chancery was also used primarily for cases that involved royal rights, but among the most important areas of litigation were the division of lands between joint heiresses, including assignment of dower, and challenges to inquisitions post mortem and feudal incidents payable on land and property – many of which will have an obvious link to your specific research.

Plea rolls of common law courts
Plea rolls record the formal processes in a common law court: until 1733 they were written in Latin, and were formulaic in the business they recorded. The details you would expect to find on a common law court plea roll include a description of the action concerned (where you will pick up details of the property or settlement under dispute), how the case proceeded within the court; and a final judgment, if one was actually made.

Records in the King's Bench can be found in series KB 27 up to 1702, continued thereafter in KB 122; indexes, in the form of docket books, are now stored in IND 1. For the Court of Common Pleas, you need to look in series CP 40, indexed by docket books in CP 60, with pleas of land in CP 43. The pleas for the Exchequer are in series E 13, with some indexes in IND 1 and a partial index of places in E 48, with additional information gleaned from repertory rolls in E 14 for certain periods. Finally, pleas before Chancery are contained in C 43, C 44 and C 206.

Records of judgment
Judgments of cases were usually recorded on the plea rolls, but by the late eighteenth century many of the cases were not filed. To find out information about the names and dates involved in a case, plus a brief outline of the

issues involved, you can consult a series of supplementary rolls that record judgments and orders. These can assist in filling in missing information for later cases, but many of these records have been destroyed or not selected for permanent preservation; therefore the following is a brief summary of where to look for surviving records of each court.

King's Bench Entry Books of Judgment are in KB 168 from 1699 onwards, while the Court of Common Pleas only retained Entry Books of Judgment from 1859 in CP 64. The Exchequer Entry Book records are equally sparse, running from 1830 in E 54; while records for Chancery are much more complete, though only for an earlier period from 1565–1785 via Remembrance Rolls in C 221 and C 222.

Supreme Court of Judicature (King's/Queen's Bench)
Following the reorganisation of the judicial system in 1875, all courts were amalgamated into the Supreme Court of Judicature, which initially had five divisions but later dropped down to only three in 1881. Each division could apply common law or equity according to the case it heard and it can therefore be difficult to locate papers of common law cases. The main place to look, though, will be among surviving King's (Queen's) Bench papers; however, many of the records have been destroyed because they were not selected for permanent preservation at a former date, and so you are likely to encounter great difficulty in finding information. For the record, cause books are in J 87 and J 168 which provide the names of parties and a brief description of the cause; indexes from 1935 are in J 88.

Civil litigation in assize courts

So far, the central Crown courts have been the subject of attention, mainly because they were also used to record or enrol property transfers as well as disputes. However, they were not the only recourse to justice available to plaintiffs who sought redress according to the common law. Records of property disputes could be heard in locally-held civil assize courts presided over by itinerant justices if a writ *nisi prius* had been issued from one of the central common law courts in London. This enabled parties to transfer the case from the central court to a more convenient local assize court, which was held at least twice a year. The records generated by the assize courts were similar to those of the central courts, and are stored in a variety of TNA series; a research guide is available both online and on-site that summarises the best place to begin your research, as the records are arranged according to the relevant judicial circuits. The main documents you will need to check are the Crown minute books, which record the basic details of the case including the names of the parties and the nature of the dispute, and are usually arranged chronologically. However, there are no indexes, so you will need to have some prior knowledge of when the case took place, such as a local newspaper report or some clue in family paperwork or title deeds.

Property records in quarter sessions

The quarter sessions were so named because they were held four times a year every three months, and were courts presided over by Justices of the Peace (JPs). Their remit was to undertake routine judicial and administrative functions in the counties, with the power to prosecute certain types of offence. More serious matters were usually – but not always – referred to the itinerant assize judges, who toured county circuits twice a year. Where they survive, quarter session records will be found in the relevant County Record Office, or sometimes among the deposited private papers of serving Justices of the Peace. But this is a problem, because the survival rate is decidedly 'mixed'. During each quarter session, many different types of document were created, including the personal working papers of the JPs; much of this material was simply discarded. The main stages of a prosecution that produced relevant records were indictments for an offence, recognisances to ensure appearance at a session, and summary convictions. In addition, the formal court sessions generated quarter-session rolls, which include writs to appear, lists of attendees, recognisances, indictments and jury lists; session and process books to record proceedings; order books to record court decisions; and session papers kept by the Clerk of the Peace, the main court official. Informal mediation and meetings to discuss routine administrative matters might be recorded in unofficial papers kept by individual JPs.

Records of prosecution

One of the key areas where you might find your property mentioned was when the owner or occupier fell foul of one of the many statutes and bylaws regarding the construction of houses. During the late sixteenth and early seventeenth centuries, overcrowding in or around towns and cities was a major concern, mainly due to the increased risk of fire or disease. Yet at the same time, population growth and urban expansion meant that there was pressure to provide sufficient accommodation for people who were drifting into urban areas. To prevent 'slums' appearing on the edges of towns, various statutes were passed that restricted new house-building. The most important was 31 Elizabeth c.7 (1588–89), stipulating that no new dwelling could be constructed without first assigning four acres of land to the site, thereby preventing overcrowding. One of the most important areas affected by this was London and the surrounding counties.

Punishment was potentially severe. An offender was liable to an initial £10 penalty, followed by 40 shillings per month for maintaining an illegal dwelling. These were not small sums of money! Furthermore, if more than one family lived in the property there was an additional penalty of 10 shillings per month. Offences against this statute were usually prosecuted at the quarter sessions, and records can be found in surviving quarter-session rolls. These can be difficult to use as, like most formal courts, they are written in Latin until 1733; but a large number have been calendared and indexed, although the name and date of a case would make searching for evidence much easier. Many of the records can now be searched on Access to Archives via The National Archives website www.nationalarchives.gov.uk/a2a, though it is probably advisable to go to the County Record Office in person as they are likely to have card indexes of catalogues relating to the records that have not yet been put online.

Records of local administration
Other matters relating to the local community fell within the remit of the quarter sessions. Repairs to roads and highways were usually the responsibility of the relevant parish, unless covered by a private turnpike trust and so, if they were not maintained, the entire parish was liable to amercement. Surviving quarter-sessions papers can often list stretches of road that needed repair, and used the names and addresses of residents as landmarks to identify the worst sections. However, the chances of finding such information about your house will be slim.

Records of other types of property can be found in the quarter-sessions papers. For example, JPs were effectively responsible for granting licences to alehouses. They issued recognisances that were valid for one year, which bound over alehouse owners to keep the peace; if law and order had been maintained, a new recognisance was issued for the following year. You will often find the name of the alehouse keeper listed, plus the names of two others who would act as sureties for the original recognisance. Usually, other alehouse keepers acted as a group and stood surety for one another and where the records survive, you can find a wealth of information about local hostelries in a community. Many of our ancestors would have run public houses, or frequented their local on the street corner. Alongside data on the ownership or tenancy of the pub, you may well find incidents of bar brawls, disturbances and other unruly behaviour that may well have included your family – a certain amount of historical colour that you may not have expected.

Chapter Ten

TRACING OCCUPANCY OF THE
ANCESTRAL HOME

M any of the documents you'll have traced in compiling your family tree
will give you a precise address for a given date – the birth or death of
a relative, the house someone was living in when they got married, or the
address where they were during a census. These are your first clues to tracing
information about the key places that your ancestors called 'home', and in
many ways tracing the history of all the houses in which an ancestor lived is
one of the most rewarding aspects of personal heritage. However, as well as
gaining a sense of where someone lived, you will also begin to uncover
information about the street and community as well, plus reveal more about
the lifestyles they would have had as you begin to empathise with the social
and economic conditions of their neighbourhood.

This chapter provides you with advice about using these same
genealogical sources, in particular census returns and wills, to put 'flesh on
the bones' and uncover more about the property in which they lived, as well
as compiling a chronology for house occupancy through a range of other
resources. One of the good things about tracking a family through the house
they were living in is that houses stay put whereas people can move around!
This means you can spot quite quickly when your family moved into, or
vacated, a particular property. Furthermore, if there is a particular dwelling
that fascinates you, it is possible to find out a bit more about the families that
followed your own into a house, and you can use a range of the survey
resources described in Chapter Seven such as the 1910 Valuation Office
survey of 1910–15 and the tithe maps and apportionments of c.1836–58, and
then use the existing census returns from 1841 to 1911 to fill in some of the
gaps.

In many ways, the events that took place inside a house would drive various changes to its fabric or décor. In particular, marriages often acted as a catalyst for constructing extensions to existing property and undertaking rebuilding schemes or major redecorations. Other unusual architectural features can be explained by looking in trade directories – houses also doubled up as places of work, and may have retained some of the original layout. It's also possible to take a peek inside the lost world of our ancestors by examining material that will show you how they used to live – the wallpaper samples, fixtures and fittings, mod cons from an earlier era and household appliances that would have filled their homes.

Genealogical Sources for House History

Although wills and census returns are covered in detail in Section One from the perspective of finding one's ancestors, they are quickly revisited here to show how the same records can be used to trace house occupancy, as well as gaining some background colour about life in the past by investigating the history of the street and neighbourhood.

Census returns

The means of access for census records are described in Section One, so the following notes are designed to help you look at census returns specifically with the history of the street in mind, or if you want to find out who lived in an ancestral home before or after your family was there.

First, you may well find that finding your family is easy, but locating the house is tricky since the property might not have a house number assigned to it – many were simply listed by the street, or even the village or hamlet. Luckily, there are a couple of techniques you can employ to get round this problem. The best place to start is the 1910 Valuation Office survey, as it links very closely with the data in the 1911 census and makes it easier to trace occupancy in 1901. Means of access to these records are described in Chapter Seven. You should be able to locate your house in the street, and then find out who lived there from the field book; but don't just stop at your property – you should aim to obtain occupancy data for the entire street, and look out for any particular landmarks such as pubs, large named houses or other substantial buildings. You can use these landmark buildings, along with the pattern of occupation, to make a reasonable attempt to locate your property in the 1901 census returns.

For example, your house in 1910 may be only two doors down from a pub, or possibly three houses in the other direction away from a named, large or identifiable house. These can be treated as fixed local coordinates to work out which unlisted property in the census is yours, particularly if the neighbours in 1901 remained the same as in 1910 or 1911. Of course, this is only a rough rule of thumb, and you should always attempt to verify the names you discover from other sources. However, once you have discovered a pattern, you can try to examine earlier census returns in the same way – bearing in mind that census enumerators often reversed the routes they took, or occasionally visited houses out of turn. You can find the route that they took listed at the start of each enumerator's schedule, with the streets they followed described in order – so you can get a sense of how they operated.

Similarly, at the start of the period for which census returns survive, you have the tithe apportionment surveys that can serve a similar purpose; these are covered in Chapter Seven as well. So it should be possible to work forward from 1841 or 1851 in the manner outlined above, although it can be a bit trickier since there won't be as many recognisable modern landmarks; in which case, see if you can use clues on an OS map to help you. The lesson to be learnt here is that one document used in isolation may be of little use, but when examined in combination with at least one other, the data it contains suddenly becomes relevant.

Apart from identifying an ancestral home, census returns will tell you a great deal more about the circumstances in which people lived. Occupations, especially when compared to neighbours, will tell you a bit about their social status or the main employment in the area; the structure of the household and the number of rooms occupied will show whether the house was large or small, especially if your family shared with more than one household in a property. Using these clues, you can look at maps, employment records and secondary sources to paint a more vivid picture of life at the time the census return was taken. Furthermore, you can work back in time, decade by decade, to spot changes in the community, street or even house – you might spot the fact that it rose or fell in social status, depending on the professions of the occupants or the number of people who lived there – or indeed the use of household servants, a sign of an upwardly mobile or more well-to-do family.

However, it is important to beware of the pitfalls of using census returns to provide a picture of who lived in your house. For a start, they record occupation on only one given day of the year: it might be the case that your house was unoccupied on that day – they were out visiting friends, perhaps – and therefore your family will not appear in the records, or could appear somewhere where they did not actually live. Furthermore, house names and numbers, and even the name of the street it was built in, were subject to change over time, so it is important to check these details in advance to ensure you are researching the correct property. Even some of the later census returns do not always include street names or house numbers, making positive identification very difficult, and it is entirely possible that your house had not yet been constructed – which is why you have to use maps and local knowledge of the community to assist in interpreting the records.

Wills and probate documents

Section One introduced wills as a genealogical resource, including the various means of access through the ecclesiastical court hierarchy, and more modern records after 1858. However, they can also contain a surprising amount of information about where your ancestors lived, through legacies that bequeathed property within an extended family, and supplement legal sources if you are trying to trace the transfer of an ancestral home from one person to the next. The background to property transfers in wills is a little complex, but nevertheless very important if you are to grasp why a house is or is not mentioned in a will. In the past, there have been restrictions on the type of property that could be transferred in a will – normally only the personal estate (personalty) of the deceased, such as cash, possessions and leases of property could be devised, and freehold land was thus excluded as realty, along with the buildings and houses constructed upon it, as discussed in the previous chapter. For a long time copyhold was also excluded on the grounds that it was not strictly inheritable.

To bypass this handicap, the 'use' or trust was employed by a landholder to establish trustees, who held the legal title to the land while permitting the landholder to enjoy the profits. As uses were considered personalty, the landholder could direct the trustees in his will to hold the land on behalf of another after his death, such as a widow, younger son or daughter. The Statute of Uses in 1535 closed this loophole, but also prevented devises by wills. This proved so unpopular that in 1540 the Statute of Wills was passed to allow the limited devise of freehold land held in fee simple via a will. The abolition of military tenure by the Tenures Abolition Act in 1660 removed the last restrictions on what could be devised, and thereafter all freehold land held in fee simple could be devised. The 1677 Statute of Frauds stipulated that only written wills could devise real estate, and they had to be signed by the testator plus three or four witnesses. People with copyhold property were still prevented from devising land until 1815, and consequently before this date you will need to check for descent in manorial records instead. The Statute of Wills in 1837 permitted the devise of all realty in a will, although all wills were to be written and signed by the testator in the presence of two witnesses who did not benefit from the will.

Despite the fact that these changes gradually made it easier to convey all property types in a will, there were still many reasons why property might not be mentioned. First, not everyone left a will, and even if one had been made there is no guarantee that there was any need to specifically mention property. If land or property was held in fee simple and was not alienated during the lifetime of the holder, then it would automatically pass to his heir at law on his death, therefore removing the need for a specific bequest in a will. The same scenario was relevant for land or property held in fee tail. In other instances, property might have been disposed of beforehand through a private agreement within the family, perhaps as part of a marriage settlement for a daughter or as part of a strict settlement. In any case, the ecclesiastical courts had no jurisdiction over realty, as this was the preserve of the common law and equity courts – all of which topics were discussed in detail in the previous chapter.

In effect, what we know today as a will was in fact two separate bequests that were combined to form one document, with a testament covering the personalty and the will bequeathing realty. Even if your property is mentioned within a will, it is rare to find street or house names specified: the usual format is to make a bequest of 'the house where I do dwell' to the relevant party. However, if you know the family was already in possession of a property, this can at least tell you who inherited the property next, and a new name can often prompt further searches in other areas. You may also find that names of occupiers are specified if a non-resident owner was bequeathing a leasehold property, and landowners with many houses can sometimes provide detailed specifications of where properties were situated and to whom they should next pass. Furthermore, if the occupier of a house was a leaseholder, the outstanding term of the lease could be bequeathed, and the name of the owner was sometimes included. You can use additional sources, listed below, to cross-reference an address or ownership particulars, with occupancy data.

Tracking Occupancy Over Time

One of the problems with putting together a timeline for your ancestors' movements is that they moved house a lot, and the main building block sources leave massive gaps in your knowledge, unless they had children on a regular basis every couple of years! Certificates generally give you an indication of where the family is living at the time of a specific event, whereas census returns – for all their detail – are one night in every ten years. Therefore how do you track down your ancestors as they moved around, or establish how long they spent in a house, neighbourhood, community or town? The following list-based sources are compiled over a long chronological period but on a regular basis, and combined with known data from genealogical resources can allow you to trace your family's residence in a place for a longer period of time.

Electoral lists

A key set of records for tracing modern houses back in time are electoral lists or poll books, as they are usually arranged by property and thereafter by the name of the eligible voters who reside at that address. Therefore it should be easy to work out from a civil registration certificate where an ancestor was living, and because electoral lists were compiled annually, you can see how long they were living at that address by working backwards and forwards from that date.

However, the right to vote has not always been as inclusive as today, and has been gradually extended throughout the twentieth century to include all men and women over the age of 18, but before 1918 not all men and very few women were eligible. From the earliest times until the nineteenth century, the right to vote was based on the amount and type of land or property that a man held, and lists of voters were compiled. From the eighteenth century these were usually based on Land Tax returns, as the right to vote was linked to holding freehold property. Therefore, early lists, often known as poll books, provide a guide to freeholders in your area, and on occasion will provide a precise address. The Guildhall Library, the Society of Genealogists'

Library, and the Institute of Historical Research all have large collections of poll books.

From 1832, electoral registers were compiled that listed the names of all those entitled to vote, with a brief description of the property that provided eligibility. The right to vote was extended from 1867, and consequently the lists became more comprehensive and provided greater details of property. Modern electoral registers from 1928, when women over 21 were enfranchised, provided street names and house numbers and can give a useful indication of who lived at your house. Most of these records are stored at the relevant local studies library, municipal archive or County Record Office, though the British Library holds a vast collection and collects all national electoral lists.

Given the fact that the records are easier to use in the modern period, it is probably easier to start with more recent family properties and work back in time. You will find that the boundaries of constituencies altered on a regular basis, so you need to keep an eye out if your house or street suddenly disappears; there are resources on hand to help you keep track of Parliamentary boundary changes. The further back in time you go, the quality of data starts to decrease: the most recent records are usually arranged alphabetically by street, but you will soon find that the lists change so that the names of eligible voters are sorted alphabetically instead. Gradually, less information about individual properties is recorded, and by the time you've worked back to the outbreak of the Second World War it can be very difficult to pinpoint the right family, as house numbers tend to disappear around this date, if not later. It is easier to track people further back in urban areas, but even then you might have to enlist the help of other sources, such as rate books which are described a bit further on.

Trade, postal and street directories

Domestic dwellings were often used as places from which occupants also traded, and from the late eighteenth century both residential street and trade directories were compiled to provide indexes to the whereabouts and occupation of tradespersons, while the private addresses of wealthier residents were often listed alongside them. The earliest lists only provide partial coverage for a town or parish, but those in the nineteenth and twentieth centuries combine street indexes that list a much higher percentage of residents and traders, with maps and plans where appropriate. Trade directories tended to cover a county or group of counties and list residents by parish, arranged under the types of occupation of the tradespersons. Street directories proliferate in urban areas, and usually give more detail. Rival directories may well give different information, so it is worth checking a variety if possible. Furthermore, they can contain incorrect data, as it was often down to the traders to inform the compilers that they had moved or ceased trading. Alternatively, the agents working for the compilers sometimes used information from earlier directories to prepare new versions. It is always sensible to corroborate your evidence from other sources.

The Guildhall Library in London has an excellent collection of London and provincial directories, as does the London Metropolitan Archives whose holdings include Buff Books, listings for the London suburbs from the late nineteenth to the early twentieth centuries. The main place to look, though, would be the County Record Office or indeed local study centre in the region where the house is located. In general you will find that there are many different directories, but the main publications to look for will be Pigot's and Kelly's, alongside the Post Office Directory, as these developed nationwide editions. You can even search for historic directories online at www. historicaldirectories.org, while a large number of trade and street directories are available from commercial dataset providers such as Find My Past and Ancestry.

Rate books

'Rates' is an umbrella term that has been used to cover various forms of local taxation, all of which were designed to contribute to the wellbeing of the community in which individuals lived, particularly aimed at the less fortunate elements of society. The levies took many shapes and forms, but can provide some basic information about property, as later documents for urban areas have been known to include assessment lists that denote house numbers. The following are the most common sources that the house historian may find to be of some use. The records were created or maintained at a parochial level, or were administered by local authorities, so the best place to find rate books and assessments would be the relevant County Record Office. The most common forms of locally-assessed rates are described below.

Poor, church and highway rates

Poor, church and highway rates were assessed on parishioners by the parochial church wardens to raise revenue for poor relief, to provide money to fund church repairs and ecclesiastical activity in each parish, or to maintain the highways within the parish. Where returns and assessments survive, they are to be found among the papers kept in the parish chest and subsequently deposited at the County Record Office or diocesan archive. Alternatively, the private papers of individuals who acted as church wardens may also yield assessment records, as will quarter-sessions records that relate to the failure of a parish to maintain a highway. They usually date from the eighteenth and early nineteenth centuries, although returns from the sixteenth and seventeenth centuries can be found. Parish rate books rarely list individuals by their place of abode, but will provide a list of eligible parishioners that can be cross-referenced with other sources. You will usually find a list of parishioners followed by the amounts they paid, and in some cases you may find an address attached. Data for towns and urban areas is often more detailed, and you will be more likely to find references to individual properties. If you do find a relative listed among these papers, it's worth considering the contribution they made to the welfare of those less fortunate than them. Of course, it's always worth checking to make sure they weren't the recipient of poor rates!

Local authority rate books

After the Poor Law Amendment Act of 1834, Poor Law Unions replaced the parochial system for poor relief administration. In consequence, new ways of financing improvements to the local community were introduced, which included assessed rates that were levied and collected by the relevant Poor Law Union. With changes to the administration of local affairs, the responsibility for raising and collecting rates gradually passed to the appropriate borough, rural, district, municipal or urban councils that were set up from the late nineteenth century onwards. The local authorities maintained rate books to record the details of the amounts levied, and these are now stored at the relevant County Record Office. Rate books normally recorded the name of the occupier, and sometimes included the name of the owner; an assessment of the value of the property in question; the amount to be collected; and, most important, the name or description of the property. They were often annotated to record changes of occupancy. If you have located an ancestral property, it is sometimes easier to work from the modern era backwards, especially if there is a good sequence of books and you know the names of the householders. Even if you do not, you can use supplementary information such as trade directories, or a comparative analysis of neighbouring returns, to work backwards. Increases in assessment data can often indicate a rise in the value of the property, usually as a result of building work or other extensions to the property. As with many tax records, they exist in long sequences – where the records survive – and allow you to chart when your ancestor first appeared in a property, and when they disappeared. Because they cover a district, you might be able to widen your search out to see if you can locate their next residence.

Sewer rate books

Sewer rate books are similar in format to local authority rate books, but exist for urban areas from the late eighteenth and particularly the nineteenth centuries where the construction and maintenance of sewers was necessary to maintain standards of public health – a topic flagged up in Chapter Seven. Local contributions were paid for sewers to be repaired and built, the terms of which were often specified in the original building lease; where sewers were maintained by the local authority, sewer commissioners were appointed to assess and collect the revenue. Their records are known as sewer rate books, and will be found in the relevant county archive or municipal, urban or metropolitan record office. In addition to the name of the contributor, they can often contain street names and house numbers. Some of the best records survive for London, when the Metropolitan Board of Works was established in 1855 to construct an ambitious network of sewers across the capital. To pay for the works, the Board was granted a £3 million loan, to be recouped from rates that were voted in 1858 to pay for the works, to be levied over the following forty years. The assessment books for these records survive at the London Metropolitan Archives.

Earlier records

Having looked at the modern period, it is also possible to work further back in time and track down property occupancy for medieval and early modern houses. There is a range of other local tax returns, such as hearth tax, that can be found at The National Archives in series E 179; you can learn about these lay subsidies, as they are called, online via a research guide. Hearth tax returns will be particularly useful if you are looking for property from the late seventeenth century, though it is often hard to link a name to a specific house. Slightly later, you can find land tax records from the late eighteenth century to 1832 enrolled in quarter-session returns, and many of the files towards the end of the period link a property to an owner or occupier. These records are based on land-ownership above a value of 40 shillings, and you can use this to start a search for documents even further back in time. Depending on the status of your ancestors, you might find that they held land or property of sufficient value or importance that it was covered by an Inquisition Post Mortem, or formed part of a marriage settlement. The relevant records are discussed here, more a curiosity than anything else due to the problems of survival, the chronological distance from the present, and difficulty linking an entry to a specific house.

Inquisitions Post Mortem

For medieval and early modern property or estates, you may find information contained in Inquisitions Post Mortem (IPMs), particularly if you are tracing a substantial property or if your house was built on land that once formed part of a large estate. The records start in the thirteenth century and continue into the mid seventeenth, and were compiled by the Crown at the death of a tenant-in-chief to determine whether an heir at law was sane, or of age (21 years) to inherit. If he was, he would pay a relief to enter into his lands; if not, then the lands would default to the Crown until they regained sanity or majority was reached, and the heir would become a ward of the Crown – the estates would be administered on the heir's behalf, but the Crown would take the profits. Royal officials known as escheators conducted the inquisitions, and they filed the returns in Chancery, the Exchequer or, from the reign of Henry VIII, the Court of Wards. At the very least, IPMs can confirm that the estate on which your house was built was passed to a descendant, thereby making a search for relevant archives that bit easier. However, the original documents are in Latin and can be difficult to interpret. The records of IPMs that have survived are now stored at The National Archives, and are arranged chronologically and according to where they were deposited. Chancery IPMs are in series C 132–C 142, and are by far the most numerous documents. Exchequer IPMs are in E 149–E 150, while records for the Court of Wards are in WARD 7. The condition of the documents varies greatly, and some Chancery copies can be very hard to read – so always check to see if there's a more legible copy in one of the other areas. Similarly, the language will be Latin and can be quite technical, though you should be able to pick out the name and age of the deceased, as well as the heir at the bottom, and a description of their property.

Assignments of dower

Since medieval times, a dower was assigned to the bride as part of the marriage agreement. Normally this took the form of money or goods, but the practice of including houses was common among wealthier classes. Furthermore, dower houses were often especially constructed for the bride, and would become her residence if her husband died before she did. Many high-status yet relatively small houses on the edge of large estates can be traced to this practice, and building accounts or personal papers in estate records can provide relevant information. Quite often such properties can contain salvage from higher-status houses that may provide misleading architectural clues. The relevant county archive is the best place to start looking for records, since in some cases, assignments of dower that involved the legal transfer of property were enrolled to provide legal evidence of title. However, if a dower was disputed, you may find traces in one of the courts described in Chapter Nine, in particular the Court of Requests.

Furnishing the ancestral home

The majority of this section of the book has examined the main sources you will need to consult if you want to trace an ancestral house through time, particularly those that relate to the people you may have picked up in your family tree. Where possible, advice has been provided about how to use information about the house to find out more about the local area and community in which the house stood. However, it is easy to forget that these same individuals considered their house as their home too, and you can uncover a surprising amount of documentary evidence that should help you place the interior of your house in its original historical context, and many of the sources that have already been described can contain additional information about house interiors, furnishings and general layout.

Frequent mention has been made already of the personal papers of past owners and occupants, and once again they will be useful if you wish to uncover more about how life would have been for former residents. These recollections can be supplemented by clues left behind in the internal architecture of your house. In addition to beams, doors, windows and stairs, which can be useful in helping you to date the construction of the house, you may find surviving fixtures or fittings that can be researched and assigned a rough date. From the mid-nineteenth century onwards there are registers of designs and representations for patents and inventions, many of which relate to everyday household objects and decorations. Similarly, probate inventories and insurance records can shed light on how a house would have been furnished, and sometimes provide detailed descriptions of the interior and layout of a property. Photographic information will also add colour to your research, and you can use a wide variety of sources in museums, both local and national, to help you gain an impression of a bygone age.

Searching for clues

The best place to start is with the interior of a property. Obviously, this is going to be hard to research if you are no longer the possessor of an ancestral home! You will need to talk to the current occupiers to see if they have uncovered any original fixtures and fittings while they were redecorating, because these can be used (via paint or style analysis) to provide a date when the interior was constructed or decorated. The internal design and layout of a house, the use of particular building materials, fixtures and fittings, and the size and décor of the rooms will also give you clues about the date of construction and the social standing of the occupants. In addition, you will find that many old household objects can turn up under the soil in the garden. Clay pipes, tiles, even remnants of contemporary household 'technology' were thrown away, and these can offer a tantalising glimpse of the lifestyles of previous owners. Similarly, bags of dateable rubbish can be uncovered in attics or cellars. Some of the contents can be matched among the design registers and representations described below, and local museums can often provide advice about assigning a date to a particular object. Furthermore, the objects that you find may be linked to a previous use of the property, which might be reflected in the current or former name of the house. Becoming a backyard archaeologist can be a very worthwhile pursuit, because the 'rubbish' that our ancestors discarded can comprise actual historical clues that reveal a great deal about their lifestyle and daily routine.

Design registers and representations
If you have managed to locate old wallpaper, dateable objects, or perhaps a photograph showing how the house was decorated at a particular period, you can attempt to match some of this material with the original designs and

sample representations that were registered by the proprietors who wished to protect their design from competitors. These records are to be found at The National Archives as part of the holdings of the Board of Trade, and cover the period 1839–1964. The records are arranged in various series, reflecting chronological periods and the type of design that was registered. There are also two areas in which to start your research – the registers, which contain the names and addresses of the design owners, the number of items registered, and the registered number; and the representations of each design, arranged by registered number.

From 1842 to 1883 the documents were given separate registration numbers according to the type of material, although you may sometimes find items misfiled in the wrong series. There is a useful research guide prepared by The National Archives that describes how to locate material, and summarises the relevant series that contain the registers and representations. Furthermore, items from this period may possess a diamond mark, which contains information that should allow you to identify the relevant registration details. Another research guide explains the conversion process, which can be a little tricky to perform.

The representations are a wonderful source if you wish to discover period wallpaper designs and contemporary household inventions, and should allow you to paint a vivid picture of how your house might once have been furnished and decorated. Some of the sketches include illustrations on how household devices would have been installed, and can explain strange alcoves or other inexplicable anomalies in the internal structure of a property.

Patents and specifications
In addition to the registers and representations, applications by inventors for patents for new inventions up to 1853, with specifications from 1711 that provide detail of the invention, were enrolled in Chancery. Copies of the letter patent sent to the applicant were enrolled on the patent rolls at The National Archives in series C 66, while the specifications of patents were enrolled in C 54 (Close Rolls), C 210 (Petty Bag Office, Specification and Surrender Rolls) or C 73 (Rolls Chapel, Specification and Surrender Rolls). After 1853, copies of patents are available from the Patent Office Sale Branch. Furthermore, printed transcripts of specifications enrolled before 1853 can be seen at the British Library, along with annual journals that provide information on the various historic trademarks that companies used, many of which appear on everyday household items. In many ways, the British Library is the best place to

investigate patents and designs, as they have designated reading rooms with publications showing the latest representations and designs that you can use to research an object or furnishing.

Copyright files

You may also wish to examine the copyright entry forms maintained by the Stationers' Company at Stationers' Hall, London, under the various Copyright Acts from 1842, which have been deposited with The National Archives and assigned the series COPY 1. A wide variety of items are covered in the records, some of which were used in domestic property. The records cover the period 1837–1912, and you can obtain the copyright number from the registers and indexes in COPY 3, which should correspond with the files in COPY 1. However, the entry forms are arranged by type of material and by date, so the copyright number will be of limited use for search purposes. The Stationers' Company has retained the registers for the period 1554–1842. COPY 1 will also be of use if you are searching for images, as part of the series is devoted to copyright of photographs. Many of these relate to individual houses or properties. However, there is no place index available in the series list, and so the records are not easily accessible.

Household inventories

Inventories are lists of possessions or property belonging to a particular person or persons, and were usually based around the contents of a household or series of properties, therefore providing a very intimate portrait of a person's possessions. They were compiled for many reasons, though the largest distinct collections relate to wills, and were drawn up as part of the probate process.

Probate inventories

Probate inventories were compiled to quantify a deceased person's estate, excluding realty, so that the executors knew the extent and value of the possessions that they were to distribute. In summary you will find that they generally listed all possessions and belongings that were contained in relevant properties or dwellings, and usually a value was assigned to the goods so that they could be sold. Consequently, you will often find a room by room list of personal possessions, furniture, clothes and paintings. For example, when the London lawyer Silvester Petyt died in 1720, the contents of his house were described in great detail: we are left with an impression of how an early eighteenth-century gentleman would have furnished his lodgings, complete with furniture from India, Dutch glassware, Turkish carpets, four looking-glasses, an eight-day clock, a musket, bayonet and sword, and nearly 200 prints and various pictures of family, royalty and judges. The inventory also lifted the lid on his business transactions, revealing a range of loans and mortgages on a string of property across the country built up from the profits of his practice. They included the great and good of the land – some of whom were included in his collection of portraits!

In general, probate inventories can be found scattered across the country archive network, wherever wills would have been proved in diocesan or Prerogative ecclesiastical courts. There is a large collection at The National Archives for the Prerogative Court of Canterbury in series PROB 2–PROB 5, many of which can be searched online. If you do find a probate inventory, make sure you look for the associated will that it relates to in the will register, so that you can find out more about the person in question.

Other inventories

Lists of possessions were made for a variety of reasons, including legal cases that were brought before the equity courts and were deposited as exhibits or documents, described in holdings of The National Archives in the previous chapter. In addition, there are a few distinct series there that contain a variety of inventories such as E 154 (goods and chattels, 1207–1721), which mainly covers premises and shops but also incorporates merchants' dwellings and private residences. Many of these refer to individuals who had been indicted for treason or other felonies, and this will lead you to other areas in which to look for inventories, as criminal cases heard by the Crown often resulted in the seizure of an indicted criminal's possessions. However, these can be notoriously difficult to track down, so unless you can find an entry listed via the online Catalogue you could waste a lot of time looking in vain. Generally, inquisitions will be fruitful, as will accounts of forfeited property that usually take the form of an inventory. Series such as E 101, 143, 163 and 199 and FEC 1 contain such information, and inventories can also be found in E 140, 219, 314 and 315; IR 59; LR 1, 2 and 5; and SP 28 and 46. Outside The National Archives, you should focus on miscellaneous and estate papers, records of house clearances for auction, and possibly quarter-session and associated legal records.

Insurance records

Fire insurance offices were established in London from the late seventeenth century, with wider coverage throughout the eighteenth century onwards. Most provincial companies restricted their practice to the local area, but the major London firms, such as the Sun, Royal Exchange and Phoenix, expanded their business to set up provincial offices. The companies insured all types of property against the risk of fire, and usually provided their own fire brigades as well. To identify an insured property, a fire mark was issued to the householder that was then fixed to the wall of the property; each company had a unique fire mark, which could also contain the policy number embossed in the corner. If you are really lucky, this may still survive today on the exterior of an ancestral home.

The main type of written record will be a policy register that details the policy number; name, status, occupation and address of the policyholder, plus the same data for tenants, if applicable; the location, type, nature of construction and value of the property to be insured; the premium paid to the company; the renewal date; and a brief outline of any endorsement. Entries in the registers were usually chronological, and each new entry was assigned a policy number. You may find that larger companies maintained concurrent registers, so the policies may not run in strict numerical order. The major companies also kept indexes to the registers, by name, place or policy number. Where contemporary indexes have failed to survive, limited indexing work has been undertaken for some companies. The registers will give a rough indication of the layout of a property, and some individuals specified in great detail what was to be insured. However, these were usually much earlier policies, and the volume of business meant that the agents restricted the detail they recorded in the registers. Other records may be of use though. For example, endorsement books, claims records and surveyors' plans and reports exist for some companies, and these can provide great detail for any property covered. Records for local companies will be deposited at the relevant County Record Office, either among the records of the company or in the personal papers of the individual agents that they employed. The Guildhall Library, London, has records of the Sun, Royal Exchange (both London and provincial business) and Hand-in-Hand (London only); the Phoenix records (London and provincial) are at Cambridge University Library, and the Westminster Fire Office records (London and limited provincial) are at the Westminster Archives Centre.

Section Three

TRACING THE HISTORY OF YOUR AREA

Introduction

The previous two sections of this book have focused on the most personal areas of personal heritage – family and home. However, it's time to widen your focus and place both into a wider historical context, that of the community and locality in which your ancestors lived. This is essentially the way you link your findings to date into the wider historical and social context of the past, and the events that you read about in history text books – the Dissolution of the Monasteries, the English Civil War, the Industrial Revolution and the two World Wars, for example – and view them through the eyes and actions of your ancestors and the communities in which they lived.

Every part of the country will have a different story to tell, depending on its own unique contribution to Britain's past. Therefore, writing a guide that goes into very specific details about records is a fairly tricky task because each area will generate its own records according to its particular history. This is always the challenge facing the local historian; however, over the next few chapters some of the main topics that would have impacted upon your community, as well as the lives of your ancestors, are introduced with an overview of the subject, and general guidance about where to go to find the most relevant information and documents.

The topics covered will allow you to add context to the lives of your ancestors, tackling wide-ranging issues such as Britain's military history, travel and communications, sport and leisure. It's not just the events that are considered; focus is also shifted to researching the physical evidence left behind – the factories, engineering works and warehouses that grew out of an industrial past that shaped whole communities; spiritual belief, different religions and the need to build places of worship; the sprawling transportation network that snaked across the land by road, rail and canals; the need to provide health, education and welfare for a growing population; and even where to research military buildings such as army barracks, air and naval bases. Each topic contains several short essays on a relevant topic, grouped under a broader theme. It is not possible to provide a comprehensive list of subjects that would cover all your enquiries, and so some advice about general local history research is provided here before you start to focus on specific areas in the rest of this section.

If you are looking to research the history of either your own, or your ancestors', local community, then you will probably be best served by heading to your local study centre (often located in a main branch library, or even a county or municipal record office), followed by the county archive or main record office for the district. Equally important will be local and regional museums, where you will find out about specific events in a local area, as well as objects and artefacts that provide colour and texture to the story. You can find the whereabouts of all resources for a region by going to ARCHON, a directory that's searchable by place, maintained by The National Archives on their website www.nationalarchives.gov.uk/archon.

The main resources you'll need are covered in the following chapters, but the principal ones will be maps, local newspapers, original manuscripts and secondary sources. Of particular use will be the *Victoria County History* series, which covers large parts of the country and contains essays about aspects of the past, from archaeology to architecture, geology to geography, and key events and people. Other antiquarian works should be available in one of the resource centres listed above, and you may find that a historical society has prepared editions and transcriptions of key collections found in local archives, or nationally that have a particular relevance to the local area.

You should also try to make contact with researchers who are operating in your area, whether they're curating or collecting a community archive, or are a recognised local history society. You can find out more about practical local history in your area by contacting the British Association for Local History (BALH), in the same way that you would (and should!) join a family history society where you live, as well as in the area that your ancestors were living. Having read these introductory notes, you are ready to start the next phase of your journey into your personal heritage. The first topic, listed here, relates to land and estates, in particular the rural way of life – and how you can find out more about the ownership and landscape of the world immediately around you.

Chapter Eleven

LANDHOLDING AND RURAL COMMUNITIES

To place your family and their houses into their historical context, you'll need to spend some time investigating the community in which they were based. An integral part of this process involves understanding the way society functioned at an administrative level, and the further back in time you go, the more likely you are to find your ancestors living and working as part of an estate, or manor – the key socio-economic unit in England and parts of Wales from the eleventh to the nineteenth century, and certainly before the general population drift into the emerging towns and cities during the Industrial Revolution. Some of the more modern resources for researching a farm or rural community have already been covered in Chapter Six, such as the National Farm Survey, the tithe apportionments and enclosure awards. However, this chapter explores the way land was parcelled up and governed by private owners and the Crown during this period, and the records that you can use to find out more about the people and places. It will also show you how to find out more about the life in a rural community, particularly as we'll all have 'agricultural labourers' somewhere in our family tree.

Researching the History of Manors and Estates

The topic of landholding and property transfers has been exhaustively tackled in Section Two when the history of the ancestral home has been examined. Most of the important records relating to the conveyance of freehold land, and the use of the court baron for the 'admission and surrender' of copyhold tenants, have been discussed in Chapter Eight; similarly, the idea of a feudal pyramid has also been explained. The aim of this section is to introduce some of the other records that were generated by the manorial system, along with an overview of the sort of material you will need to examine if you want to obtain a better understanding of how life in a manor worked, especially for rural tenants who would have found seasonal work in the fields as employees of the various owners of farms and estates that controlled so much of the British countryside for centuries.

I've described in Chapter Eight how land law evolved after the Norman Conquest, and that the manor was the basic administrative unit and way of regulating landholding, work and local justice. Nevertheless, it is important to stress once again that manors were not always compact geographical entities, and were often united only by the social and economic ties that bound each individual to the lord of the manor; collectively these social and economic ties were known as the customs which would vary according to each manor and region. You can find out the names, and rough boundaries, of the manors in the area in which your family lived from sources such as the *Victoria County History*, where manorial descents – the way a manor passed from owner to owner from the Domesday-book to the nineteenth century – show you who were the lords of the manor, and whether they had any larger estates that incorporated more than one manor in the area. These people would have been the major landowners and played a central role in community life – chief employers, important donors of money to charity, sponsors of schools and patrons of the local church. A resident 'Lord of the Manor' would live in the capital messuage, or chief house; of course, as estates became larger and revenue grew accordingly, the estate owners built grander and grander houses until they grew into the stately homes we see today.

Nevertheless, at a basic level, village life would revolve around key moments in the seasonal agricultural cycle, such as ploughing and sowing, tending to crops and of course the harvest. The success or failure of the annual crop played a vital role in the wellbeing of a manor or community – indeed it was literally a matter of life and death. Essentially, the population was predominantly wedded to the land prior to the industrial changes in the nineteenth century, though there were important shifts in the way agriculture was managed from the sixteenth century onwards (with enclosures creating larger farms and better land management techniques), and a particular emphasis on the eighteenth and nineteenth centuries when technological advances replaced the need for intensive human labour. As a consequence, the nineteenth century saw a real change to the way local communities operated, with many people facing poverty in the face of increased mechanisation; as a result, protests in the form of the Swing Riots of the 1830s and the Luddite movement showed the passion that agricultural workers held for their 'people-based' rural way of life, although the repeal of the Corn Laws in 1846 meant that even more people were forced from the land as cheaper corn was imported from abroad. Many people were encouraged to move to the towns and cities to find work in factories; others joined emigration schemes and left Britain forever. The ties of the manor became looser, until the introduction of enfranchisement and changes to property laws effectively ended manorial importance in local life by the start of the twentieth century.

However, if you are looking for information about local rural life, the formal administration of the rules and regulations of the manor generated many types of record that lift the lid on the minutiae of life, and local issues that were important to contemporaries. These manorial records should not be confused with estate management records, which are described below. The most informative series are the official records of the manorial court, where the lord of the manor, through his appointed deputy, the steward, regulated tenants' entry into land and collected revenue generated by the feudal ties. These records have already been described in some detail in Chapter Eight with particular relevance on the system of land transfer. However, routine administrative matters were also considered – the repair of fences and hedges, drainage of ditches, upkeep of roads and highways, maintenance of properties. The manorial courts had jurisdiction over a range of other day-to-day matters that formed part of the customs of the manor, including elements of law and order, plus the resolution of disputes between manorial tenants. All of these issues were addressed in the manorial court, and the records allow you to see what sort of tensions existed at this local level, as well as the measures that the manorial courts took to ensure the continued smooth running of the community. Some are amusing, others very sad; many are mundane. However, it's this patchwork of everyday events in a rural society that formed the day-to-day routine of our ancestors, so the records are well worth browsing if only to gain an empathy with the pace of life.

In addition to court rolls, the steward and his officials would have created a range of subsidiary documents to assist with the administration of the manor – and where they survive, they can tell you about the structure of society and the key members of the community who held land and employed agricultural labourers. One document was the 'extent', which tended to list all the tenants for the manor, regardless of tenure, which meant that freeholders and leaseholders were recorded, as well as the copyhold tenants who appeared in the court rolls. A type of manorial survey, the extent would typically provide the date that it was made, and then describe all land and its rent value to the lord, assigning the type of land to the name of a tenant, with a brief description of the property. However, extents were created only at the whim of the lord of the manor, usually when a manor changed hands. They became less popular by the fifteenth century and were gradually replaced by rentals, which tended to be less detailed but still covered all types of manorial tenants, and were created on a far more regular basis, often annotated with details of deaths or changes of occupancy. These were the most prevalent form of survey until the sixteenth and early seventeenth centuries.

Later surveys from the sixteenth century onwards took on new and varied forms, and included far greater detail than earlier list-based surveys. They were more formal, often the product of special manorial courts of survey, and conducted by appointed commissioners. Tenants would be asked a series of questions so that the commissioners could compile a detailed assessment that commonly included a description of the boundaries of the manor, the customs of the manor and a rent roll or rental. A rent roll commonly listed all tenants who held property in the manor, plus a note of the rent they paid and the land or property they held. Increasingly, they were linked to maps that were specifically produced to accompany survey documents thus providing a visual aid to the lord of the manor, and often contained a separate reference book that would list all the tenants for each holding. Not only will a map and associated survey provide an indication of the manorial boundary, and the list give details of all the plots of land and associated tenants (plus the value of the land and rent), but it can also provide a link to other later records such as tithe apportionments of the 1840s. The only downside is that the survival rate of these associated reference books is not good, and the location of maps can be very diverse. They are usually found among County Record Office cartographic collections, or have passed into private hands and thus appear in some unlikely places, such as on the walls of offices or private houses. Many rentals and surveys can be found in national collections as well, such as The National Archives for manors that fell into Crown hands, or formed part of the royal estates.

In addition to surveys, the records generated by financial transactions can contain information about the changing nature of a manor, the profitability of the land, and general information about life in communities throughout the pre-industrial period. Stewards' account books are a good place to begin looking, as they recorded money paid or owed, as well as expenditure that had been ordered on behalf of the lord. The records are arranged according to the 'charge and discharge' system, which first lists all revenue accruing to the manor and then details expenses and payments made from this revenue. The balance was the amount paid to the lord of the manor. Collectively, these records are known as ministers and receivers accounts. Other material that can be of use includes rent-rolls or rentals, not to be confused with the survey version, which provide lists of tenants who had paid money to the lord, as opposed to how much they owed. Most of these records will now be found in the relevant County Record Office, though The National Archives has a large collection of associated manorial records in their holdings.

Estate management and the rural way of life

In addition, manorial documents formed part of larger collections of documents generated by the management of larger private estates, of which one or more manors may have formed an important constituent part. Aside from the court rolls, estate owners produced a variety of other documentary sources to assist them with the management of their financial arrangements. It is important to remember that these were private documents created for a private purpose. Sometimes this material has been deposited in the public domain, usually the relevant County Record Office, but there is no guarantee that it has. If this is the case, and the papers are still in the possession of the current owners of the estate or a family archive, you might be able to make a written approach, especially if land agents are employed to manage the collections, but don't be surprised if you receive a negative response. After all, how would you feel if someone wrote to you asking to look through your private papers?!

Estate owners would employ stewards and land agents to administer their affairs, both practical in terms of negotiations with tenants and establishing patterns of employment within the lands they farmed directly; and also financial. Consequently, you may find a complementary array of estate management material that is linked to, but stands a level above, that of the manor. This will include rentals and surveys, maps and plans, and accounts;

but also a range of subsidiary documents such as correspondence, employment books, expense accounts and purchase ledgers for the estate. This is where you will pick up a better sense of the quality and pace of life – you'll find implements used in the fields, expenditure on the beasts of burden (horses, oxen) that were the staple 'technology' for centuries, construction of barns (many of which doubled up during harvest as accommodation for the seasonal labourers) and other purchases around the estate. Where this material has survived – and has been deposited – it's usually to be found in the relevant County Record Office, sometimes with restrictions placed on access depending on the sensitivity of the material. You might also want to double up your research in the local museum, where physical objects may survive – a far more vivid way of empathising with a long day's work in the field!

The whereabouts of these estate and family papers are usually listed on websites such as Access to Archives, or a report prepared by the Royal Commission for Historic Manuscripts (whose archives are now available for consultation at The National Archives). Equally, The National Archives has a large collection of private estate papers, as will other international research institutions with manuscript collections such as the British Library. You should also think of consulting university libraries, which will have the papers of locally important figures including much estate material.

One of the largest landowners in Britain was the monarchy, owning vast swathes of land in its own right and often taking control of private estates. The National Archives is the natural place of deposit for records relating to the administration of Crown lands, as well as areas outside normal county jurisdiction, such as the Duchy of Lancaster and the Palatinates of Chester, Durham and Lancaster. You might also find that the Royal Archives has some additional information about royal estates, but essentially this is a 'private' archive and reserves the right to refuse entry. Just like any private estate owner, the Crown generated administrative records as part of the management of its lands and manors, creating documents similar to the ones described above. Indeed, the survival of records tends to be far greater than for most private estates, as separate Government departments were created to assist with the management, in particular relating to the financial aspects. Consequently, there are many more places in which to start your research, such as the Crown Estates Office (all record series beginning CRES), the Office of Auditors of Land Revenue (series LR) and the Office of Land Revenue Records and Enrolments (series LRRO). If you are unsure whether your property once formed part of a Crown estate, then you can try looking at CRES 2/1613, which includes a list of Crown manors in 1827; and CRES 60 contains annual reports from all bodies that administered Crown estates between 1797 and 1942.

In addition to the Crown, the other major landowner outside private hands was the Church, and you can find out more about the workings of its estate management via the diocesan record office (usually the same as the county archives), where many of the administrative files have been deposited. For example, the Bishop of Winchester created a series of financial accounts known as pipe rolls, many of which have been transcribed. These show in great detail how estate management changed over time during the medieval period, as well as show the type of crops grown, the names of the tenants that leased land and the geographical spread of its territories. Furthermore, the network of monasteries that were dismantled in the sixteenth century under Henry VIII owned vast estates, mainly through bequests and gifts from private citizens. They too kept estate records, as well as a list of the various deeds and legal proofs of title (known as cartularies): some are to be found in local archives, but the vast majority of monastic records relating to land, leases and finance are at The National Archives in the deposited collections of the Exchequer, which oversaw the dissolution of the monasteries and subsequent land sales following the Crown's seizure of former monastic possessions via the Court of Augmentations. This is a very rich area for the local and social historian to explore if they want to find out more about their local area, especially if there's a ruined monastery in the vicinity – the chances are that it once owned a large proportion of the land in the area. The records at The National Archives, or elsewhere, will show you what life was like living and working on an ecclesiastical estate.

Even if you have located an estate that was a key employer in your local area in times gone by, finding an agricultural labourer in the family tree will be the end of the road in terms of occupation records, simply because of the seasonal and therefore casual nature of the work, and the fact that people would move from estate to estate depending on where work could be found. As described above, some estates kept better records than others, and so you might be fortunate in discovering a steward's payment book for casual labour, or another form of pay list that names your ancestors. However, for the vast majority, there simply won't be a written record that survives and so you will have to simply paint a picture of what life was like from other resources. There are a range of institutions across Britain that can help you do this. Local museums have already been mentioned, but there are also research centres and regional museums that have larger collections of both written records and materials that are relevant to a rustic existence. The Museum of English Rural Life, part of the University of Reading, is a leading institution in England, while you'll find many county shows still focus upon traditional techniques that our ancestors used. The West Dean estate in Sussex also has a centre that teaches traditional rural skills and crafts. You could also try the National Farmers' Union for further information about twentieth-century working conditions and possible family records, as well as engagement in public and community life by organisations such as Young Farmers. There are national collections in other parts of the British Isles, such as St. Fagan's National History Museum, Cardiff; the Scottish Life Archive, part of the National Museum of Scotland, Edinburgh; and the Ulster Folk and Transport Museum near Belfast.

Chapter Twelve

TRADE AND INDUSTRY

One of the key events to impact upon the lives of our ancestors would have been the Industrial Revolution, and this topic introduces three of the main key sectors that evolved throughout the late eighteenth century into the nineteenth – and were perhaps the largest source of employment for many communities. You are likely to find evidence of miners, factory workers and mill employees in your family tree, especially if you hail from one of the key industrial zones that emerged. Equally, the impact these momentous changes had on the local communities – often turning villages into towns, and towns into cities – have left their trace in the built environment. Here, you can find out not only where your ancestors worked, but the history of the local industry and its legacy over time.

Industrialisation

Britain's economy and landscape was primarily agricultural until the 1700s when the development of industry and the manufactured export trade gradually started to overtake agricultural output. Different regions of Britain were shaped by the raw minerals they provided and the physical landscape they embodied. Wales, rich in coal seams and close to the factories of the West Midlands, became riddled with mine shafts, while the rivers flowing through Sheffield and coal from nearby mines powered the machinery in workshops processing locally-extracted iron ore for the once-famous Sheffield steel and cutlery.

The Black Country, comprising the area covering West Bromwich, Oldbury, Blackheath, Cradley Heath, Old Hill, Bilston, Dudley, Tipton, Wednesfield, parts of Halesowen, Wednesbury and Walall, gained its name from the smoke belted out by thousands of iron foundries and forges working with the help of the coal mines beneath ground. The Black Country Living Museum next to Dudley Castle is the perfect place to get a feel for life in the Industrial Age. Historic industrial buildings from all over the Black Country have been moved and re-built at the open-air museum, from tightly-packed terraced houses to a colliery complete with underground mine trips, a rolling mill, lime kiln and canals.

Local museums, libraries and archives will have an abundance of information about the various trades and industries that emerged in their area during the industrialisation of Britain – how they came about, how they evolved, how they shaped the local communities and environment, and how long they lasted. The history of the Industrial Revolution in the West Midlands from 1700 to 1830 can be explored on the Revolutionary Players website at www.revolutionaryplayers.org.uk. Here, themed articles on the history of the Birmingham brass industry, Derby porcelain and the Kidderminster carpet industry will be found alongside images of people and places that shaped the industrial age, and a digital library of published and unpublished archive material.

The Industrial Revolution of the nineteenth century witnessed a dramatic explosion in urbanisation, as a growing population migrated from villages to towns in search of work. The sudden increase in the populations of once small towns, which had inadequate sanitary provisions to deal with large numbers of people moving into overcrowded tenements and terraced houses, resulted in slums taking over inner-city centres. Working conditions were no better than the poor living conditions endured by industrial workers in the eighteenth and nineteenth centuries, as shifts were long with few or no breaks from monotonous, dangerous work and pay was low.

The Working Class Movement Library contains a large collection of books, pamphlets, archive material dating from the 1760s and photos detailing the history of the trades and lives of working-class people who organised themselves to give their communities a voice in an attempt to raise living and working standards. In many ways, this is one of the few places where the true characters of ordinary working men and women are revealed in their own words and actions. The WCML holds a wealth of information about forgotten trades that left few employment records, such as the blacksmiths, metalworkers, brush makers, gas workers, shipwrights and textile workers. The Library is open to all researchers and can be visited at 51 The Crescent, Salford, M5 4WX (tel: 0161 736 3601).

The trades of the industrial age have mostly died out in modern Britain, yet many of the buildings and landscapes they created remain. Most of the trades our working-class ancestors were employed in were privately-run enterprises, and if all you have is a census return stating an occupation then you may not be able to find out much more about the exact place in which they worked. If you don't already know which building your industrial forebear worked in, then the best step forward is to have a look at the town your ancestor lived in on a map of roughly the same date as a census return providing their occupation. Most working-class people rented accommodation within walking distance of their place of work, and some employers provided accommodation for their workers. Working days were long and shifts started early, so the less time that was spent travelling to and from work, the better. Locating your ancestors' address on a contemporary street map will give you an overview of the nearest factories (or pit) to where they were living. Ordnance Survey (OS) maps drawn at regular intervals from the mid-1800s to the present day label the names of industrial buildings. The County Record Office will have any other maps that were drawn before the first OS map, but the detail they include will vary.

You might be lucky enough to find or already know the name of the factory, pit or company your ancestor worked for, in which case you can look the name up on the Access to Archives database at www.nationalarchives. gov.uk/a2a to find descriptions and locations of any surviving records. The National Register of Archives is an index to the location of business and family estate records, and can be searched at www.nationalarchives. gov.uk/nra. It's particularly worth trying the NRA if your ancestor's family owned a factory or a mine, as there is more chance that a record of their ownership will have survived than any employment records for their employees. Even if you are unable to find any business records, it's still possible to research how the trade impacted the local community, whether there were any localised booms or busts that might explain a change in circumstances, what working conditions were like locally and what kind of reputation the manufacturing employers in the area had. Local history books at the library are often a fruitful source of information, and the evidence given at Royal Commissions on working conditions in the mid-nineteenth century can also provide evidence about specific areas. Workers' statements recorded by the Royal Commissions were published in newspapers, and the full final reports can be found at the British Library or the Parliamentary Archives.

Mills

Early factories were called mills because they needed to be located near running water for a power supply. Lancashire was famous for its cotton mills, and urban areas that grew up around the mills that dotted the countryside became known as mill towns. The textile industry had formerly been one of the many cottage industries performed at home by women and their children. The formation of mills meant that a whole production line could work together under one roof, and under the watchful eyes of the foreman and manager. Huge steam-powered machinery made the mills a noisy and dangerous place to work, and the smoke they belched out created dark, gloomy landscapes.

Mills produced cotton, wool and worsted, and the age-old industry of flour milling was also industrialised in the 1880s. Textile mills were enormous buildings that dominated the surrounding landscape and grew in size as the industry expanded, some of them as tall as six or seven storeys to accommodate the various lines of production. Huge chimneys to disperse smoke generated by the steam-powered engines were a characteristic feature of the mill. Lots of light was needed so the workers could inspect the quality of the cloth and work long hours even during dark winter days, so lights were hung from the ceilings and the mills lit up the surrounding neighbourhood with their many rows of windows. The mill buildings were not the only physical impact on newly-developing mill towns. Turnpikes and canals were initially dug to transport the finished manufactured products from the mills across the country and to the ports where they would be exported overseas. Later in the nineteenth century a railway network spread across the countryside as an even faster way of feeding the nation's demand for manufactured goods.

Many mills were demolished throughout the twentieth century but the National Trust, which has taken an interest in preserving industrial landscapes, has restored the Quarry Bank Mill and impressive Styal Estate in Wilmslow, Cheshire, to show how an entire industrial community lived, from the mill owner's picturesque private garden down to the Apprentice House. Many of the mills that survive are now being converted into apartments through regeneration schemes, so there's the possibility that the local mill where your ancestors worked may still exist, even though it went out of business decades ago. John Rylands University of Manchester Library is home to the Greater Manchester Textile Mills Survey Archive, which contains maps identifying over 2,000 mill sites. The findings of field surveys over 1,000 sites combined with archive research have been published in *Cotton Mills in Greater Manchester* (1992). The Rylands Library also contains some business records and papers of local industrial organisations.

The Spinning the Web website at www.spinningtheweb.org.uk provides an in-depth history of the Lancashire Cotton Industry, with a section on the places where the industry had a strong environmental and cultural impact, the products that were made and the history of mill designs and layouts. Every industry experienced highs and lows, which impacted on the local community who were employed in the trade, and the cotton industry was no different. In the early 1860s the mills in Lancashire were forced to grind to a halt during the American Civil War as blockades on raw cotton exports from the southern ports of America were enforced. The Lancashire Cotton Famine ensued following mass unemployment, and the industry struggled to recover to its once famed levels of cotton production. Evidence of how the famine and riots over relief affected your local area can be found in regional newspapers at the local studies centre. Contemporary history books written at the time, such as *The History of the Cotton Famine*, by R.A. Arnold (London, 1864) and *The Facts of the Cotton Famine*, by John Watts (London, 1866), may also be found in the County Library or at the British Library.

Factories

Factories sprang up throughout the nineteenth century close to the source of raw materials and fuel, either near to streams, rivers or coal pits. The minerals extracted from Britain's rich land were shaped into decorative ornaments and new-fangled household implements to meet the demands of a new Consumer Age. The use of coal meant that factories no longer needed to be near a water supply and started to be built closer to small towns where there was already a large workforce to meet labour demands and communication networks to transport the finished products. Match and tobacco factories were found in London, toy factories in Birmingham and cutlery factories in Sheffield.

As Britain's industrial export trade grew stronger and more factories opened up, more people migrated to the ever-expanding towns to seek employment. The number of jobs in agriculture decreased as machines could do the work faster and more efficiently, so displaced workers in the countryside left for the town in search of employment. Throughout the nineteenth century the various industrial trades experienced ups and downs, but as one factory closed down, another would open elsewhere, attracting unemployed masses to its environs. Towns that before the Industrial Revolution were relatively small and rural, suddenly exploded in size and were transformed into major cities, like Manchester and Sheffield. Nineteenth-century factory models continued to be used for production lines and mass-manufacture well into the twentieth century, and in the mid-twentieth century power stations added their chimneys to the industrial landscapes of Britain.

The pollution emitted by factories and power stations had an unprecedented impact on the urban communities of which they were at the heart. Smog, pumped out as one of the many toxic by-products of the industrial age, blackened surrounding buildings and half a decade on from the Clean Air Acts of 1956 and 1968 surviving buildings are still scarred. The Great London Smog of December 1952 contributed to 4,000 more deaths than usual, which were attributed to high levels of sulphur dioxide from industrial pollution in the fog that settled over the capital for five days. Such smog regularly settled over British industrial towns and was the focus of the Clean Air Acts, which encouraged the use of cleaner fuels. Clean-up operations in major cities have started to wash the surface dirt from important public buildings, but evidence of the environment our forebears lived in can still be seen in the black soot coating ordinary houses.

Satanic industrial landscapes provided a source of inspiration for nineteenth- and twentieth-century artists who have left us with a lasting image of the scenes our ancestors were confronted with on a daily basis. Joseph M.W. Turner, born in the last year of the eighteenth century, painted famous industrial landscapes as he witnessed the changes taking place during the Industrial Revolution, such as the transformation of provincial manufacturing towns like Leeds. L.S. Lowry brought his landscapes to life with colours and people, and was a notable industrial landscape painter for over thirty years from around 1912. Lowry's work, which documented the changes brought about by mill closures and redevelopment in the North West of England in the early twentieth century, can be seen at the Lowry Centre in Salford, Lancashire.

Most factories were utilitarian buildings with no redeeming features to warrant them being saved from the demolition squad once their use had been fulfilled. Rare examples of factories that have been reincarnated are the 1920s Oxo Tower, now used as a restaurant and shop units, and mid-twentieth-century Bankside Power Station, home to the Tate Modern art museum, both in London. In Bedminster, Bristol, the old Robinson paper bag factory survives, as does the factory of tobacco makers W.D. & H.O. Wells, and in Newcastle upon Tyne the old Biscuit Factory is open to the public as an art gallery. A great deal of information on factory life in the nineteenth century can be found in the Energy Hall at the Science Museum in South Kensington, London, which celebrates the history of steam power. Next door the Victoria & Albert Museum houses examples of the products created during the Consumer Age and paintings of industrial landscapes, such as those by Turner. After all, the Great Exhibition of 1851 was Prince Albert's dream-child, bringing all the great industrial powers of the world under one roof to show off their wares and amazing technological achievements in nearby Hyde Park. The history of the Crystal Palace and the Great Exhibition is celebrated at the V&A, along with some of the geniuses of the industrial era.

Researching the working lives of individual factory employees is not as easy. The Factory Act of 1833 was passed after the findings of a Royal Commission, which published evidence of child exploitation in British factories. The 1832 Report of the Select Committee on the Bill for the Regulation of Factories provides a window into the lives of ordinary young workers from the beginning of the nineteenth century, containing evidence from children who worked long hours in squalid conditions. The People's History Museum in Manchester is home to the Labour History Archive & Study Centre where the history of trade union movements led by working people in ordinary industrial towns can be researched.

Mining

England's mining history can be traced as far back as the Domesday-book. Tin and copper mines once littered the landscape of Devon and Cornwall, and men continued to work these mines right into the twentieth century, though they did not employ as many as the huge coal-mining enterprises that emerged during the Industrial Revolution. The country was heavily dependent on coal, right from the earliest days of the Industrial Revolution until the recent development of greener fuels. Thousands of men across the country, of all ages, relied on the pits for work either below or above ground. The work of the miners was so vital to the survival of the country's economy that they did not have to join the Army during either of the World Wars. Despite the hard and dirty work done underground, vibrant mining communities sprang up around the pits, particularly in Wales, the Midlands and the North of England.

Large landowners set up the first mines, and family estate records of the local landed gentry may contain information on the early mining history of the area, including plans and drawings of how the mines once looked. The location of family papers can be found using the National Register of Archives at www.nationalarchives.gov.uk/nra. The Royal Commission on Mines published a report in 1842 containing evidence on working conditions from miners all over the country, which is an interesting insight into the daily routine and hard toil done by men, women and young children. Mines were mostly privately run until the nationalisation of coal by the Coal Industry Nationalisation Act of 1946, when the newly-formed National Coal Board (NCB) took control of the assets of private collieries. Employment records for miners who worked for the Coal Board between 1947 and the 1990s are held by Iron Mountain Records Management at Rumer Hill Industrial Estate, Rumer Hill Road, Cannock, WS11 8EX (tel: 01543 574 666). When the Conservatives started to re-privatise the coal industry in the 1980s the mining communities pulled together and organised strikes that affected the whole country. Miners' strikes were common throughout the mid/late twentieth century as the rest of the country and industry could not function without coal, so the bargaining power of the trade unions was strong. Evidence of the local politics and extent of strike action affecting small and large mining communities will be found in local newspapers at the library or County Record Office.

The mines had a huge impact on the physical landscape of Britain. The local pit could be easily distinguished from miles around by its distinctive mine shaft, tightly-packed rows of colliery workers' cottages can be found close to the entrance of many pits, and slag heaps created man-made hills in the surrounding area, most of which are now covered in grass and look unremarkable today except to the locals who remember what lies beneath the green surface. The Cornish and West Devon Mining Landscape has been declared a World Heritage Site, and the remains of a large number of its mining buildings are now protected. The website at www.cornish-mining.org.uk has a wealth of information about how the mineral mining industry impacted the local environment from 1700 to 1914 and what remains of the infrastructure that it created, such as the quays, harbours and ports that were purposefully built so the mined products could be easily exported from the peninsula.

Since the demise of the UK coal industry in the 1980s, museums have been set up to preserve the memory of mining communities and the buildings and entrapments that were once a familiar sight, but have since rapidly disappeared with hardly a reminder that the industry ever existed. The National Coal Mining Museum for England is in Wakefield (www.ncm.org.uk) but there are also many smaller local mining museums, such as Durham Mining Museum, where you can learn about how the industry impacted the area where your ancestors lived. The Welsh Coal Mines website at www.welshcoalmines.co.uk was set up by an ex-miner and contains a wealth of historical information about individual mines across the country: when they were opened, who ran them, when they closed, photos of the mine buildings and details of any pit disasters that affected the community.

Local history study centres and County Record Offices for areas that were dominated by the mining industry will have photos of mining communities, pits and villages, and may hold the records of any private mining companies if you're searching for employment records for an ancestor. The National Archives in Kew holds some records relating to individual mines dating back to the 1700s, and a guide to finding these has been published on the website at www.nationalarchives.gov.uk under the title *Coal Mining Records in The National Archives*. Many post-nationalisation coal mining records are kept at the Mining Records Office in Mansfield, which is particularly worth a visit if you'd like to research the history of a specific colliery. The collection includes plans showing the location of mine entrances and extent of coal mining operations going back to the nineteenth century. The Mining Records Office is at 200 Lichfield Lane, Berry Hill, Mansfield, Nottinghamshire, NG18 4RG and can be contacted on 01623 637233. The online Coal Mining History Resource Centre at www.cmhrc.co.uk has digital copies of maps showing the names and locations of pits across the UK, as well as photos, and information on mining disasters. *My Ancestor was a Coalminer* by David Tonks (Society of Genealogists, 2003) is an in-depth research guide to finding records for individuals who worked in the mines.

Chapter Thirteen

WAR AND PEACE

M ost of us in Britain are lucky enough to have lived peacefully, free from the fear of war on our doorsteps. It's difficult to believe that within living memory bombs were dropped on nearby streets and the threat of invasion was a real one. We're reminded of less peaceful times when an overgrown lookout is stumbled upon during a country walk, or the stumps of metal railings cut down for the war effort are spotted. Researching how the First and Second World Wars, and even earlier conflicts, affected your local community is an invigorating reminder of just how privileged most of us are to be able to live freely on our island. Learning about what life was like for those of our ancestors who were less lucky can teach a lot about their lives and may help us better understand their characters and appreciate some of the choices they made. Records survive in the archives to help you discover the battles your army ancestors were involved in, the places they visited during the course of their military career, the medals they were awarded, and their conduct while serving abroad or on home turf.

Army

The Army was one of the major employers in British history, and the chances are very high that one of your ancestors enlisted and saw service at some point. You can use the surviving records generated and preserved by the War Office to trace an outline service history, as well as find out more about the campaigns in which they fought and possibly lost their lives. Service papers from the nineteenth century onwards provide physical descriptions of the men, their ages, occupations, addresses, names of next of kin, marriage details and the reasons for discharge; while musters and pay lists can fill in the gaps, showing where they served and what their general conduct was like. The National Archives holds military records dating back to 1660 mainly in the War Office series (WO), though personnel records for people in the army after 1922 are still held by the Ministry of Defence. The surviving service records and discharge to pension papers for soldiers who fought in the First World War are arranged alphabetically at The National Archives in series WO 363 and WO 364, and these papers are gradually being digitised at www.ancestry.co.uk. Unfortunately over 60 per cent of the First World War personnel files were destroyed during the Blitz, including those of officers. Discharge papers for soldiers in the Army between 1760 and 1913 can be found at The National Archives in series WO 97; between 1760 and 1854 and from 1883 these records can be searched by name. The discharge papers for 1855–82 are still arranged by regiment, however. Records of associated branches of service, such as the militia, can also be researched at The National Archives.

Surviving First World War officers' files can be found in series WO 339, an index to which is in WO 338, with further records in WO 374. Officers' careers dating right back to 1660 can be traced using the published Army Lists found on open shelves at TNA, as well as a range of documentation found largely in series WO 25 and WO 76. The Documents Online pages on The National Archives website feature digitised collections of a selection of First World War records, including Campaign Medal Index cards, selected War Diaries, prisoner of war interviews with British soldiers, and service records for the Women's Army Auxiliary Corps. In addition, the regimental museum may have some further personal information, albeit limited, and possibly a collection of group photographs.

However, it is also important to understand more about the campaigns in which they fought, as well as details about what life was like in the Army at various times. Campaign records for the period 1660–1914 are contained in State Papers and War Office papers, and a subject, name and regiment index to these is provided in the *Alphabetical Guide to War Office and other Military Records* (Kraus Reprints, 1963), which can be found at The National Archives where the original records are held. Military campaigns of the First and Second World Wars and any other conflicts or military occupations during that time can be tracked through daily unit War Diaries at TNA. War Diaries are useful for finding out the daily movements of a regiment. They are held in various War Office series and are arranged by unit, regiment and date, but rarely name individuals. Specialist military hospitals also kept War Diaries.

The National Archives have started to digitise some War Diaries from the First World War, which are mostly held in series WO 95 and can be downloaded on the Documents Online pages at www.nationalarchives. gov.uk/documentsonline/war-diaries.asp. A copy of the War Diary would have been retained by the regiment and may have survived with other regimental records either still held by the relevant regimental office, the County Record Office or kept at the regimental museum. War Diaries were replaced in 1946 by Quarterly and Unit Historical Records and Reports, also held at TNA in the War Office series.

The archives at the Imperial War Museum (IWM) in London and the Imperial War Museum North in Salford contain supplementary material for taking your research further once the main records at Kew have been searched. Personal diaries, pamphlets and published material can be viewed in the IWM Reading Room, and its collection can be searched by keyword, such as a name, place, unit or event, at www.iwmcollections.org.uk. The archive is open to all researchers who make a prior appointment. Further art, photograph, audio and moving image collections are available for researchers to access, and can also be searched by keyword on the website. The local regimental museum will contain more detailed historical information and records about the impact of the regiment on the local community, their actions and the conflicts they saw. Some regimental museums have an archive attached, and contact details can be found on the ARCHON directory at www.nationalarchives.gov.uk/archon.

After the Great War of 1914–18 a war memorial was erected in most parishes commemorating the names of lost husbands, brothers, fathers and sons who left the village to fight for peace in Europe, but who never returned. More were added after the losses of the Second World War. War memorials are marked on Ordnance Survey maps, so their location is easy to find. The Commonwealth War Graves Commission, responsible for maintaining over 1 million war graves of those fallen in battle, compiled the Debt of Honour Register containing the names marked on memorials across Europe. The names have been put on a free online database at www.cwgc.org, providing vital details such as age, date of death, regiment, rank and next of kin, so individuals can be identified. Each person's entry details on which memorial their name can be found, or where they were buried, including plot numbers and a link to a picture of the memorial site. The names include men and women who were in the forces, as well as civilians caught up in raids. The Debt of Honour Register also enables searches for the names of cemeteries or memorials, so you can obtain a list of the people named on a particular memorial, which will include more details than the actual memorial (such as age, service number, rank, regiment and next of kin). The Royal British Legion organises trips to war cemeteries (visit www.remembrancetravel.com).

Navy

Traditionally viewed as the senior service in the armed forces, the Royal Navy has also provided employment for our ancestors over the centuries; an organised navy can be traced back to the time of King Alfred (the Great), although King John was credited as establishing the first major 'fleet' in the first decade of the thirteenth century. A strong navy was always particularly important for an island nation, and today we have access to a massive amount of information that allows us to trace the ships your naval ancestor sailed with, the places they went to, any promotions they received and the military engagements they took part in using Royal Navy records. The majority of records created by the Royal Navy are kept at The National Archives in the Admiralty series (ADM). Officers' careers can be traced from 1660 using published naval biographies and the Navy List, which began in 1796. Service records for ratings start in 1853, though a rating's career can be traced using muster lists and pay rolls if you know which ships he served on. The Documents Online sources on The National Archives website include a large number of the principal records for tracing Royal Naval careers. The digitised collections so far cover Royal Naval officers' service records in series ADM 196 for 1756–1917, Registers of Seamen's Services in ADM 139 and ADM 188 for 1853–1923, Wills of Royal Naval seamen written 1786–1883 in ADM 48, Royal Naval Division (RND) service records in ADM 339 for officers and men who joined 1914–19, First World War Royal Naval Volunteer Reserve (RNVR) service records in ADM 337, First World War Women's Royal Naval Service (WRNS) records in ADM 318 and ADM 336, and Royal Marines service records in ADM 159 for 1842–1936. If your ancestor fought at the Battle of Trafalgar in 1805 then his name and biographical details should be found on the Trafalgar Ancestors database at www.nationalarchives.gov.uk/trafalgarancestors. Detailed advice on locating Royal Naval records that have not yet been put online can be found among The National Archives research guides under Royal Navy. The Caird Library at the National Maritime Museum in Greenwich holds additional records documenting seafaring history, including diaries of prominent naval officers.

Equally important are the operational records stored at The National Archives, as well as museums elsewhere. These will include Admiralty correspondence, (including captains' letters about actions and engagements, as well as any outbreaks of indiscipline on board), ships' logs (for movements around the globe), reports of proceedings, surgeons' journals (which can make for gruesome reading!), and further advice about how to access material at The National Archives relating to operations can be found via another research guide. In addition, you can visit one of the many museums that offer a glimpse into the realities of life on the ocean wave, such as the Royal Naval museum at Portsmouth where you can also find HMS *Victory*; alternatively, HMS *Belfast*, moored on the River Thames near Tower Bridge, is also open to the public to experience a more modern naval vessel. It is also worth investigating life in one of the Royal Dockyards that also employed many of our ancestors, mainly on the south coast at institutions such as Chatham or Portsmouth. Records are split between The National Archives and the National Maritime Museum, Greenwich, and there are research guides available online to explain the location, content and function of the records.

You may also want to investigate the possibility that your naval ancestor went on to enjoy further service in the coastguards, which recruited many former naval employees to provide important protection and rescue services for Britain's coastline. There is no single name index to records of the coastguard, but evidence of service can be found among papers of the Admiralty at The National Archives in series ADM and the Board of Customs in series BT. Admiralty records for the coastguard from the early nineteenth century to the mid-twentieth century are in series ADM 175, and are arranged chronologically according to when an individual was employed in the service. There are also records of coastguard stations and bases at The National Archives. In addition, you may also find locally-held records relating to coastguard service, particularly if your ancestor performed acts of gallantry and assisted with rescue operations.

RAF

The Royal Air Force was created on 1 April 1918 following the amalgamation of the Royal Flying Corps (RFC) and the Royal Naval Air Service (RNAS), which were established in 1912 and 1914 respectively. Service records for airmen who died before April 1918 or were discharged from the RFC before the RAF was established will be found among those of the regular Army, and biographies of the first 1,400 men to join the RFC can be found in *The Contemptible Little Flying Corps* by Webb and McInnes. RNAS records for airmen who served up to March 1918 are in ADM 188, and the officers' records are in ADM 273, which can be searched on the online Catalogue by name. The records of the first 329,000 airmen in the RAF from April 1918 are in series AIR 79, which is indexed in AIR 78. Records for RFC officers are in AIR 76, along with those of officers who were with the RAF until 1920. Thereafter all RAF airmen's and officers' records are still kept by the RAF. The careers of officers can be traced using the Air Force Lists from March 1919.

Operational Record Books (ORBs) and Accident Reports can be used once the airman's squadron is known, and these provide a fascinating insight into the flights they made and operations they worked on. They have the added advantage of covering the Second World War as well, so even though the service record might not be in the public domain, information about the missions flown can be recovered from these records. They are not just limited to squadrons; there are base ORBs as well, which are particularly useful if your ancestor worked in one of the support services rather than as a pilot. You can find out more about locating Air Force and pension records from The National Archives research guides for the Royal Air Force.

There are also records at The National Archives about aviation technology, with blueprints for some of the very earliest planes used prior to and during the First World War. However, the best place to research aviation history is the Imperial War Museum, in particular the aviation collection at Duxford, Cambridgeshire and the RAF Museum in Hendon, which has its own library and research facility.

Conflicts and Military Architecture

Even though the Norman Conquest is technically the last time the country was invaded – though French forces landed in Wales during the Napoleonic Wars, the 'Glorious Revolution' was actually an invasion by William III that was legitimised by 'invitation', and the Channel Isles were occupied by the Nazis during the Second World War – there have been many threats of invasion over the centuries which have resulted in the construction of military defences, many of which stand today. Furthermore, these green and pleasant lands have witnessed horrific battles of their own, from the slaughter of the Wars of the Roses and the English Civil War to the Jacobite uprisings of the eighteenth century. This section examines ways you can investigate the military history of your local area, and especially how you can combine archaeology with documentary research to gain a greater understanding of the construction techniques behind prominent architectural constructions.

Our more distant past is littered with archaeological evidence that we can research today – from Iron Age hill forts to the Roman construction of Hadrian's Wall to keep out the Picts, with Offa's Dyke to the west preventing Welsh incursions. The Normans constructed castles as military outposts in the years following Hastings, as they attempted to establish their rule through force of arms against native opposition – the grassy hills that formed part of the motte and bailey earthwork fortifications still dot the landscape, as do the subsequent stone castles that became bastions of both royal and private authority. One of the greatest castle-builders of the medieval age was Edward I, whose 'ring of stone' enforced his own conquest of Wales, and still provides stunning examples of military architecture that stand today – Harlech and Caernarvon, for example. However, he was also instrumental in establishing the bastide, a type of fortified town that withstood French raids during the Hundred Years' War in the following century. Fear of French incursions shaped early Tudor military defences, with squat forts appearing in south coast ports that embraced new technology – the cannon. With the perceived threat shifting south with fears of Spanish invasion towards the end of the century, a system of defensive beacons were introduced on a chain of prominent hilltops. Many of these sites are listed buildings, or protected by English Heritage or The National Trust: you can find full listings, and more details on specific sites, from their websites. Similarly, the National Monuments Record will have photographs and data about many military buildings in your area, as will the nearest museum and archive. It's also worth looking for archaeological digs or reports into the pre-history of the region, and there are a range of professional societies that can help. Written records about castle-building and military expenditure can be found at The National Archives; for example, the names of some of the workers on Edward I's castle-building programme can be found in Exchequer records of the age.

It wasn't just military fortifications that were constructed for defence. Following the Jacobite revolts in 1715 and 1745, and their brutal suppression, a network of roads and forts were constructed in the Highlands of Scotland to prevent further insurrection, and a ready means of moving troops around in case of future trouble. Fort William is an excellent example of eighteenth-century military architecture, as were the peel towers that were built towards the end of the century, along with the Grand Military canal that snaked across Kent, as part of defensive measures intended to prevent – or at least slow down – French invasion during the Napoleonic Wars, when there was a very real fear that troops would cross the Channel and import the ideology of the Revolution.

Men in the Army needed accommodation as they travelled around the country training and defending British towns from invasion or rioters. Soldiers were initially put up in lodging houses, inns and even private dwelling houses, but as the Army grew this system became increasingly impractical. A systematic barrack-building programme began throughout England in the late eighteenth and early nineteenth centuries, though barracks had been built around major cities and ports such as Plymouth during the eighteenth century to defend against invasion from the French and Spanish, and around forty barracks were built in and around London for the same reasons. Barracks are typically plain, uniform structures. The location of most barracks has remained unchanged for a couple of hundred years, though examples of the early buildings are few and far between. Ravensdowne Barracks in Berwick-upon-Tweed was one of the first purpose-built Army barracks, and the east block of it is now open to the public housing an exhibition about living standards for the first soldiers to live there. One of the most spectacular is Weedon Barracks, which was intended as a military base for the Government in case Napoleon's invasion plans ever succeeded. Maps and plans of forts, barracks and bases dating from the seventeenth through to the twentieth century can be found at The National Archives in series WO 78, WORK 43, and WO 153.

Battlefields are similarly important places in our national consciousness, and you can often find associated walking tours of these historic sites. Many of the fields that saw great loss of life during the English Civil War are mostly unrecognisable now, but there are clues in the archives to show where events took place in the 1600s – state papers, militia lists, contemporary accounts and personal records can reveal a great deal about the course of events during a battle. It's also possible to follow up the fate of both prominent combatants and supporters of both sides via records held at The National Archives – state papers for the period include the various Parliamentary committees that dealt with the seizure of both Crown lands and the estates of Royalist supporters for sale or re-grant (which in turn generated a huge amount of business in the equity courts after the Restoration in 1660 – often taking decades to sort out). Parliamentary surveys were commissioned, now deposited in the Exchequer in series E 317, which often provide a detailed analysis of property in the middle of the seventeenth century, as well as the names of the winners and losers of the Civil War.

However, the most poignant battlefields are often overseas, and the cemeteries along the Western Front in France and Flanders bear testimony to the horrific loss of life, on both sides, during the First World War. Tracing an ancestor who was buried in one of these mass graves has been tackled earlier, but you can also trace the testimonies of those who witnessed war from the battlefield. The Imperial War Museum holds many testimonies from the conflict, both written and recorded, while trench maps of the First World War (mostly held at The National Archives) can be found in *Armageddon; A British trench map atlas of the Western Front, 1914–1918*, by Peter Chasseaud (Lewes, 1991).

Of course, there are many battlefields across the world where British troops will lie, with those of the Second World War very much in the public attention as time marches by and the number of veterans starts to decrease. Of course, it was not just military personnel who saw the devastation of war first hand: air raids during the Second World War took the lives of over 60,000 civilians. Very early in the war, Anderson shelter kits were distributed for people to erect in the back garden. These were basic structures that were made of sheets of corrugated steel and could accommodate six people. The shelters were half buried in the ground with earth piled on top, so when the war was over some homeowners simply filled them in. The remains of Anderson shelters can still be found in back gardens today. The air-raid warden's papers for your local area may survive at the district archive or County Record Office. You can also find details of civil defence plans at The National Archives, along with some records of the Home Guard – immortalised as 'Dad's Army' – and quite chilling accounts of the tension felt in 1940 when invasion seemed to be a matter of days away, prompting many false alarms and maybe even an actual incursion onto British soil at Shingle Street.

In September 1940 the Ministry of Home Security began compiling a bomb census to provide a picture of bombing raid patterns across the UK as quickly as possible. The location of bombs dropped on houses and buildings was plotted on Ordnance Survey maps as accurately as possible, with corresponding notes on the date and time the bomb fell, what type and size of bomb had been dropped, whether the bomb exploded, the level of damage caused, and how far the damage extended to neighbouring properties, as well as the size of the crater and the number of casualties. The descriptive detail of each attack was recorded in Report Forms, kept at The National Archives in series HO 198. The forms were filed with a sheet of tracing paper containing a basic plan of the locality and a mark for where the bomb dropped. The tracing papers have Ordnance Survey map references on them, so when the tracing is placed over the OS map the exact location of the bomb can be found. Bomb census maps are found at TNA in series HO 193 and some detailed air-raid damage reports subsequently carried out for some raids are in HO 192. Local authorities also compiled incident reports and maps for bombs dropped in their area, and if these survive they may have been retained by the Local Authority, or have been deposited at the County Record Office or local archive. The London bomb census has been published in the book *London County Council bomb damage maps, 1939–1945* edited by Ann Saunders (2005).

Chapter Fourteen

TRANSPORT AND COMMUNICATIONS

Modern Britain is criss-crossed with road, rail and canal networks, allowing us to rush around our crowded land to see places of interest, visit friends and family, or research for our ancestors in far-flung archives! We jump on planes and rush off around the world, or enjoy the benefits of being an island by joining a cruise or ferry to cross the seas to other lands. Travelling around Britain, or indeed the world, is only possible because of the communication networks that began to appear in the late eighteenth century onwards – in particular canals and railways, but also an increasingly organised road system as well. The aim of this chapter is to look at the impact that travel networks had on communities, as they can explain various anomalies in your family's story. It's often a puzzle, when you examine census returns, why the places of birth for a brood of children are different, often covering a variety of seemingly unrelated places. The answers may lie in a simple examination of a contemporary map and then spotting the main transport route that they travelled up or down. Often it was a job that created a need to move around – you see the various towns that a railwayman might have lived in when you look at the company they worked for, and the stations that were along the route. Often, looking at your personal heritage with reference to the means of contemporary travel will tell you a lot about your family's story, and why you ended up being born where you were! Alternatively, if you want to see at a glance how an area changed over the course of time, and the impact that transportation had in driving that change, simply examine a series of maps from the late eighteenth to the early twentieth centuries, and you will see an emerging picture of canals, railways and roads that altered the traditional boundaries of older communities, often out of all recognition.

Railways

It is fair to say that the creation of a railway network in Britain was both a result of, and a driving force behind, the Industrial Revolution and for the first time opened up new possibilities for travelling substantial distances from one's place of birth to find work – although beware generalisations that state the coming of the railways created mass internal migration. Most people lived their entire lives no more than 10 miles from their place of birth, though would travel around their locality in search of work when times were hard. Railways found an immediate market for freight, linking ports and factories so that goods could be moved across Britain and then around the world. The great railway builders such as Brunel imagined an integrated global transport network, providing links between the Great Western Railway and the *Great Britain* and *Great Eastern* vessels that would carry passengers and goods to exotic destinations. Passengers were also moved around in great numbers, though not necessarily to find new lives in other parts of Britain. Social mobility was still limited, even if regional movement was increased and the ability to gravitate to a large town through the rail networks was heightened.

The development of a national railway network was piecemeal. The first railways were very local, and often linked to specific industrial ventures – moving coal from mine to factories, or local transportation of goods. The first inter-city line, the Liverpool to Manchester Railway, was only built in 1829 and was used to test the various types of locomotive systems – with Stephenson's *Rocket* famously winning the Rainhill Trials. From this point onwards, private companies were formed to build and run railway tracks across the country, obtaining Acts of Parliament for the compulsory purchase of private land – for which the landowners were often handsomely compensated – and building stations, often drastically altering the towns and cities that were along the route or acted as final destinations. Some companies were amalgamated, for example after 1921 when the Big Four were left to operate (Great Western Railway, London and North Eastern Railway, Southern Railway and London, Midland and Scottish Railway); from 1948 all railways were nationalised to form British Rail, and a process of rationalisation then ensued, led by Dr. Beeching who has forever been held responsible for closing many of the local branch railways.

If you are looking to trace the history of a local railway, then first of all you need to work out which company used to own the line or operate its services along the track, as the surviving records – collected by the British Transport

Historical Commission and largely deposited at The National Archives (with Scottish material at the National Archives of Scotland) – are arranged by the name of the former private company. The House of Lords Record Office will hold material relating to the Acts – including maps and plans showing the proposed route – while the National Railway Museum Library and Archives, York, holds a large collection of related railway material, as well as providing access to historic rolling stock.

In terms of surviving material, there are two main branches of research you can follow – tracing a railway ancestor who worked on the railways in construction and engineering, as part of a train crew, or administrative roles in stations, support services or running the railway company; or tracing the actual impact of the railway on the community through the construction of stations, track and rolling stock. In terms of staffing records, you can find salary registers, personnel records and staff registers which survive for some railway companies whose records have been deposited at The National Archives in the RAIL series, though there is no unified index and records for some railway companies are not indexed at all. It helps to know which railway your ancestor worked for to begin a search, as the records for different companies are separated. Edwards' *Railway Records: A Guide to Sources* (2001) provides a guide to the companies that operated in different areas at various points in time to help you narrow down the company records you need to search. The records are generally arranged by department, so you'll need to use the occupation descriptions provided on census returns and certificates to work out which department your ancestor worked for. Men who worked as engine drivers, firemen, engine men or wagon repairers were employed by the Locomotive Department, for example. Some railway records are deposited in County Record Offices across the country, which are detailed in Edwards' guide.

You can also find out more about life working on the railways from these and other records. Accident reports provide an account of some of the casualties that occurred, not just crashes that caused loss of life but more mundane matters that happened from time to time, many of which will have impacted upon your local community (collapsed embankments, for example); railway publications are also important in adding colour, such as the *Railway House Journals* and *The Railway Gazette*, which can be seen at the National Railway Museum Library and Archives. You can also add colour by looking for photographs, maps, timetables and other miscellanea. In terms of company records, you can find construction plans, designs and drawings relating to the railways and stations themselves, records relating to land and property, company records showing the expansion of business throughout the nineteenth century, legal material about the formation and governance of the companies, and even the construction of cottages for railway workers.

Canals

Britain's inland waterways were a major source of transportation of goods as well as people centuries before railways were invented, though there was an increase in man-made waterways from the seventeenth century onwards. By the early nineteenth century, the waterways network covered a staggering 4,000 miles and provided employment for both construction workers – navigational engineers, shortened to 'navvies', who subsequently found work on railways and roads in the nineteenth century onwards – and those conducting trade and passenger services along the canals and rivers that made up the network. Where it was available, water-borne transport was often quicker and safer than using the overland road network which was plagued by poor maintenance, seasonal disruption and danger from accidents and robbery. In many ways, canals were the cutting edge transport technology of the eighteenth century, with a massive network being built to link emerging industry with the ports, and were only eclipsed in the mid-nineteenth century by the railways. As you might expect, vast quantities of archival material survive relating to the companies who funded and constructed the canals and employed people to run and maintain the network, plus associated records of the bargemen and hauliers who used the canals to transport goods and people around the country.

Possibly the best place to start if you want to investigate the history of a canal that passes through your town or village is to explore the Waterways Archive, which is a unified collection of records stored in several county archives under the administration of the Waterways Trust (which maintains the canal network today). There are also three visitor centres for the National Waterways Museum at Ellesmere Port, Gloucester Docks and Stoke Bruerne, the first two of which also hold archival material. You can find records of boat owners, names of the registered boatmen, records of the tolls that were levied around the network, as well as various photographs and oral histories from workers and tradesmen. In addition, there will be official company archives deposited there which you can use for more technical material about construction. Also there are many records at The National Archives among the railway company files, as they began to take over the canal companies throughout the nineteenth century; many of the records stretch back to the seventeenth and eighteenth centuries. As with the railway companies, construction of new canals required Parliamentary permission, so you will find material such as maps and plans accompanying compulsory purchases in the House of Lords Record Office. There has also been a resurgence in canals in modern times, with trusts and charities set up to maintain and preserve these waterways – you can find out more about them from your nearest local study centre, or from the Waterways Trust.

There are associated records for river transportation as well, often stretching back into earlier periods of time with licences to operate ferry crossings (before the large-scale construction of bridges in the eighteenth and nineteenth centuries to carry roads and rail tracks). The Company of Watermen was formed to regulate the trade, with licences issued to authorised operators; records are now in the Guildhall Library, London mainly relating to the Thames. Many records relating to the regulation of river trade and ferries can be found in county archives, or municipal archives where a town or city was built on a major river.

Roads

There has always been a rudimentary road network in Britain, mainly focused on local routes connecting villages and towns so that trades folk could travel and trade within the orbit of a major market town so that goods would remain fresh; it's important to strip away modern refrigeration when you consider how far people could travel with their produce, which is why so many villages retained local dairies, fishmongers, butchers, bakeries and greengrocers – all products had a limited shelf life! From Roman times, the need to connect places that were further apart – for Government (or conquest) purposes – led to the creation and maintenance of a wider network that was suitable for troop movements and larger vehicles, bearing in mind that for most of history the main means of propulsion for vehicles remained the horse.

The maintenance of local roads fell to the individual parishes through which they ran, and you may well find local residents hauled up before the quarter sessions by the Justices of the Peace for failing to properly keep the roads up to scratch. Because this was such a problem, turnpike trusts were set up in 1663 to regulate the system, with the support of local Acts of

Parliament. From this date onwards, piecemeal road improvements took place, with the construction of new roads, so that there was in the region of 22,000 miles of turnpike roads across the country by the middle of the nineteenth century. To fund the roads, tolls were introduced – with gates and tollhouses established to regulate the system. With greater control over the roads – and better surfaces and facilities – it became safer, and more pleasant, for travellers to make longer journeys, with coaching routes finding greater popularity in the eighteenth century and private companies operating out of major provincial centres often 'buying' coaching inns along the way to provide overnight accommodation for longer journeys. Indeed, during this period it is almost impossible to disentangle the history of roads from the history of coaching inns and pubs; a glance at the early trade and commercial directories, as well as local newspapers, will reveal coaching times, suitable coaching inns and pubs offering accommodation, and the times and routes taken. Maps were also commissioned and produced to show the road networks, many of which are now stored in county and regional archives, as well as a large number in the British Library's map collection.

In terms of regulation, there are many records that survive for the turnpike trusts, and their successors in the nineteenth century, the Highway Boards (from 1835) – maps, plans and legal agreements for the establishment and expansion of the roads under the trust's jurisdiction; accounts and payments relating to the income derived from tolls, and expenditure on the maintenance of the roads; plus routine minutes and memoranda when the trustees met to discuss policy. Since many were prominent local landowners, these minutes provide a fascinating glimpse into local self-governance – with the possibility that you might discover why roads took a certain route, particularly if the land of some of the trustees was involved! The bulk of turnpike trust and Highway Board material will be found locally in county archives, though some material will be found in The National Archives. Later road-building programmes, including transport policy in the era of the motor car and the development of the motorway construction network, are to be found there among a variety of series, including the Ministry of Transport in MT files. It's also important to remember the role played by the Post Office in the communication network, as the means of delivering and distributing the Royal Mail from 1635 was reliant on the road networks. Many people also used the mail coaches as a means of public transport; you can find out more about the Post Office and its role in the development of public transport via the Post Office Archives in London.

Maritime travel

As an island nation, Britain has enjoyed a unique relationship with the sea – protector and food provider, a place of employment but fraught with danger. The development of a Merchant Navy, alongside the Royal Navy, is as old as the need to travel abroad and embraces both local fishing fleets and global shipping companies. There is every chance that an ancestor ventured into this world at some point, especially if they lived in a community near the sea – and bearing in mind that in Britain you are never more than about 60 miles from a stretch of coast, that would include more people that you would first imagine – and thousands more worked in the industry building ships, working in ports, or providing official services for the influx and export of the goods that connected to the global economy that was emerging in the nineteenth century. All of these varied connections with the sea can be researched.

In terms of general resources, there are a number of places where you can research the history of Britain's maritime past. The most obvious starting place would be the National Maritime Museum, in particular the Caird Library which holds a massive collection of prints and photographs, letters and correspondence, official publications and gazettes, and various official records relating to ships and shipping. There is also a range of regional maritime museums, many focusing on the specific terms of trade for the places that they cover. For example, the archives at Bristol examine the city's relationship with the slave trade; the maritime museum at Liverpool focuses on the trade links with America, especially the tobacco trade that helped create a massive labour market for dockers and traders at the city's famous docks, as well as the passenger liner industry that saw millions of people travel across the Atlantic in the nineteenth and twentieth centuries. The Port Cities website aims to help people discover more about port life using archive material to tell the history of the people and cultures that have thrived around the UK's major ports. The site at www.portcities.org.uk explores Bristol, Hartlepool, Liverpool, London and Southampton's architecture and physical landscape using photos, archival documents and historical narrative. For example, you can discover the story of building Hartlepool's harbours and docks, why and how they evolved, and learn all about the people who planned and designed them. Shipyards – where the construction and maintenance of the increasingly huge vessels took place – are another rich source of social history, particularly in the nineteenth century when iron replaced wood, steam took over from sail, and Britannia truly ruled the waves. Employment records, used alongside newspaper reports and company papers, show just what incredible feats of engineering these ventures were, and how many people found work there – from humble riveters to chief naval architects. Alongside specialist maritime museums and archives, the County Record Office network will feature collections relating to the sea and the fishing industry, for example, while technical information on shipbuilding and construction can be found in the holdings of the Institution of Civil Engineers, London. The private papers of some of the great shipbuilders can also be accessed, such as Brunel's letter books and working papers at Bristol University, for example. You can also trace the history of specific vessels, if you so wish, via collections at places such as the National Maritime Museum, the company records for the organisations that owned them, and official sources such as Lloyds Lists, which were originally set up to assist with insurance but became an invaluable reference work in the nineteenth century for the shipping industry, listing the name and dimensions of the ship, its owners, its home port and the captain (among other data).

If you suspect your ancestor served in the Merchant Navy – bearing in mind that many people swapped between the Royal Navy during times of war, and then went back to private practice – you should consider the vast amount of material that now resides in The National Archives, predominantly in the Board of Trade series (BT) as that Government department inherited responsibility for regulating the industry. In terms of service records, Registers of Seamen were kept from 1835 until 1857, indexed by name and found in series BT 120, BT 112, BT 113, and BT 116, detailing the ships each seaman sailed with as well as brief biographical information. However, the system was abandoned because it quickly became unworkable, and consequently merchant seamen who served between 1858 and 1913 can only be traced on Agreements and Crew Lists if the names of the ships they served with are known. Some of these are available at The National Archives in series BT 99, though others are now scattered in county archives, with some at the Caird Library at the National Maritime Museum, London, and the remainder deposited in the Maritime History Archive, University of Newfoundland. The Register of Seamen was reinstated in 1913 and can be used to trace the careers of merchant seamen until 1972, but unfortunately the records between 1913 and 1918 were destroyed; most of the records from the 1940s up to 1972 are intact and available to view in series BT 382, with pouches searchable online by name and date of birth in BT 372. Masters in the Merchant Navy can be traced using similar registers for the later period, as well as a series of certificates of competency that officers were required to obtain, and Lloyds' Captains' Register from 1851 to 1947. Documents Online records cover medals issued to Merchant Seamen for the Second World War in series BT 395, and World War II Merchant Shipping Movement Cards in series BT 389. To locate detailed instructions on how to trace a seaman's career, look up 'Merchant Seamen' in The National Archives online subject research guides.

Chapter Fifteen

MIND, BODY AND SOUL

Today, for most of us, it is hard to imagine living in grinding poverty, given that we have access to welfare state resources such as income support, old age pensions and tax credits. Yet these are very modern manifestations of the way we've struggled to cope with those less well-off in our society, and you can research the gradual change from local provision of healthcare and poor relief to a national system. It's highly likely that some of your ancestors faced a struggle to survive, and might have spent time in one of the institutions set up to look after the infirm, poor or elderly – the poor house or workhouse.

Hand in hand with improvements in healthcare during the nineteenth century came an increasing interest in reforming education for children, mainly because of attempts to cut down on the number of hours that children were working on the factory floor and replace it with equivalent time in the classroom to improve literacy rates.

It is possible to shed some light on the circumstances our ancestors faced by examining the changing ways the state has dealt with the issue of poverty through the ages, and the records generated during this time, as well as look into the establishment of a national school system, and the buildings and playing fields that were constructed in the same era.

Poverty and Social Care

The history of society's attempts to care for its poor makes rather sorry reading. Until the Poor Law Amendment Act was passed in 1834, assistance to those unable to support themselves was essentially the responsibility of the local community where they lived, and consequently there were no national standards of care. The basic administrative unit was the parish, since it was considered an ecclesiastical duty to offer alms and charity to the poor – a function traditionally embraced by the monasteries, until their dissolution in the mid-sixteenth century. To compensate for the loss of this function, an Act was passed in 1601 which created a system whereby each parish was required to offer poor relief to those in need, which was essentially levied as a local tax and administered by the overseers of the poor for each parish church. As part of the scheme, the revenue collected was distributed to the needy, while those capable of toiling in the fields were put to work, along with abandoned children and orphans.

While this sounds like an early forerunner of the welfare state, conditions facing the poor were harsh, and there was great resentment among the taxpayers. Stringent efforts were made to check the credentials of claimants, and in 1662 a further Act empowered the parochial authorities to move on any newcomer or stranger who was not from their jurisdiction and who claimed poor relief. In 1697, even more draconian steps were taken, when an Act decreed that the poor were to be badged with a large letter P to identify them as receiving poor relief, preceded by a letter identifying the name of their parish so that they could not claim from more than one source. Twenty-five years later, the main component of the Victorian system was put in place when the first workhouses were initially mooted, the idea being that the deliberately harsh regimes imposed on the unfortunate inmates would act as a deterrent for those who found it easier to live off the poor relief. Consequently, conditions varied wildly from parish to parish, and by the 1830s it was recognised that changes had to be made.

With the introduction of the Poor Law Amendment Act in 1834, the system was overhauled and given a national administration and policy. Various Government-sponsored schemes had been attempted in the past; initiatives had been set up in the 1820s and 1830s to move the rural poor from areas such as East Anglia to the newly-industrialised north, with the aim of finding work for former agricultural labourers and redundant artisans in rural professions in the emerging factories. However, this often transferred the problem from one part of the country to another, with the mill towns quickly becoming overcrowded and areas of extreme poverty and deprivation creeping into the growing cities. Consequently, events such as the cotton famine in the 1860s – triggered by the American Civil War, which disrupted the flow of raw materials to Britain's factories in the North West – created havoc, with thousands out of work and relying on charitable donations. It was during this period that cooperative societies were established to cater for the starving poor.

Under the terms of the 1834 legislation, Poor Law Unions were created across the country that replaced the old parochial parishes, and at a stroke secularised the business of charity. A nationwide policy was imposed on the poor, rather than the piecemeal local approach. At the centre of the policy were the workhouses, which operated on the thesis that the undeserving poor would never willingly take up a place within the workhouse because the conditions were so harsh; while the 'deserving' poor – those without any means of support, the elderly or infirm – had no choice in the matter. The Poor Law Unions continued until 1930.

There are a variety of ways in which you can identify a relative who had fallen on hard times. The best place to start is with official records, such as birth, marriage and death certificates – the product of official registration, introduced in England and Wales in 1837, Scotland in 1855 and Ireland in 1864 – and census returns. Certificates often provide an indication of a person's social status, particularly if they list an official residence. The birth of a child might be recorded in a workhouse or paupers' hospital, indicating that the parents were unable to afford a place of their own, or were reliant on state support for their survival. The place where someone died can also reveal a great deal about their final circumstances – in the days before state pensions, the elderly and infirm had to rely on their families to support them, or work for as long as possible, and often ran into difficulties if there was no-one left to look after them. Consequently, many moved into the workhouse or almshouses, where they ended their days.

You can also use the census returns from 1841–1911 to locate an ancestor, and start to make some judgments about their relative wealth. Institutions such as workhouses, pauper hospitals and charitable establishments are listed, with the name, age, place of birth and – on occasion, occupation – of each inmate. These can also be used to establish whether someone spent some time inside; though it is important to bear in mind the fact that these were only snapshots taken on a single night every ten years, so the vast majority of a person's life would be unrecorded. Since people moved in and out of such institutions, you would need to look elsewhere for clues. In particular, you should try to track down admission and discharge registers, as well as burial records for each institution. Further advice about where to find the records of workhouses is provided elsewhere in this chapter.

Maps can also reveal a great deal about the conditions where someone lived: for example, the maps produced by the philanthropist Charles Booth for various districts within the sprawling Victorian metropolis of London used colour to shade the poorest parts of town at given dates, and can be used today to work out whether our ancestors lived in relative luxury or poverty. Even standard Ordnance Survey maps provide a useful research resource – they can reveal in great detail the location of houses that no longer stand, providing a visual indication of the historic status of the area. Things to look out for are crowded streets, often built back to back in a fairly rapid period of time and usually linked to the construction of factories – which you can determine by examining and comparing a sequence of maps from various dates. Many urban areas were required under a series of property Acts in the late nineteenth and early twentieth centuries to demolish the sprawling slums that had grown unchecked throughout the period of industrial expansion, which through poor sanitation and low standards of living were a health risk to the residents; plans and planning papers can usually be found in local archives, which provide excellent historical context to the lost world of the Victorian poor.

Applications to the various bodies responsible for poor relief should yield results, provided you know where your ancestors were living and feel confident that they had fallen upon hard times. Minute books created by the Poor Law guardians are a good place to start, usually deposited in the relevant county archive, while earlier papers concerning the administration of poor relief are arranged under the name of the relevant parish, usually among the papers of the overseers of the poor in the local archives. However, there are other collections as well. The National Archives has correspondence generated by the Poor Law Unions, which can be searched for information about those claiming poor relief, and there are thousands of names tucked away in these documents, though few are indexed.

One of the great institutions that emerged from the changes to the Poor Law was the workhouse, intended to provide for those who had fallen on hard times – but at the same time act as a deterrent. Consequently, to enter the workhouse was a last resort and was a grim fate, one shared by many people who were unable to support themselves through lack of work, sickness or infirmity. Workhouses are usually associated with the Victorian period, and indeed became the main method of dealing with poverty under the terms of the 1834 Poor Law Amendment Act. However, they had been first created under an earlier piece of legislation in 1722, and had already gained notoriety for being places to avoid at all costs.

It was the deliberate intention of the authorities to make workhouses as unpleasant, brutal and feared as possible, so that people would take whatever steps necessary to ensure they did not end up inside. The Dickensian impression of cruelty was often well founded; beatings were common, and in many cases sanitary conditions were poor, leading to epidemics of disease such as cholera, dysentery and tuberculosis. Many workhouses split the inmates into male and female dormitories, which meant that entire families were split up. The daily routine was hard and monotonous, and the inmates faced long days and little time to themselves. In the summer months they rose at 6 a.m., started work an hour later and continued until midday. After a brief break, they returned to work until 6 p.m., when they ate dinner; two hours later they went to bed. The regime was only slightly easier during winter conditions, with an extra hour in bed and a later start at 8 a.m. Food was of poor quality, the basics required to sustain life, and from time to time scandals emerged in the press about the appalling levels to which people stooped. One of the worst concerned the Andover workhouse in 1845, when inmates took to stealing the bones of dead animals they were meant to be crushing, and sucking the marrow from them for food. One of the problems was that unscrupulous workhouse masters and mistresses siphoned funds off for personal gain, leaving the inmates the bare minimum to survive.

Amazingly, paupers were free to leave the institution at any time, yet the inability of so many to do so is a damning indictment of the lack of alternative support available to the more vulnerable sections of society. Many people returned to the workhouse time and time again, often becoming institutionalised, while these grim places were often the first port of call for orphans, foundling children, the elderly or infirm who had no families to support them. Throughout the nineteenth century, there was a growing recognition that conditions had to improve – highlighted by Charles Dickens' critique in works such as *Oliver Twist* – but change was slow to arrive. At the start of the twentieth century, a Royal Commission took four years to consider the evidence put before it by campaigners for and against the continuation of the workhouse system, and the best way to tackle poverty and the unemployed. Although it was recognised that the terms of the original 1834 Poor Law Amendment Act were out of date, no firm decision was made as to the way forward. Options ranged from creating separate institutions for the sick, mentally ill and elderly, while other commissioners preferred to tackle the problem head on, by urging the Government to address the causes of destitution. Consequently, neither view gained ascendancy and workhouses continued, though under a new name, the 'Poor Law Institution'. In 1929, responsibility for running the system was once again devolved locally, this time to county and borough councils. It took the creation of the National Health Service and the welfare state after the Second World War to finally eradicate the dreaded workhouse. Many of the former workhouses still stand, converted to other uses. You can find out more about researching them via www.workhouses.org.uk.

Healthcare

In addition to poverty and social care, the monasteries also served as hospitals, taking in the sick and infirm. On their dissolution in the sixteenth century, responsibility for treating disease and sickness passed once again to the local community. Hospitals were set up, particularly in towns and cities; pesthouses appeared on the outskirts of villages, which were essentially isolation hospitals where people would be locked up to avoid infecting others in the area – particularly during outbreaks of epidemics such as the plague or smallpox. Many of these sites still stand, and research at the local record office can pinpoint their location. The establishment of the National Health Service in 1948 created a central means of administering the range of voluntary, charitable or municipal hospitals that had appeared over the previous centuries. Cottage hospitals were essentially an extension of the pesthouse, and would serve small or rural communities. Charitable hospitals were often founded with a grant of land and a trust fund to support them – again, local records can help trace any surviving records, with details of the trust funds often to be found enrolled at The National Archives in the close rolls in series C 54. You can also discover more about many of the municipal hospitals from the relevant archive, and information about teaching hospitals linked to a university can be traced via the university archives, where they survive. Public hospitals were often established to separate out the infirm and sick from the workhouse, and are often referred to as county hospitals; indeed, many workhouses continued to maintain infirmaries of their own which became de facto hospitals, and were brought under the control of local authorities under the Local Government Act of 1929.

There is a centralised index to both modern and historic hospital records, maintained by The National Archives, called HOSPREC. It links you to an estimated 2,800 hospitals and the whereabouts of their surviving records (usually with the modern NHS Trust). Relevant material can also be found at The National Archives, which holds NHS policy files in a wide range of MH record series – you can consult the online Catalogue or research guides for further information. The Wellcome Trust library in London is a specialist archive with a vast range of material relating to hospital administration and policy, as well as medical tracts and files relating to the ways our ancestors used to treat a range of diseases. You can also search records of Parliament for the various commissions and enquiries that were conducted into public health, particularly nineteenth-century epidemics such as cholera that led to massive changes in public health and sanitation, such as the construction of sewer networks and slum clearances that shaped the cities that we live in today.

Care for the mentally ill was often haphazard, with no real state support until the mid-nineteenth century. In theory, people would be placed in an asylum, meaning place of safety; but in practice this was only the preserve of the well-to-do, who could afford the fees. For most people, they found themselves grouped with the poor, elderly and infirm in a workhouse because there was no statutory requirement for a separate state institution to be maintained. In 1808, the County Asylums Act encouraged the voluntary construction of state asylums to care for the mentally ill, but it was only when the 1845 Lunacy and County Asylum Act was passed that a large scale construction programme was embarked upon. Previously, licences were granted for private asylums under the 1774 Madhouse Act, with JPs providing grants of licence via the quarter session records (and only changed for private asylums under the 1959 Mental Health Act). You can find out more about county asylums post-1845 via hospital records – such as the HOSPREC database – and administrative files, as well as personnel records for admission and discharge (though usually closed for 100 years for confidentiality reasons) held locally in the County Record Office or metropolitan archive. Some policy files and case studies can be found in the archives of the Ministry of Health, especially in record series MH 12 for those held in workhouses, and some patient files in a variety of other MH series, at The National Archives.

Schools and Education

The subject of the development of education for all has long been a thorny issue, with the richest and most privileged tending to enjoy the greatest benefits in the more distant past. Many private or independent schools can trace their origins back to a medieval grant or foundation, with countless more being established in the centuries afterwards as charitable trusts or religious schools. Most were fee-paying, though bursaries and scholarships were also available depending on the terms of admission, or the original foundation charter or grant. In terms of reading and writing, these functions had traditionally been linked to religious houses and monasteries, which obviously disappeared when they were suppressed by Henry VIII. The use of Latin as the official language of court meant that formal education was linked to religion – the word 'clerical' derived from the ecclesiastical 'clerk', for example, and many of the early professions such as law or accountancy (useful in the various local manorial or royal courts, or as an administrative estate steward) were the result of a religious education. The university system was similarly designed to attract scholars who practised in theology, divinity or other related subjects to prepare the student for a life in the Church.

Many schools within the independent sector have published lists of their former students (or alumni, as they are called), as have long-established universities such as Oxford and Cambridge. Indeed, if you are researching the history of one of these institutions, you will usually find that they have their own archives as well as lists of former students and teachers, often running 'old pupil' associations. The history of school buildings may also be traced through the school's own records, as well as deposited material at a County Record Office or archive.

Although formal education generally remained the preserve of the elite and professional classes prior to the eighteenth century, other forms of vocational education were often preferred by large sectors of society – an apprenticeship in a craft, particularly if it was linked to a family trade, was a standard line of education for many townsfolk. Indeed, many trades and crafts required formal training before a member could be admitted into a guild. Records of apprentices and guilds are usually held locally, although there are some apprenticeship indentures available at The National Archives, while records of some of the major guilds are either retained by the modern organisation, or deposited at a municipal record office. The Guildhall Library holds many records relating to guild membership and activity, and can be found in London.

It was primarily the work of philanthropists and religious organisations that provided a rudimentary education system. Joseph Lancaster, a non-conformist, founded the Monitorial System for educating children (with older, more able students teaching younger children), with the creation of the Royal Lancastrian Society in 1808 to extend his programme across the country. In response, the National Society was founded in 1811 by the Church of England to provide a system of church schools, where basic numbers and letters, as well as an appreciation of the Bible, were taught. Government grants were given to various educational societies, though the bulk of money was used to fund the construction of National Schools up and down the country – in theory, one for each parish and generally built fairly near to the church. Meanwhile, other means of gaining an education might come from orphanages, foundling hospitals and charities, some religious and others philanthropic (such as Dr. Barnardo's), where the children in the care of these institutions through lack of parents were given rudimentary reading and writing skills.

However, it was really from the impact of the Industrial Revolution, when large numbers of children were employed for long hours, that the requirement to provide a more formal education system gathered momentum. Much of this incentive came, ironically, from some of the factory owners themselves, in particular those who followed the Unitarian faith, who welcomed the 'half time' system where children's shifts were split between time on the factory floor, and periods of study at schools often built at the expense of the factory owners themselves. The Elementary Education Act was introduced in 1870 to begin the process of regulating the education system, with the creation of local Boards of Education that could raise funds and build new Board schools to provide elementary education for 5 to 12-year-olds, alongside the various voluntary and church schools. Indeed, state funding to the National Schools and other society schools gradually decreased, and they were often taken over by the local Boards. In 1902 the Education Act abolished the Boards, creating instead a series of Local Education Authorities to run the education system for both primary and secondary schools.

If you are looking to research the history of a local school, or track down where your ancestor was educated, there are a variety of places you'd need to go. First, many school records – including registers or establishment lists

– have been deposited in the relevant archive for the Local Education Authority (often the county or municipal archive). You will also find The National Archives holds a range of policy files relating to the various Acts and their provisions, along with curriculum developments and some records of individual schools from the 1850s onwards (though most are post-1870). The Institute of Education will also be an important place to approach for information.

Mind, Body and Soul

It's all very well to focus on where our ancestors lived and worked, but it's also important to remember that they were people like us, who held religious beliefs, read books, or enjoyed sporting activities on their days off. There are a wide range of places you can start looking for detail about the human side of your ancestors, leading you to consider them as real members of your family – as well as engaging in community life on one level or another. This section takes a quick look at the places where your ancestors reflected on eternal mysteries – churches, chapels, meeting rooms and non-Christian places of worship. It also looks at the lighter side of life – the various ways in which they would have relaxed, from community events and ancient rituals linked to festivals, to the development of organised sport. Finally, it considers some of the developments in civic life during the Victorian period, such as the establishment of communal facilities such as parks and open spaces, libraries and museums, and some of the ways in which they celebrated or commemorated the past. Many of the topics covered here are linked to places you can visit rather than records you can use for research, but this is all part of your journey into the past. It will also enable you to view your community in a different way, and might even inspire you to get involved in more projects that are taking place in your local area – helping to maintain a village green or memorial park that your great-grandparents perhaps assisted in founding, or simply because there is a strong possibility that they walked or played in the same places when they were alive.

Although the role of the Church is very much under debate in the modern world, it was central to the entire way of life in towns, villages and communities for centuries, especially in a quintessentially rural Britain before the Industrial Revolution changed the shape of society in the nineteenth century. The church was at the very heart of everyday life – not just from cradle to grave to perform baptisms, marriages and burials (or 'hatch, match and dispatch' as it's quaintly known in genealogical circles), but also to provide a place of spiritual comfort, moral codes of conduct and a focal point for community life during festivals and holidays. These were close ties, and your ancestors would have taken part in harvest festivals and other communal celebrations regardless of their private faith. Records relating to genealogical searches have been described elsewhere, and this is not the place to provide a full history of the whereabouts of sources for non-Anglican material, or the various other religious faiths. However, you can trace the history of ecclesiastical buildings in your local area. The dissolution of the monasteries in the sixteenth century has often been referred to in the context of the impact this had on the community, but many of the former abbeys and priories still stand, maintained for the public by organisations such as The National Trust, with many more incorporated into private houses. You can also investigate the history of churches, many of which have been standing virtually unaltered for centuries – though the colour and beauty of the medieval interiors and artwork might have been stripped out during the Reformation throughout the sixteenth century. Many new churches were built, particularly in the nineteenth century when urban expansion saw the creation of new parishes and places of worship. The relevant records will either be with the church, or deposited with other documents from the 'parish chest' in a county or diocesan archive. You can also look at the history of other places of worship, such as non-conformist meeting houses (which were often set up and maintained through charitable trusts), as well as places of worship for non-Christian faiths such as mosques and synagogues.

The health and wellbeing of our ancestors was not just linked to the spiritual side of life. It's also important to look at what they did to relax and let off steam during the times they were not working. Much as members of the cloth might have disapproved, the public house rivalled the church for a central position at the heart of the community: it was a place to meet and discuss local events, have a meal and a drink, or get a good night's rest if travelling from outside the village. It also fulfilled many public duties, such as inquests and inquisitions, sales, auctions and even exhibitions – there's a recorded case of a local entrepreneur 'buying' an Egyptian mummy in the early nineteenth century and then displaying it in pubs across the country, with people paying money to view the curiosity from the past! Entertainment took many forms, often separated by one's 'class' – pubs were often the site for less savoury pastimes such as cock and dog-fighting, bear-baiting or boxing matches. Other sporting activities were often linked to training and skills related to the art of war – archery practice was made a parochial requirement during the medieval and Tudor periods when the need for soldiers was great, and swordplay and horse-riding were encouraged among the aspiring knightly classes. Of course, organised sports were often linked to local traditions – the origins of football are linked to local rivalries between communities at annual feast days, only developing into the game we recognise today (with codified rules) in the nineteenth century, though the tribal nature has survived with fierce local rivalries still marking modern derbies. You can trace the history of many football clubs through their own archives, as well as newspaper reports and local sources. The same applies to other sports, such as golf, rugby, tennis and cricket – most have origins in the medieval period through village games, but were codified later on in the eighteenth or nineteenth centuries by their embrace by the public – or by the echelons of society that 'civilised' the game.

In many ways, the nineteenth century was a civilising age, with a range of civic initiatives being introduced to encourage better standards of living for the population at large to improve mind, body and soul. Dr. William Penny Brookes, for example, examined the fate of the labouring classes, especially those who would sign up for the Army without any proper training. He devised ways in which they could exercise – but linked it to a programme of education as well – and established the forerunner of the modern Olympic Games at Much Wenlock, Shropshire. Brookes was typical of a range of Victorian visionaries and philanthropists who strove to improve the fate of their fellow man, particularly those of a lower social status, and the era was marked by a range of initiatives that we take for granted today – public libraries, parks and swimming pools, for example. All of these can be researched locally in the libraries and record offices that our ancestors helped to create, fund, stock and use.

Section Four

CREATING AN ONLINE
PERSONAL ARCHIVE

The previous sections of this book have shown you how to research various aspects of your personal heritage. Most of your research will have gathered together documents and photographs of the places you have visited, and it can be challenging to organise it. Equally, you should also include your own story as part of your work, particularly if you are planning to pass it around the family, or onto the next generation. Advice about creating online family trees has already been provided in Section One, but the aim of this section is to introduce a new resource, Arcalife, that enables to you create a unique community that preserves and brings together your memories, life experiences, events, stories, family tree and family history. The website allows you to look back into the past as you can with other family history sites, but uniquely it also helps you create and archive your own living history today and then pass it on to future generations.

Why Create a Personal Archive?

Most of today's family history sites are effective in allowing you to look back and research your ancestors. However, what about the records and memories of today? What are we doing to capture and secure our lives today for the benefit of future generations? People believe that technology will take care of that at some later date, and eventually it will. Right now, it might sound like the stuff of science fiction films, but there may come a time when all the machines and appliances that we interact with on a daily basis – PCs, mobile phones, MP3 devices, chip and pin cards – will act as information collectors and classifiers about us in an almost endless stream of data about our lives. This combined with the miniaturisation of these technologies will mean that we will barely notice it is happening. Sounds scary? We are probably at least thirty years away from this point, but technology has a habit of marching on ever more quickly. However, it does have some very important advantages too, like not having to get out the video recorder or camera to capture those key moments in our lives. Equally important, we will start to automatically collect and store the interpersonal communications that we don't bother to archive – we no longer sit down and write letters to one another any more, relying on phone calls, texts and e-mails that are often deleted instantly once they are read. Of course, there are social networks out there – Twitter, MySpace, Flickr and of course, Facebook – that encourage you to upload personal data, and record your daily feelings, thoughts and interactions with friends and family. However, this tends to be everyday, mundane material, most of which will not be of interest or relevance in years to come. What's needed is a storage facility where you can select and manage your content – not just the here and now, but the events and documentation that have happened throughout your life.

The concept of archiving is not new of course, but today more than ever with the technology that we already have, there is plenty of opportunity to leave a much richer legacy than any of our ancestors previously have. What we can do personally is think of our life experiences as a potential source of historical and cultural record, as well as taking pleasure in being able to re-live those moments at a time of our own choosing. When we are living busy lives it's sometimes hard to imagine dedicating a few minutes to contributing to the cultural record of the human race, our country or even our locality. However, consider how much value your future family will place on really knowing you – not second-hand through anecdotes and stories, although that would be nice – but by your own hand. You can ensure the legacy of your personal archive by putting your life archive onto a site that is properly set up to deal with the privacy and longevity issues associated with personal history – contributing to the cultural record is a by-product if you choose it to be. Arcalife (www.arcalife.com) gives you the ability to capture your personal or life archive today and to share it if you choose; if you sign up to a lifetime membership they will also ensure, for a reasonable fee, that your legacy is delivered onto the next generation of your family should something untoward happen to you. Furthermore, Arcalife allows you to publish selected memories and personal archival material into www.memorybank.me, a people's archive that everyone can contribute to and comment on each other's memories while allowing content to aggregate to create our timeline of historical events from 'the bottom up'.

The great thing about these sites is that they really bring your experiences, memories and stories to life. They essentially let you get creative with your material and turn it into something that others can see and enjoy. Or, if the idea of sharing doesn't appeal to you, you can keep them private in your own Arcalife account, safe in the knowledge that you can visit and update them whenever you want to, while reminding yourself of your favourite moments in life.

How Does Arcalife Work?

Getting started is pretty straightforward, and there are instructions on the site, but here are a few tips about how to begin creating your own life archive on Arcalife:

Step 1 – Open your account, which will automatically create your life archive and you at the centre of your family circle and family tree. If you want to ensure that your material is passed on to an executor, you'll need a lifetime account.

Step 2 – Gather the files, documents, scans, photographs, video or audio from your computer into one folder and decide what you think is worth uploading and naming. If you want to name after you upload, this is also possible. Most social network sites have a place where you can upload, organise and play/view files, which in Arcalife is called your media archive. A tip for uploading larger files like home movies – start the upload just before bed and it will be done in the morning!

Step 3 – Invite other family members to join the family archive. From materials that you have uploaded you can make showcases like timelines, time capsules and photo galleries for yourself and your ancestors. These can be kept completely private, shared with other family members or made public. Nothing is made public unless you say so.

Step 4 – Write your memories, events and experiences using the guided material and questions. This will allow you to leave a written legacy to allow future family to really know you. Or use one of the Arcalife tools like 'messages beyond the grave' or 'family stories interview' to leave an audio record of your thoughts.

Personal Archiving and Contributing to the People's Historical Archive

There are some obvious parallels between researching local and community history and looking back into your own personal or family history. Hamlets, villages, towns and cities of the past were obviously smaller than they are today. It's quite likely that someone of notoriety in the local community will also turn out to be a relative. Historical events and occurrences are often surrounded by documentation that was generated at the time. Some are held in archives, churches, parish centres, libraries or other places that were the focus of the community. There is plenty of opportunity for cross-referencing in your research. For example, a historical record or reference to a fire might lead you to information about the heroic act of a long-dead ancestor.

Today sites like Memorybank and Arcalife are working together to allow material that is made public in your personal archive to become part of the overall cultural archive of your locality. In addition, historical material generated at Memorybank can provide a useful local backdrop and timeline of events that can assist family history researchers in fleshing out detail about their ancestors, the kind of place they lived in and the events of the day.

Many schools have a strong interest in the personal historical and local historical record. From a student's point of view the local history of their area probably holds far more interest and therefore attention than the history of another part of the UK. To most of us, despite the rise of global travel and the Internet, our locale is still a critical part of who we are. We see reminders of our local and personal history all around us every day. We may not consciously notice them, but they are there, and it's still fascinating to many to learn the stories behind them. Memorybank are working with Arcalife to create resources for schools, so that teachers have access to a wide range of relevant personal material, as well as lesson plans, case studies and other content, while students can experience the fun of the detective process that lies at the heart of history, as well as contributing projects, interviews and new content that feeds back into the Memorybank community for others to use, enjoy and contribute to.

How do I ensure the longevity of my personal archive?

If you have material in older non-digital formats there are a few ways that you can get this material into modern format for upload and ongoing storage for the future.

Various high street shops in the UK will convert your VHS tapes, Hi 8 or digital video into files that won't degrade with time and that you can upload to the Internet for safe keeping. This can be a little pricey, but worth it to secure all those family memories for future generations. Sites geared up for personal archiving like Arcalife will take care of ensuring that your format is accessible in the future as part of their terms of use.

Of course it all depends on the volume of photographs you are planning to digitise, but there are a number of photo-scanning companies out there that will scan your photos at a cost. If you are happy sending them away, search the Internet for the most cost-effective. After all, if you take them to the high street, they will do the same. If you do decide to send them yourself by post, of course use registered post or a courier with a tracking number, to make sure your photographic assets are protected, and if possible retain any negatives.

Alternatively, if you don't wish to risk sending precious photos you can start selectively and if you have a scanner, scan these yourself. Most desktop printers today are all in one and include a printer, scanner and fax. Soon these services will also be available through the archiving sites. These should be good value as they can leverage bulk scanning and do all the work for you.

The ethos behind Arcalife

Arcalife was born from the most basic of human needs, to leave a lasting imprint of our experiences. Ever since the earliest humans scrawled pictures of themselves and their hunted quarry in cave paintings, we have always strived to document and record our lives in a safe place where they will remain forever.

That basic desire hasn't changed, and as we've seen, the empowering technology available to us today may be more physically enduring, but raises issues of volume and permanence. Many of our interactions are through the Internet, in e-mail, Instant Messaging, blogging, or in mobile SMS, digital video or camera footage. They are available at the click of a button. That's what we do: click+save, click+save and click+save. But it can almost be overwhelming with the sheer volume of material we can accrue through new media technology, and as a consequence we overlook the importance of selection and preservation of our own personal records, often not recognising their potential interest in years to come.

Knowing that we can record or 'save' these important moments does not necessarily mean that we know how or what to record if we want to leave future generations with a rich and engaging life history. Arcalife was crafted to provide this guidance and to bring the experiences of yesterday, today and tomorrow to life, as well as to be shared and enjoyed. In many ways, as a member of a family, you have a responsibility for creating this rich history and securing your family's personal emotional heirlooms, and the rewards are significant. Being a part of the Arcalife online community means that you are adding an emotional asset to your future family, contributing to a private digital estate that will be treasured for generations to come.

Many family history researchers have enjoyed looking back and discovering their ancestors, but one of the most striking realisations people tend to experience was how little there survives that had endured time, and how hard it can be to derive a sense of who that person was. Living in the Information Age gives us the unique opportunity to change this. In the past, memories and experiences were kept on papers that have never been formally preserved or archived, or perhaps passed on by word of mouth, leaving massive gaps in recorded cultural and family history. The family shoebox passed on from generation to generation will still exist for a few more years to come, but its time is limited.

Personal archiving for the family historian or genealogist

In many cases people start by building a family tree or conducting a family history search, but probably the best thing you can do before you do anything at all is to think about what you want to get out of the pursuit of your heritage. You can spend years tracing your genealogy, going back generation after generation through your lineage. Some people find this alone a satisfying hobby and also get a great deal of fulfilment, knowing something about where they come from. The key question is this: do you want to spend all your efforts looking back, when some of the richest rewards are in your more recent history?

Within the living memories of your present-day family, you probably have a wealth of fantastic history with which you can identify. Try picking a relatively recent ancestor, who seems interesting and about whom you think you may be able to gather material. This can be a motivational place to start researching your family history, before you immerse yourself in records and certificates. Moving across your tree and fleshing out the details about an ancestor has the added benefit of allowing you to connect with your living relatives today. This can aid your search later when you start to move back in time.

You may also want to think about capturing some of your own or your family's living history and preserving it for the next generation. What better gift could you give to a son or daughter when they come of age, than their own personal archive, rich with all the experiences, images and memories from their childhood? For example, an online copy of all of their childhood art, pictures of their favourite childhood toys that have long since been purged to the charity shop, not to mention family videos and photographs all stored safely away from any potential damage.

What makes a personal archive?

Inputs from regular online sources – today you might have accounts at sites like Twitter, Facebook, MySpace, Flickr, YouTube or other social networks, and these accounts might have material you would want to bring in and store in your personal archive. Any site that you choose should be able to permit you to transfer your personal content via an application, or via downloading onto your PC which can then be uploaded back into Arcalife.

Uploads from your 'unclassified' archive – we all have a dumping ground on our PC, or perhaps in drawers and boxes for paper material in our house. This is not a very practical way or safe way of storing what could be some of our most important emotional and informational heirlooms, and you can digitise or transfer this material into Arcalife.

Sharing – being able to share the memories, stories and photographs with other family members or close friends will motivate you and give you enjoyment in return for the efforts you have made. You can import shared data from friends and family into your account, especially if you are keen on adding your memories to the public community in Memorybank.

Animation – the emotion and honesty you put into capturing your unique perspective on life makes your archive buzz with life and engaging to readers, present and future. You can use many of the animation tools to bring your material to life, and generate new ways to display content.

Tools and resources

To help you secure your legacy and pass this on to future generations of your family, Arcalife has designed a range of tools and organisational devices to allow you to easily upload, manage and publish your personal archives online. They are described here.

Products on Arcalife

Events & Experiences

 Arcalife has provided a set of guide rails to help you record the most interesting and important parts of your life, so you don't have to think about what you should record. You can also attach family photos to events, to bring them to life. Essentially they are a set of structured but customisable set of categories that allow the user to capture their life experiences, life stories and life events in a fun way that can be shared with current family members or future generations.

Memories

The site has an amazing set of resources for anyone who is looking for ideas about how to archive their life. The **guided life surveys** within the memories section will help you to bring out the best stories of the key times in your life. In the future, these life stories will become your legacy. The questionnaires are easy to use and are designed to help you capture what's important to you. No question is compulsory, and they have a tracker that helps you to remember what you have done and what to do next. The surveys are based around the key points in peoples lives, designed to draw out anecdotal stories of childhood, child-rearing, the good old days and twilight years.

Life Cube ™

A 3-D Cube allowing the user to play video clips, pictures and images in a sequence with audio of their choosing.

Makes the best moments of your life flash before your eyes. Build and send to your friends, so they get to know the real you.

TimeLine

Display and share the lives of your ancestors or yourself on a multimedia timeline. Play from birth to the present day with audio. A unique view of your life.

Timecapsule

A grouping of stories, memories, events, pictures and audio that can be put together and timed to be kept locked away until a predetermined date and then released to family, the Arcalife community or the Internet.

Social network via Family Tree

Your family legacy can be built out easily and quickly in the Family Tree and Friends network. The family tree follows all of the standard genealogy conventions and can do all the things that a standard family tree does but you can also build fast and flexibly showing all types of relationships (step, ex, friends, etc), and still filter back to just your bloodline only. You can quickly print, build and add family history. The concept of a family tree being a network has been extended and a completely new dimension has been added to allow the hierarchy of the family tree to co-exist with a friends network, allowing users to maintain a close family and friends environment as well as a wider network in the same graphic, to view and search for information and more; gedcom file upload is also available.

Unique to Arcalife: from each person identified in the family tree, you can drill down to their life experiences archive and find out all about your past and current family members.

Family History records search

If you want to trace your ancestry and establish your genealogy, use Arcalife's family history search to trace your heritage. You can search for death records, marriage records, birth records, birth certificates, obituaries, war records and other vital records or information about your ancestors to help you build up a picture of your family heritage. The record search includes more than 1 billion records!! Uniquely you can also build and share your family history for current and future generations, all in a free and secure environment. So if you already have a lot of existing research you can bring it on to the site and share the pieces you want to with other family members.

Family History interviews

Arcalife.com will soon offer a family history telephone interview hosted by an interviewer trained in active listening and facilitation skills to help your family capture bygone moments for posterity.

Privacy and information ownership – do's and don'ts of online archiving

Do – make sure that the site you choose stores the information in a safe location – this means that the site you choose should have a good reputation and their hosting provider has a good reputation. If you are not sure, ask their customer service this question before you sign up.

Do – read the privacy statement before you join – the Internet is truly international, but there will be regulations about privacy that you should note when you sign up to any social network account. Even if the company running the website or network is not based in the country where you live, you will still be protected against invasion of privacy regardless of where the storage facility is physically located.

Do – think about what kinds of information you want to share in your archive and what you want to keep to yourself. Pick a site that can support your need for sharing or privacy and has security permissions that you can change according to your needs.

Do – think about whether you or the site owns the data that you add. Most established sites like Facebook, MySpace, Flickr and others have policies that mean that they essentially own your account and the data in it. Facebook hit the news lately when they took ownership of a memorialised account. Choose a site designed for future archiving, or see if they operate under laws of creative commons licence, which allows you to retain a say over the use of your content.

Do not – share personal family information on Facebook, MySpace and open-acquaintance based social networks like this. If you add this kind of material to open sites you are certainly risking some kind of identity theft. We the participants need to increase our social portfolios by choosing appropriate networks for the kinds of information we are sharing.

Do not – let worries about identity theft stop you from archiving online – it's a question of picking the right kinds of site for the right information. Even with the risks it's preferable to put stuff online rather than storing your family material on a computer or hard drive where the data can be lost or irreparably damaged so easily. Choosing a site with lots of security at all levels within the site is a good way to stay in control. Some good advice here is to visit the security or privacy options page, and set the options before you start to add materials. Many of the sites have preset defaults to make it easy to get started right away and you may be happy with that, but it's always worth checking.

INDEX